T0144493

Applied Quantum Cryptanalysis

RIVER PUBLISHERS SERIES IN DIGITAL SECURITY AND FORENSICS

Series Editors

ANAND R. PRASAD
Deloitte Tohmatsu Cyber LLC,
Japan

R. CHANDRAMOULI
Stevens Institute of Technology,
USA

ABDERRAHIM BENSLIMANE
University of Avignon,
France

The "River Publishers Series in Security and Digital Forensics" is a series of comprehensive academic and professional books which focus on the theory and applications of Cyber Security, including Data Security, Mobile and Network Security, Cryptography and Digital Forensics. Topics in Prevention and Threat Management are also included in the scope of the book series, as are general business Standards in this domain.

Books published in the series include research monographs, edited volumes, handbooks and textbooks. The books provide professionals, researchers, educators, and advanced students in the field with an invaluable insight into the latest research and developments.

Topics covered in the series include-

- Blockchain for secure Transactions
- Cryptography
- Cyber Security
- Data and App Security
- Digital Forensics
- Hardware Security
- IoT Security
- Mobile Security
- Network Security
- Privacy
- Software Security
- Standardization
- Threat Management

For a list of other books in this series, visit www.riverpublishers.com

Applied Quantum Cryptanalysis

Author

Alexei Petrenko

Innopolis University, Russia

Editor

Sergei Petrenko

Innopolis University, Russia

LONDON AND NEW YORK

Published 2023 by River Publishers

River Publishers

Alsbjergvej 10, 9260 Gistrup, Denmark

www.riverpublishers.com

Distributed exclusively by Routledge

4 Park Square, Milton Park, Abingdon, Oxon OX14 4RN

605 Third Avenue, New York, NY 10017, USA

Applied Quantum Cryptanalysis / Alexei Petrenko and Sergei Petrenko.

Routledge is an imprint of the Taylor & Francis Group, an informa business

ISBN 978-87-7022-793-3 (print)

ISBN 978-10-0087-946-9 (online)

ISBN 978-1-003-39287-3 (ebook master)

While every effort is made to provide dependable information, the publisher, authors, and editors cannot be held responsible for any errors or omissions.

Contents

Foreword

Dear readers!

The modern development level of information and communication technologies (ICT) realizes the opportunity to take industrial production and scientific research in information security to a fundamentally higher plane, but the effectiveness of such a transition directly depends on the availability of highly qualified specialists. About *5000* Russian information security specialists graduate every year, whereas the actual industrial demand is estimated at 21,000 per year until 2025. For this reason, the Russian Ministry of Education and Science, along with executive governmental bodies, has created a high-level training program, which they continually develop, for state information security employees. This initiative includes *170 universities*, *40 institutions* of continuing education, and *50 schools* of secondary vocational training. In evaluating the universities' performance *over 30 academic disciplines*, information security has scored the highest for three consecutive years on the Russian Unified State Examination. In addition, employee training subsystems operating in the framework of the *Russian Federal Security Service*, the *Russian Ministry of Defense*, the *Russian Federal Protective Service*, *Russian Federal Service for Technical and Export Control*, and the *Russian Emergencies Ministry of Emergency Situations* are similar to the general system for training information security specialists at the *Russian Ministry of Education and Science*, which trains personnel according to the specific needs of individual departments.

Yet, there remains the well-known problem that the vast majority of educational programs in information security struggle to keep pace with the rapid development in the ICT sphere, where significant changes occur every *6 months*. As a result, existing curricula and programs do not properly train graduates for the practical reality of what it means to efficiently solve modern information security problems. For this reason, graduates often find themselves lacking the actual skills in demand on the job market. In order to ensure that education in this field truly satisfies modern industrial demands, *Innopolis University* students and course participants complete

ix

actual information security tasks for commercial companies as well as governmental bodies (e.g., for the universities *over 100 industrial partners*).

Also, *Innopolis University* students participate in domestic and international computer security competitions, e.g., the game *Capture the Flag (CTF)*, considered to be among the most authoritative in the world.

Currently, *Innopolis University* trains information security specialists in *"Computer Science and Engineering" (MA program in Secure Systems and Network Design)*. The program is based on the *University of Amsterdam's "System and Network Engineering" program with its focus on information security*. In 2013, it was ranked as the best MA program for IT in the *Netherlands (Keuzegids Masters 2013)*, and in 2015, it won the award for best educational program (*Keuzegids Masters 2015*). The University of Amsterdam is one of the partners of Innopolis University and is included in the top 50 universities of the world (*QS World university rankings, 2014/2015*).

An essential feature of this program is that *Innopolis University* students take part in relevant research and scientific-technical projects from the beginning of their studies. In solving computer security tasks, students have access to the scientific-technical potential of *3 institutes, 14 research laboratories*, and *5 research centers* engaged in advanced IT research and development at *Innopolis University*. This partnership also extends to *Innopolis University's* academic faculty, both pedagogic and research-oriented, which numbers more than *100 world-class specialists*. The information security education at *Innopolis University* meets the core curriculum requirements set out in the *State Educational Standards for Higher Professional Education 075 5000 "Information Security"* in the following degrees: *"Computer Security," "Organization and Technology of Information Security," "Complex Software Security," "Complex Information Security of Automated Systems,"* and *"Information Security of Telecommunication Systems."* At the same time, high priority is given to practical security issues of high industrial relevance; however, given the relative novelty of these needs, they remain insufficiently addressed in the curricula of most Russian universities and programs. These issues include the following:

- applied quantum cryptanalysis;
- quantum and post-quantum cryptography;
- quantum computers and computing;
- quantum communications;
- computer emergency response team (CERT) based on groundbreaking cognitive technologies;

- trusted cognitive supercomputer and ultra-high-performance technologies;

- adaptive security architecture technologies;

- intelligent technologies for ensuring information security based on Big Data and stream processing (*Big Data + ETL*);

- trusted device mesh technology and advanced system architecture;

- software-defined network (SDN) technology and network functions virtualization (NFV);

- hardware security module technology (HSM);

- trusted "*cloud*" and "*foggy*" computing, virtual domains;

- secure mobile technologies of *5G and 6G* generations;

- organization and delivery of national and international cyber-training sessions;

- technologies for automated situation and opponent behavior modeling (*WarGaming*);

- technologies for dynamic analysis of program code and analytical verification, etc.

The current edition of the "**applied quantum cryptanalysis**" was written by *Alexei Petrenko, Ph.D., Associate Professor, Innopolis University*. The work of this author has significantly contributed to the creation of a national training system for highly qualified employees in the field of computer and data security technologies. This book sets out a notion of responsibility in training highly qualified specialists at the international level and in establishing a solid scientific foundation, which is prerequisite for any effective application of cybersecurity technologies.

Professor Alexander Tormasov
Rector Innopolis University,
Dr. Sc. (Phys. Math.)

Dear readers!

Today, we can witness an explosive growth of attention to Q-computing. Q-computing technologies, along with artificial intelligence (AI) and machine learning (ML) technologies, cloud and foggy computing, as well as technologies for collecting and streaming processing of Big Data and ETL, are constantly leading the lists of "end-to-end" information technologies for the digital economy of technologically developed countries of the world. One of the main reasons for this state of affairs is the potential ability of quantum computers to solve some computational problems more efficiently than any of the most modern classical computers of the von Neumann architecture (supercomputers). The most expressive and interesting, from an applied point of view, examples of such problems are integer factorization, effectively performed by Shor's quantum algorithm, as well as record search in an unordered database, effectively solved by Grover's algorithm.

In 1994, the mathematician Peter Shor, who worked at AT&T Bell Laboratories at that time, developed an algorithm solving the factorization problem in polynomial time (hence, the number of gates is polynomial) and on a polynomial number of qubits, while classical algorithms solve it in superpolynomial (subexponential) time. Therefore, as soon as a quantum computer with a sufficient number of qubits is created, all modern cryptography will be at risk of compromise. Actually, it will be compromised immediately, since any information, hidden using this approach, can be opened by any person who has access to such a quantum computer.

Shor's algorithm differs from other well-known quantum algorithms in terms of having serious applied significance and is more complex in terms of mathematics and architecture. Two computational paradigms are involved in its implementation – the classical part prepares input data for the Shor algorithm and also manages cycles and returns in order to find the desired result; the quantum part executes a linear sequence of unitary transformations over specially prepared states of input qubits. The essence of the Shor factorization algorithm is to reduce the factorization problem to the problem of finding the period of the function. If the period of the function is known, then the mentioned factorization is carried out using the Euclid algorithm in polynomial time on a classical computer. The quantum part of the factorization algorithm is just looking for the period of the function. And the classical part of the algorithm first prepares the function in a special way and then checks the period found by the quantum part for sufficiency to solve the problem. If the period is found correctly (the algorithm is probabilistic; so it may not find what is required), then the problem is solved. If not, then the quantum part of the algorithm is to be run again. And, since checking the solution correctness for the factorization problem is simple enough (multiplication of two numbers and comparison with the third), then this part of the algorithm can be ignored when calculating complexity.

It should be recognized that among the known quantum algorithms (more than 40), Shor's algorithm has generated a huge stir, and it can even be argued that because of the mentioned algorithm, a new computational model based on the laws of quantum mechanics has received such wide development. The thing is that numerous modern algorithms and cryptography systems are based on the hypothesis of algorithmic complexity of the number factorization problem. At the same time, scientists working in the cryptography believe that the National Security Agency (NSA)[1] and other intelligence agencies around the world have accumulated a huge amount of encrypted data from the Internet, which today cannot be decrypted by modern means. These data are stored and replenished, and it would be reasonable to assume that the NSA will be able to decrypt them when they get the appropriate quantum computer at their disposal. In such a scenario, not only the personal correspondence of citizens several decades ago will be at quantum threat, but the current correspondence, which we previously considered to be reliably protected, will be at risk. Gilles Brassard, a well-known computer science professor at the University of Montreal, is even more categorical[2] – "It would be absolute madness to believe that somewhere there is no one, and maybe a lot of those who record all network traffic and just wait for a technique that can crack all the old ciphers to appear. Therefore, although there is not yet a quantum computer sufficient for these purposes, and even if it is not developed within the next 5-10 years, as soon as it appears, all your correspondence that you sent from the first day using these classical encryption methods will be compromised, i.e., available to someone to whom it was not intended."[3]

Thus, Shor's quantum algorithm solves factorization and discrete logarithm problems and can be used for cryptanalysis of most practically applicable cryptosystems (RSA, DSA, ECDSA, and GOST R 34.10). It is expected that in the next five years, quantum computers will surpass classical computers of the von Neumann architecture in solving the cryptanalysis problem, including cryptanalysis of the RSA cryptosystem (one of the most common systems of asymmetric encryption, named after its authors – Ron Rivest, Adi Shamir, and Leonard Adleman). By 2025, quantum computers will be able to

---

[1] https://www.nsa.gov

[2] http://www.iro.umontreal.ca /~brassard/web/en/

[3] https://spkurdyumov.ru/uploads/2016/04/kvantovyj-vzlom.pdf

effectively crack RSA with a key length of 2048 bits (the minimum recommended by international cryptographic standards).

At the moment, using the Shor algorithm, the numbers $15 = 3 \times 5$ and $21 = 3 \times 7$ have been successfully factorized on quantum computers.[4] Also, a 4-qubit adiabatic quantum computer was successfully adapted to solve the factorization problem, factoring the number $143 = 11 \times 13$ and the number $56,153 = 233 \times 241$.[5] Curiously, the factorization of a larger number at first went unnoticed by researchers, and only two years later was it shown that a whole class of numbers was factorized during the experiment. Next, the number 200,099 was factorized by quantum annealing on a D-Wave 2X computer.[6] The next interesting result was the factorization of the number 291,311[7] using a quantum computer based on the principles of nuclear magnetic resonance. And the record factorized number at the current time is the number $1,099,551,473,989 = 1,048,589 \times 1,048,601$.[8]

Note that the practical results of applying Grover and Simon algorithms to the analysis of model cryptosystems are still poorly understood, since the implementation of such systems requires a large number of quantum gates, which is not available at the current level of development of Q-technology. However, selective examples of the implementation of the Grover method on model problems and its implementation, including on the IBM cloud quantum computer, are presented in many works.[9],[10] The implementation of Simon's algorithm is described in the technical guidance on quantum algorithms.[11] It is also interesting that the most impressive results on factorization were obtained using quantum computers implementing models that were previously considered not quite suitable cryptanalysis problems, such as, for example, the quantum annealing model.

Thus, the development of the algorithmic base is able to shorten the time of the appearance of efficient quantum computers relative to our estimate. Moreover, the prospects for the appearance of a "practical" quantum

---

[4] https://research-information.bris.ac.uk/en/publications/experimental-realization-of-shors-quantum-factoring-algorithm-usi

[5] https://arxiv.org/abs/1411.6758

[6] https://arxiv.org/abs/1604.05796

[7] https://www.researchgate.net/scientific-contributions/Richard-Tanburn-2079794789

[8] https://4627su41pzrvhaad34118k3y-wpengine.netdna-ssl.com/wp-content/uploads/2020/12/Analyzing-the-Performance-of-Variational-Quantum-Factoring-on-a-Superconducting-Quantum-Processor.pdf

[9] https://cis.temple.edu /~boji/papers/REU2018.pdf

[10] https://arxiv.org/pdf/1804.03719.pdf

[11] https://qiskit.org/textbook/ch-algorithms/simon.html

computer capable of performing cryptanalysis tasks become even closer, if we take into account the results of IBM's development of quantum processors. So, in November 2021, IBM introduced the 127-qubit Eagle processor, and by 2023 predicts overcoming the 1000-qubit limit.[12] At one time, Google researchers showed that about 20,000,000 physical (available at the current level of technology) qubits are enough for effective cryptanalysis of RSA.[13] Taking into account the possibility of efficient parallelization of calculations between several devices with a significantly smaller number of qubits, demonstrated in this work, IBM's achievements convincingly demonstrate the realism of the quantum threat.

The foregoing raises the urgency of the presented "**Applied Quantum Cryptanalysis**" monograph. I hope that this book will be a very valuable tool for the development and formation of highly qualified specialists of a new class in the field of information technology and cybersecurity.

Professor Sergei Petrenko
Head of the Information Security Center at Innopolis University
Dr. Sc. (Tech.)

---

[12] https://newsroom.ibm.com/2021-11-16-IBM-Unveils-Breakthrough-127-Qubit-Quantum-Processor
[13] https://arxiv.org/pdf/1905.09749.pdf

Preface

"Quantum computers will make modern cryptography methods hopelessly obsolete. And then what will happen?"

American science and nature writer. Editor at Discover Magazine.
"Series editor" of The Best American Science and Nature Writing
yearly anthology since 2002.
Tim Folger

This monograph contains the best practice of solving problems of quantum cryptanalysis to improve cybersecurity and resilience of the digital economy. The book discusses the well-known and author's software implementations of promising quantum Shore algorithms, Grover, Simon, and others. Shor's algorithm provides exponential acceleration of solving factorization problems, discrete logarithm (DLP), and elliptic curve discrete logarithm problems (ECDLP). The mentioned tasks are widely used in TLS, SSH, or IPsec cryptographic applications of Internet/Intranet and IIoT/IoT networks, communication protocols based on Diffie–Hellman key agreements (depend on the strength of DLP or ECDLP), digital signature algorithms (DSA, ECDSA, and RSA-PSS), public key encryption algorithms (El Gamal and RSA-OAEP), etc. In other words, Shor's quantum algorithm is potentially capable of violating these algorithms, and with them, all the mechanisms of public key cryptography deployed in cyberspace.

The book will be useful for chief information officers (CIO) and chief information security officers (CISO), certified information systems auditors (CISA), managers of the top echelon of companies responsible for ensuring security and cyber resilience of business, as well as teachers and students of MBA, CIO, and CSO programs, students, and postgraduates of relevant specialties.

Acknowledgments

The author would like to thank Professor Alexander G. Tormasov (Rector Innopolis University) and Professor Sergei A. Petrenko (Head of the Information Security Center at Innopolis University) for the foreword and support.

The author would like to sincerely thank Professor Nikolai A. Moldovyan (Russian Academy of Sciences, RAS), Professor Alexander G. Lomako, and Professor Igor A. Sheremet (Russian Foundation for Basic Research, RFBR) for their valuable advice and comments on the manuscript, the editing of which contributed to the improvement of its quality.

The author would like to thank Professor Alexander G. Lomako and Professor Alexey S. Markov (Bauman Moscow State Technical University) for the positive review and semantic editing of the monograph.

The author would like to thank his friends and colleagues: Alexander Romanchenko, Sergei Grebnev, and Aleksey Fedorov (qapp. tech), Vladimir Belsky and Ivan Chizhov (Kryptonite.ru), and Dmitry Khovratovich and Sergei Tikhomirov (Chaincode Labs.) for their support and attention to the work.

The author would like to express special gratitude to Nikolai Nikiforov – Minister of Informatization and Communication of Russian Federation, Roman Shayhutdinov – Deputy Prime Minister of the Republic of Tatarstan, Minister of Informatization and Communication of the Republic of Tatarstan, and Prof. Dr. Alexander S. Holevo – Academician of the Russian Academy of Sciences (RAS).

The author would also like to thank Elvira Khismatullina for translating the original text into English as well as Rajeev Prasad – publisher at River Publishers for providing the opportunity to publish the book and Junko Nagajima – production coordinator who tirelessly worked through several iterations of corrections for assembling the diverse contributions into a homogeneous final version. The reported study was funded by RFBR, project number 20-04-60080 *"Models and methods for ensuring the sustainability of society's social and technical systems in the face of viral epidemics such as the COVID-19 pandemic based on acquired immunity."*

Alexei Petrenko
Associate Professor Innopolis University, Ph.D.
fatawl1b@gmail.com

List of Figures

List of Tables

List of Abbreviations

AES	Advanced Encryption Standard (as specified in FIPS 197).
AES-CMAC	The AES cipher-based MAC mode (as specified in SP 800-38B).
ASN.1	Abstract Syntax Notation One.
C(i_e)	Notation for a category of key-establishment schemes in which i ephemeral key pairs are used, where $i \in \{0, 1, 2\}$.
C(i_e, j_s)	Notation for a subcategory of key-establishment schemes in which i ephemeral key pairs and j static key pairs are used. In this recommendation, schemes in the subcategories $C(0_e, 2_s)$, $C(1_e, 2_s)$, $C(1_e, 1_s)$, $C(2_e, 0_s)$, and $C(2_e, 2_s)$ are defined.
CA	Certification authority.
CDH	The cofactor *ECC Diffie–Hellman* key-agreement primitive.
CSP	Critical security parameter.
DH	The (non-cofactor) *FFC Diffie–Hellman* key-agreement primitive.
DLC	Discrete logarithm cryptography, which is composed of both *finite field cryptography (FFC)* and *elliptic curve cryptography (ECC)*.
EC	Elliptic curve.
ECC	Elliptic curve cryptography; the public key cryptographic methods using operations in an elliptic curve group.
FF	Finite field.
FFC	Finite field cryptography; the public key cryptographic methods using operations in a multiplicative group of a finite field.
ID	The bit string denoting the identifier associated with an entity.
KC	Key confirmation.
KDM	Key-derivation method.

KM	Keying material.
KMAC	The *KECCAK*-based MAC (as specified in SP 800-185).
len(x)	The bit length of the shortest base-two representation of the positive integer x, i.e., $\text{len}(x) = \lfloor \log2(x) \rfloor + 1$.
MAC	Message authentication code.
MAC (*MacKey*, *MacData*)	A MAC algorithm with MacKey as the key, and MacData as the data.
MacOutputBits	The length of the MAC output block in bits.
MacTag	An MAC tag.
MacTagBits	The length of the MacTag in bits.
MQV	The Menezes–Qu–Vanstone key-agreement primitive.
Null	The empty bit string.
RBG	Random bit generator.
SHA	Secure hash algorithm (as specified in FIPS 180 and FIPS 202).
$T_{\text{bitLen}}(X)$	A truncation function that outputs the most significant (i.e., leftmost) bitLen bits of the input bit string, X, when the bit length of X is greater than bitLen; otherwise, the function outputs X. For example, $T_2(1011) = 10$, $T_3(1011) = 101$, $T_4(1011) = 1011$, and $T_5(1011) = 1011$.
TTP	Trusted third party.
U, V	Represents the two parties in a (pair-wise) key-establishment scheme.
{ }	In this recommendation, the curly braces { } are used in the following three situations: (1) $\{x\}$ is used to indicate that the inclusion of x is optional; for example, the notation "Input: w $\{, x\}$, y, and z" implies that the inclusion of x as an input is optional. (2) If both X and Y are binary strings, the notation of binary string "$Y\{\|X\}$" implies that the concatenation of string X is optional. (3) $\{x1, x2, ..., xk\}$ indicates a set with elements $x1, x2, ..., xk$.
X ‖ *Y*	The concatenation of two-bit strings X and Y. For example, $11001 \| 010 = 11001010$.
[a, b]	The set of integers x, such that $a \le x \le b$.
$\lceil x \rceil$	The ceiling of x; the smallest integer $\ge x$. For example, $\lceil 5 \rceil = 5$, $\lceil 5.3 \rceil = 6$.
$\lfloor x \rfloor$	The floor of x; the greatest integer that does not exceed x. For example, $\lfloor 2.1 \rfloor = 2$, and $\lfloor 4 \rfloor = 4$.

Z	A shared secret (represented as a byte string) that is used to derive secret keying material using a key-derivation method.
Z$_e$	A component of the shared secret (represented as a byte string) that is computed using ephemeral keys in a Diffie–Hellman primitive.
Z$_s$	A component of the shared secret (represented as a byte string) that is computed using static keys in a Diffie–Hellman primitive.
GF(p)	The finite field with p elements, where p is an (odd) prime number. The elements of *GF(p)* can be represented by the set of integers $\{0, 1, ..., p - 1\}$. The addition and multiplication operations for *GF(p)* can be realized by performing the corresponding integer operations and reducing the results modulo p.
GF(p)*	The multiplicative group of non-zero field elements in *GF(p)*.
g	An FFC domain parameter; the selected generator of the multiplicative subgroup of prime order q in *GF(p)*.
k mod p	The modular reduction of the (arbitrary) integer k by the (positive) integer p (the modulus). For the purposes of this recommendation, $j = k \bmod p$ is the unique integer satisfying the following two conditions: $0 \leq j < p$, and $k - j$ is a multiple of p. In short, $j = k - \lfloor k/p \rfloor p$.
p	An *FFC* domain parameter; an odd prime number that determines the size of the finite field *GF(p)*.
counter	An optional *FFC* domain parameter; a value that may be output during domain parameter generation to provide assurance at a later time that the resulting domain parameters were generated using a canonical process.
q	When used as an *FFC* domain parameter, q is the (odd) prime number equal to the order of the multiplicative subgroup of *GF(p)** generated by g. Note that q is a divisor of $p - 1$.
r_U, r_V	The ephemeral private keys of party U and party V, respectively. These are integers in the interval $[1, q - 1]$. (In some instances, r_U and/or r_V may be restricted to a subinterval of the form $[1, 2N - 1]$.
t_U, t_V	The ephemeral public keys of party U and party V, respectively. These are integers in the interval $[2, p - 2]$.

SEED	An *FFC* domain parameter; an initialization value that is used during domain parameter generation that can also be used later to provide assurance that the resulting domain parameters were generated using an approved process.
x_U, x_V	The static private keys of party U and party V, respectively. These are integers in the interval $[1, q-1]$ (in some instances, x_U and/or x_V may be restricted to a subinterval of the form $[1, 2^N - 1]$).
y_U, y_V	The static public keys of party U and party V, respectively. These are integers in the interval $[2, p-2]$.
a, b	ECC domain parameters; two elements in the finite field $GF(q)$ that define the (*Weierstrass*) equation of an elliptic curve, $y^2 = x^3 + ax + b$ when q is an odd prime p *or* $y^2 + xy = x^3 + ax^2 + b$ when $q = 2^m$ for some prime integer m.
avf(Q)	The associate value of the elliptic curve point Q.
$d_{e,U}, d_{e,V}$	The ephemeral private keys of party U and party V, respectively. These are integers in the interval $[1, n-1]$.
$d_{s,U}, d_{s,V}$	The static private keys of party U and party V, respectively. These are integers in the interval $[1, n-1]$.
FR	Field representation indicator (an *ECC* domain parameter); an indication of the basis used for representing field elements. If a polynomial basis representation is used for a field of order 2^m, then *FR* indicates the reduction polynomial (a trinomial or a pentanomial); otherwise, *FR* is null.
G	An *ECC* domain parameter, which is a distinguished (affine) point in an elliptic curve group that generates a subgroup of prime order n.
GF(q)	The finite field with q elements, where either q is an odd prime p, or q is equal to 2^m for some prime integer m. The elements of $GF(q)$ are represented by the set of integers $\{0, 1, ..., p-1\}$ in the case that q is an odd prime p, or as bit strings of length m bits in the case that $q = 2^m$.
h	An *ECC* domain parameter; the cofactor, a positive integer that is equal to the order of the elliptic curve group, divided by the order of the cyclic subgroup generated by the distinguished point G. That is, nh is the order of the elliptic curve, where n is the order of the cyclic subgroup generated by the distinguished point G.

n	An *ECC* domain parameter; a prime that is the order of the cyclic subgroup generated by the distinguished point G.
Ø	The (additive) identity element of an elliptic curve group; also called the "neutral point" of that group. $Ø$ is the unique element satisfying $Q + Ø = Ø + Q = Q$ for each Q in the group. For the (*Weierstrass*) elliptic curve groups considered in this recommendation, a special "*point at infinity*" serves as $Ø$.
q	When used as an *ECC* domain parameter, q is the field size. It is either an odd prime p or equal to 2^m for some prime integer m.
$Q_{e,U}, Q_{e,V}$	The ephemeral public keys of party U and party V, respectively. These are points on the elliptic curve that is defined by the domain parameters.
$Q_{s,U}, Q_{s,V}$	The static public keys of party U and party V, respectively. These are points on the elliptic curve that is defined by the domain parameters.
SEED	An optional *ECC* domain parameter; an initialization value that is used during domain parameter generation that can also be used later to provide assurance that the resulting domain parameters were generated using an approved process.
x_P, y_P	Elements of the finite field $GF(q)$ representing the x and y coordinates, respectively, of a point P.

Glossary

Common Terms and Definitions

Active entity: A user or a process acting on behalf of a user. It is also referred to as a subject.

Algorithm: A clearly specified mathematical process for computation; a set of rules that, if followed, will give a prescribed result.

Approved: FIPS-approved or NIST-recommended. An algorithm or technique that is either (1) specified in a FIPS or NIST recommendation, or (2) adopted in a FIPS or NIST recommendation and specified either (a) in an appendix to the FIPS or NIST recommendation, or (b) in a document referenced by the FIPS or NIST recommendation.

Assumption: Used to indicate the conditions that are required to be true when an approved key-establishment scheme is executed in accordance with this recommendation.

Assurance of private key possession: Confidence that an entity possesses a private key corresponding to a public key.

Assurance of validity: Confidence that either a key or a set of domain parameters is arithmetically correct.

Big-endian: The property of a byte string having its bytes positioned in the order of decreasing significance. In particular, the leftmost (first) byte is the most significant byte (containing the most significant eight bits of the corresponding bit string) and the rightmost (last) byte is the least significant byte (containing the least significant eight bits of the corresponding bit string). For the purposes of this recommendation, it is assumed that the bits within each byte of a big-endian byte string are also positioned in the order of decreasing significance (beginning with the most significant bit in the leftmost position and ending with the least significant bit in the rightmost position).

Binding: Assurance of the integrity of an asserted relationship between items of information that is provided by cryptographic means. Also see "Trusted association."

Bit length: The length in bits of a bit string.

Bit string: An ordered sequence of 0s and 1s. Also known as a binary string.

Byte: A bit string consisting of eight bits.

Byte string: An ordered sequence of bytes.

Certificate authority (CA): The entity in a public key infrastructure (PKI) that is responsible for issuing public key certificates and exacting compliance to a PKI policy. Also known as a certification authority.

Cofactor: The order of the elliptic curve group divided by the (prime) order of the generator point (i.e., the base point) specified in the domain parameters.

Confidentiality: The property that sensitive information is not disclosed to unauthorized entities.

Critical security parameter (CSP): Security-related information whose disclosure or modification can compromise the security of a cryptographic module. Domain parameters, secret or private keys, shared secrets, key-derivation keys, intermediate values, and secret salts are examples of quantities that may be considered CSPs in this recommendation. See FIPS 140.

Cryptographic key (key): A parameter used with a cryptographic algorithm that determines its operation.

Cryptographic module: The set of hardware, software, and/or firmware that implements approved security functions (including cryptographic algorithms and key generation). See FIPS 140.

Destroy: In this recommendation, an action applied to a key or a piece of secret data. After a key or a piece of secret data is destroyed, no information about its value can be recovered. Also known as zeroization in FIPS 140.

Domain parameters: The parameters used with a cryptographic algorithm that are common to a domain of users.

Entity: An individual (person), organization, device, or process. "Party" is a synonym.

Ephemeral key pair: A key pair, consisting of a public key (i.e., an ephemeral public key) and a private key (i.e., an ephemeral private key) that is intended for a very short period of use. The key pair is ordinarily used in exactly one transaction of a cryptographic scheme. Contrast with a static key pair.

Fresh: Newly established keying material that is statistically independent of any previously established keying material.

Hash function: A function that maps a bit string of arbitrary length to a fixed-length bit string. Approved hash functions are expected to satisfy the following properties: (1) one-way: it is computationally infeasible to find any input that maps to any pre-specified output; (2) collision resistant: it is computationally infeasible to find any two distinct inputs that map to the same output.

Identifier: A bit string that is associated with a person, device, or organization. It may be an identifying name or may be something more abstract (for example, a string consisting of an IP address).

Integrity: A property whereby data has not been altered in an unauthorized manner since it was created, transmitted, or stored.

Key agreement: A (pair-wise) key-establishment procedure in which the resultant secret keying material is a function of information contributed by both participants so that neither party can predetermine the value of the secret keying material independently from the contributions of the other party. Contrast with key-transport.

Key-agreement transaction: An execution of a key-agreement scheme.

Key confirmation: A procedure to provide assurance to one party (the key-confirmation recipient) that another party (the key-confirmation provider) possesses the correct secret keying material and/or the shared secret from which that keying material is derived.

Key-confirmation provider: The party that provides assurance to the other party (the recipient) that the two parties have indeed established a shared secret or shared keying material.

Key-derivation function: As used in this recommendation, a function used to derive secret keying material from a shared secret and other information.

Key-derivation method: As used in this recommendation, a method used to derive secret keying material from a shared secret and other information. A key-derivation method may use a key-derivation function or a key-derivation procedure.

Key-derivation procedure: As used in this recommendation, a multi-step process that is used to derive keying material from a shared secret and other information.

Key establishment: The procedure that results in secret keying material that is shared among different parties.

Key-establishment key pair: A private/public key pair that is used in a key-establishment scheme. It can be a static key pair or an ephemeral key pair.

Key-establishment transaction: An instance of establishing secret keying material using a key-agreement or key-transport transaction.

Key-transport: A (pair-wise) key-establishment procedure whereby one party (the sender) selects a value for the secret keying material and then securely distributes that value to another party (the receiver). Contrast with key agreement.

Key-transport transaction: An execution of a key-transport scheme.

Key-wrapping: A method of protecting keying material (along with associated integrity information) that provides both confidentiality and integrity protection by using symmetric-key algorithms.

Key-wrapping key: In this recommendation, a key-wrapping key is a symmetric key established during a key-agreement transaction and used with a key-wrapping algorithm to protect the keying material to be transported.

Key-wrapping algorithm: An algorithm for protecting keying material that provides both confidentiality and integrity protection using a symmetric key-wrapping key.

Key-wrapping key: A symmetric key used with a key-wrapping algorithm to protect the keying material to be transported.

Keying material: Data that is represented as a binary string such that any non-overlapping segments of the string with the required lengths can be used as secret keys, secret initialization vectors, and other secret parameters.

MAC tag: Data obtained from the output of an MAC algorithm (possibly by truncation) that can be used by an entity to verify the integrity and the origination of the information used as input to the MAC algorithm.

Message authentication code (MAC) algorithm: A family of cryptographic functions that are parameterized by a symmetric key. Each of the functions can act on input data (called a "message") of variable length to produce an output value of a specified length. The output value is called the MAC of the input message. An approved MAC algorithm is expected to satisfy the following property (for each of its supported security levels): it must be computationally infeasible to determine the (as yet unseen) MAC of a message without knowledge of the key, even if one has already seen the results of using that key to compute the MACs of other (different) messages. An MAC algorithm can be used to provide data-origin authentication and data-integrity protection. In this recommendation, an MAC algorithm is used for key confirmation; the use of MAC algorithms for key derivation is addressed in SP 800-56C.

Nonce: A time-varying value that has at most an acceptably small chance of repeating. For example, the nonce may be a random value that is generated anew for each use, a timestamp, a sequence number, or some combination of these.

Owner: For a static public key, static private key, and/ or the static key pair containing those components, the owner is the entity that is authorized to use the static private key corresponding to the static public key, whether that entity generated the static key pair itself or a trusted party generated the key pair for the entity. For an ephemeral public key, ephemeral private key, and/or ephemeral public key pair, the owner is the entity that generated the ephemeral key pair and is authorized to use the ephemeral private key of the key pair.

Party: See "Entity."

Prime number: An integer that is greater than 1 and divisible only by 1 and itself.

Primitive: A low-level cryptographic algorithm that is used as a basic building block for higher-level cryptographic operations or schemes.

Private key: A cryptographic key that is kept secret and is used with a public key cryptographic algorithm. A private key is associated with a public key.

Protocol: A set of rules used by two or more communicating entities that describe the message order and data structures for information exchanged between the entities.

Provider: A party that provides (1) a public key (e.g., in a certificate); (2) assurance, such as an assurance of the validity of a candidate public key or assurance of possession of the private key associated with a public key; or (3) key confirmation. Contrast with recipient.

Public key: A cryptographic key that may be made public and is used with a public key cryptographic algorithm. A public key is associated with a private key.

Public key certificate: A data structure that contains an entity's identifier(s), the entity's public key (including an indication of the associated set of domain parameters) and possibly other information, along with a signature on that data set that is generated by a trusted party, i.e., a certificate authority, thereby binding the public key to the included identifier(s).

Public key validation: The procedure whereby the recipient of a public key checks that the key conforms to the arithmetic requirements for such a key in order to thwart certain types of attacks.

Random nonce: A nonce containing a random-value component that is generated anew for each nonce.

Receiver: The party that receives secret keying material via a key-transport transaction. Contrast with sender.

Recipient: A party that (1) receives a public key; or (2) obtains assurance from an assurance provider (e.g., assurance of the validity of a candidate public key or assurance of possession of the private key corresponding to a public key); or (3) receives key confirmation from a key-confirmation provider.

Scheme: A set of unambiguously specified transformations that provide a (cryptographic) service when properly implemented and maintained. A scheme is a higher-level construct than a primitive and a lower-level construct than a protocol.

Security properties: The security features (e.g., replay protection, or key confirmation) that a cryptographic scheme may, or may not, provide.

Security strength (also, "bits of security"): A number associated with the amount of work (that is, the number of operations) that is required to break a cryptographic algorithm or system.

Sender: The party that sends secret keying material to the receiver in a key-transport transaction. Contrast with receiver.

Shall: This term is used to indicate a requirement that needs to be fulfilled to claim conformance to this recommendation. Note that shall may be coupled with not to become shall not.

Shared secret: A secret value that has been computed during a key-establishment scheme, which is known by both participants and is used as input to a key-derivation method to produce keying material.

Should: This term is used to indicate an important recommendation. Ignoring the recommendation could result in undesirable results. Note that should may be coupled with not to become should not.

Static key pair: A key pair, consisting of a private key (i.e., a static private key) and a public key (i.e., a static public key) that is intended for use for a relatively long period of time and is typically intended for use in multiple key-establishment transactions. Contrast with an ephemeral key pair.

Store and forward: A telecommunications technique in which information is sent to an intermediate station where it is kept and later sent to the final destination or to another intermediate station.

Support (a security strength): A security strength of s bits is said to be supported by a particular choice of algorithm, primitive, auxiliary function, parameters, etc., for use in the implementation of a cryptographic mechanism if that choice will not prevent the resulting implementation from attaining a security strength of at least s bits. In this recommendation, it is assumed that implementation choices are intended to support a security strength of 112 bits or more (see SP 800-57 and SP 800-131A).

Symmetric key: A cryptographic key that is shared between two or more entities and used with a cryptographic application to process information.

Symmetric-key algorithm: A cryptographic algorithm that uses secret keying material that is shared between authorized parties.

Targeted security strength: The security strength that is intended to be supported by one or more implementation-related choices (such as algorithms, primitives, auxiliary functions, parameter sizes, and/or actual parameters) for the purpose of instantiating a cryptographic mechanism. In this recommendation, it is assumed that the targeted security strength of any instantiation of an approved key-establishment scheme has a value greater than or equal to 112 bits and less than or equal to 256 bits.

Trusted association: Assurance of the integrity of an asserted relationship between items of information that may be provided by cryptographic or non-cryptographic (e.g., physical) means. Also see "Binding."

Trusted party: A party that is trusted by an entity to faithfully perform certain services for that entity. An entity could be a trusted party for itself.

Trusted third party: A third party, such as a CA, that is trusted by its clients to perform certain services. By contrast, the two participants in a key-establishment transaction are considered to be the first and second parties.

Introduction

Currently, the national quantum programs supporting exploratory research in the field of quantum technologies are being implemented in 17 technologically advanced countries around the world; 12 of them financially support the mentioned programs. The leading scientific institutes and foundations as well as best public and private universities in the field of natural sciences are involved in the advanced research and program implementation. For example, the National Quantum Initiative (2018) is being implemented in the USA, which is aimed at maintaining the technological leadership of the USA in the field of quantum technologies in the medium and long term. A series of more than 80 dual-use R&D projects has been deployed under the management of the US National Security Agency, the NSA, the US Agency for Intelligence Advanced Research Projects Activity in the Field of Military Intelligence (IARPA), the Defense Advanced Research Projects Agency of the US Department (DARPA), the US National Science Foundation (NSF), the US Department of Energy, etc. At the same time, the US budget for the development of quantum technologies in 2021 exceeded $2.5 billion. Other countries are actively participating in international programs for the development of quantum technologies. At the same time, all national quantum programs have been identified by governments as highly important for the state national security and economic competitiveness.

In most national quantum programs, the four following directions of exploratory research are identified:

* quantum computers and computing;

* quantum communications (near-term perspective);

* quantum cryptanalysis (near-term perspective);

* quantum and post-quantum cryptography.

Therefore, the following key technologies have been identified in a quantum cryptography:

- quantum key distribution (QKD) and quantum encryption in fiber-optic communication channels and in open space;

- quantum hashing and quantum digital signature;

- quantum super-dense encoding of information using "entangled" and "hyper-entangled" particles (one quantum bit (qubit) can carry up to two ordinary bits), which increases the bandwidth of the quantum communication channel;

- encoding in quantum information transmission systems, etc.

In quantum cryptanalysis, Shor's algorithm provides exponential acceleration of solving factorization problems, discrete logarithm problem (DLP), and elliptic curve discrete logarithm problems (ECDLP), widely used in cryptographic applications in cyberspace. Therefore, the well-known protocols TLS, SSH, IPsec, etc., rely on Diffie–Hellman key agreements (which depend on the strength of DLP or ECDLP), digital signatures (DSA, ECDSA, or RSA-PSS) or public key encryption (El Gamal or RSA-OAEP). Shor's quantum algorithm can potentially crack most protocols and schemes of asymmetric encryption (public key cryptography). In general, all known quantum algorithms can be divided into two groups: providing exponential gain (for example, Shor's algorithm) and providing quadratic gain (for example, Grover's algorithm).

Particular attention is paid to the Shor quantum algorithm and other polynomial algorithms capable of solving cryptanalysis problems with the required reliability and complexity in polynomial time. Grover's quantum search algorithm is also quite interesting; it speeds up algorithms for solving some NP-class problems, for which a better algorithm than a direct search is unknown: for example, to speed up the key search for crypto systems such as the well-known DES algorithm. The quantum Fourier transformation is also the subject of high interest, which solves the problems of calculating the discrete logarithm and factorization and crack many cryptosystems using a quantum computer, for example, RSA. According to the reports of the American National Institute of Standards (NIST), the AES, SHA-2, SHA-3, RSA, ECDSA, ECDH, and DSA crypto algorithms used in the USA and NATO countries are subject to quantum threat. The quantum computers compute at completely different speeds than modern fifth generation supercomputers, which makes the reading of encrypted texts a very real threat.

For quantum computing, all cryptographies are divided into quantum-secure and quantum-insecure. Algorithms and cryptosystems of symmetric encryption (including AES or GOST R 34.12-2015) are attributed to quantum-secure but with at least twice the key length increased (it is difficult to say exactly what length will be sufficient). Algorithms and cryptosystems of asymmetric encryption based on the complexity of integer factorization (for example, RSA) or discrete logarithm (for example, El Gamal or elliptic curves) should be classified as quantum insecure. Quantum computers also pose a real threat to the security of most well-known blockchain platforms, which universally use asymmetric cryptographic algorithms to create a public–private key pair and an address that is obtained using hashing operations and a checksum of the public key. As a result, in a number of countries, like the USA and the European Union, it is already planned to switch to the use of stable quantum cryptography. Therefore, the mentioned NIST is in the process of developing the quantum cryptography standards, and the NSA recommends its suppliers to implement SHA-384 instead of SHA-256.

This monograph contains the best practice of solving problems of quantum cryptanalysis to improve cybersecurity and resilience of the digital economy. The book discusses the well-known and author's software implementations of promising quantum Shor algorithms, Grover, Simon, and others. Shor's algorithm provides exponential acceleration of solving factorization problems, discrete logarithm (DLP), and elliptic curve discrete logarithm problems (ECDLP). The mentioned tasks are widely used in TLS, SSH, or IPsec cryptographic applications of Internet/Intranet and IIoT/IoT networks, communication protocols based on Diffie–Hellman key agreements (depend on the strength of DLP or ECDLP), digital signature algorithms (DSA, ECDSA, and RSA-PSS), public key encryption algorithms (El Gamal and RSA-OAEP), etc. In other words, Shor's quantum algorithm is potentially capable of violating these algorithms, and with them, all the mechanisms of public key cryptography deployed in cyberspace.

The book will be useful for chief information officers (CIO) and chief information security officers (CISO), certified information systems auditors (CISA), managers of the top echelon of companies responsible for ensuring security and cyber resilience of business, as well as teachers and students of MBA, CIO, and CSO programs, students, and postgraduates of relevant specialties.

The book contains four chapters, dedicated to the following topics:

- The relevance of practical issues of quantum cryptanalysis aimed to improve cybersecurity and resilience of the digital economy.

The analysis of the well-known national quantum programs of technologically developed countries of the world is conducted. The main prerequisites and scientific foundations for solving practical problems of quantum cryptanalysis based on the algorithms of Shor, Grover, Simon, etc., are revealed. The basic requirements for promising quantum cryptanalysis software packages are determined.

- Possible implementations of the Shor factorization algorithm on a quantum circuit to develop requirements for quantum cryptanalysis algorithms. The applicability of Fourier transforms to determine the periodic structure of finite-length sequences is analyzed. The classical factorization problem has been reformulated to solve it on modern quantum computers with 16 or more qubits. A modification of the basic Shor factorization algorithm is proposed for the possibility of its execution on a quantum computer. The complexity of the quantum factorization algorithm is estimated to determine the necessary and sufficient computing resources. An example of a possible implementation of the Shor factorization algorithm on a quantum circuit is presented. The estimation of the limiting capabilities of the quantum factorization algorithm for solving quantum cryptanalysis problems is carried out.

- Quantum cryptanalysis algorithms based on factorization and discrete logarithm problems in various algebraic structures. The stability of the modern cryptographic algorithms has been evaluated to clarify the tasks of cryptanalysis of asymmetric encryption schemes (RSA or El Gamal) and digital signature (DSA, ECDSA, or RSA-PSS) based on factorization and discrete logarithm problems (DLP and ECDLP) in various algebraic structures in a quantum computing model. The necessary and sufficient conditions have been determined for the effective solution of cryptanalysis problems of asymmetric encryption schemes (RSA or El Gamal) and digital signature (DSA, ECDSA, or RSA-PSS) in a quantum computing model. A basic quantum Shor factorization algorithm is proposed. A quantum Grover search algorithm has been developed. A quantum algorithm for symmetric encryption key recovery based on the message text and ciphertext has been developed. A quantum algorithm for cryptanalysis of the RSA asymmetric encryption system has been developed. A quantum algorithm for cryptanalysis of the El Gamal system has been developed.

- Examples of the developed promising software package for quantum cryptanalysis of asymmetric encryption and digital signature schemes. The well-known quantum emulators Quantum Development Kit, Quantum Computing Playground, jQuantum, QuEST, Quantum Programming Studio, Q-Kit, etc., are considered. The main advantages and limitations of the mentioned quantum emulators are shown. A practical implementation of the Shor algorithm based on the IBM Q platform and the specialized programming language Qiskit is proposed. This made it possible to test a number of possible combined schemes based on the promising IBM Q System One quantum computers with a 20-qubit system, as well as a number of simulations on classic fifth generation supercomputers. The results obtained indicate the feasibility of practical use of the modified Shor algorithm to improve the cryptographic protection of digital economy applications.

Alexei Petrenko
Associate Professor Innopolis University, Ph.D.
May 2022

1

The Relevance of Quantum Cryptanalysis

The first chapter shows the relevance of solving practical issues of quantum cryptanalysis to ensure the required cybersecurity digital economy. The analysis of the well-known national quantum initiatives and programs in technologically advanced countries of the world (*USA, China, EU countries, Russia*, etc.) is carried out. The role and place of applied quantum cryptanalysis in modern cryptology search studies are shown. The main prerequisites and scientific foundations for solving practical problems of quantum cryptanalysis based on the algorithms of *Shor, Grover, Simon*, etc., are revealed. The potential vulnerabilities of modern blockchain systems to typical quantum crypto attacks are considered. The basic requirements for promising methods, algorithms, and software of quantum cryptanalysis are defined. Possible verbal statements of the problem of research aimed at improving the effectiveness of known methods and algorithms of quantum cryptanalysis are formulated.

1.1 National Quantum Programs

Currently, national quantum programs that support exploratory research in quantum technologies are implemented in 17 technologically developed countries (*CIFAR. A Quantum Revolution: Report on Global Policies for Quantum Technology, 2021*[1]). In **12** of them, such programs are directly funded by the state, while leading research institutes and advanced research foundations, as well as leading public and private universities in the natural sciences, are involved in their implementation. Other countries are actively participating in international programs for the development of quantum technologies. At the same time, all national quantum programs (Table 1.1) have been identified by governments as critically important for the national security and economic competitiveness of the state [5–7, 24, 27–29, 39, 54–56, 71, 74–76, 109–113, 115–139, 167–169].

---

[1] https://cifar.ca/wp-content/uploads/2021/05/QuantumReport-EN-May2021.pdf

Table 1.1   List of well-known national quantum programs.

Country	Name of the national quantum program	Budget and deadlines
USA	National Quantum Initiative (2018)	More than **$2.5 billion.** **2018–2023**
China	Quantum Technology R&D as Strategic Industry in Five-Year Plans and "Made in China 2025"	**$15.3 billion** (creating an experimental center) 2020–2025
Russia	Roadmap for the development of quantum technologies (2019)	$691 million (**51.1 billion rubles**) 2019–2024
The EU Program	Quantum Technologies Flagship (2018)	$181 million 2018–2021
France	National Strategy for Quantum Technologies (2021)	More than **$1.2 billion** 2021-2026
Germany	Quantum Technologies — From Basic Research To Market (2018)	**$2.4 billion** 2018–2023
India	National Mission on Quantum Technologies & Applications (2020)	More than **$1.08 billion.** 2020–2025
Israel	National Program for Quantum Science and Technology (2019)	$380 million 2019–2025
Japan	Quantum Technology Innovation Strategy (2020)	$206 million 2020–2025
Netherlands	National Agenda for Quantum Technology: Quantum Delta NL (2019)	$850 million 2019–2024
Singapore	Quantum Engineering Program (2018)	$90.9 million 2018–2025
South Korea	Quantum Computing Technology Development Project (2019)	$40.9 million 2019–2024
Great Britain	National Quantum Technologies Programme (2013)	More than $1.23 billion 2019–2024
Australia	"Growing Australia's Quantum Technology Industry" (2020)	98.6 million of dollars 2019–2024
Canada	Quantum Canada Strategy (in development since 2016)	$149.7 million 2017–2022

The main objectives of the mentioned national quantum programs are the cooperation of interested parties in academia and industry to conduct promising dual-use R&D in the field of quantum technologies, as well as to facilitate the translation of exploratory research into practice. An additional goal is the development of human capital (or resource). A number

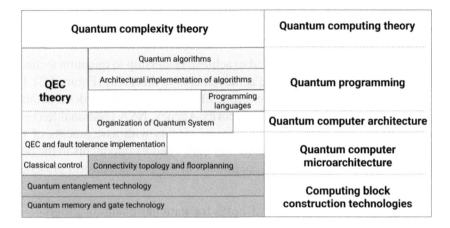

Figure 1.1   The main directions of quantum computing development.

of programs have set clear medium-term goals, for example, to develop a working industrial prototype of a "practical" quantum computer by 2030 (or earlier), as well as to develop scenarios for its use to create an eco-system of quantum computing [8–16, 19–21, 25, 41–47, 57, 65–68, 72, 77–82].

The primary objectives of the national quantum programs include:

- creation of scientific and technical centers of excellence in the field of quantum technologies;

- organization and implementation of promising dual-use R&D on a given topic;

- provision of direct financing of special dual-use projects;

- provision of public investments or seed capital to enterprises producing new quantum technologies.

In most national quantum programs, four main directions of exploratory research are identified (Figure 1.1) [8, 9, 14, 15, 21, 24–29, 38, 40, 43–47, 73, 77–80, 82–97, 166–169]:

- quantum computers and computing;

- quantum communications (near-term perspective);

- quantum cryptanalysis (near-term perspective);

- quantum and post-quantum cryptography.

Consider the structure and content of these programs in detail on the example of the National Quantum Initiative of the USA in 2018 (*National Quantum Initiative, 2018*[2]) (Figure 1.2).

In early 2018, the US decided to achieve leadership in quantum technologies (ahead of China's scientific achievements in this area) (Figure 1.3). On the instructions of the US Congress (one of the three highest federal authorities of the United States) National Security Agency, NSA (National Security Agency, NSA[3]) has prepared a number of reports with assessments of the military-technical potential of the United States and its opponents in the field of quantum technologies. These documents in the expanded form presented the following:

- structure and comparison of costs for national quantum programs in technologically advanced countries of the world;

- quantity and quality of previously conducted scientific and technical research;

- evaluation of the practical significance of the obtained scientific results;

- assessment of the potential capabilities of the relevant experimental base;

- assessment of the quality level of training of specialists in the direction of quantum technologies, etc.

Further, a Memorandum (2018) on the budget priorities of the US presidential administration in the field of dual-use R&D was developed. At the same time, the following areas of search research were identified: *artificial intelligence (AI), quantum technologies (Q), autonomous robotics*, and *high and ultra-high performance machine computing* (up to 10 or more Exaflops). In terms of quantum technologies, the task was set to maintain the technological leadership of the United States in the medium and long term.[4] In 2018, a draft version of the law "*National Quantum Initiative Act*" was prepared,[5] in which the allocation of significant financial resources was planned for the following organizations:

- National Institute of Standards and Technology (NIST) in the amount of $400 million (80 million per year) for the organization and conduct of scientific events on specified topics[6];

[2] https://www.congress.gov/115/plaws/publ368/PLAW-115publ368.pdf
[3] https://www.nsa.gov
[4] https://www.quantum.gov/wp-content/uploads/2022/02/QIST-Natl-Workforce-Plan.pdf
[5] https://www.congress.gov/115/plaws/publ368/PLAW-115publ368.pdf
[6] https://csrc.nist.gov/projects/post-quantum-cryptography/post-quantum-cryptography-standardization

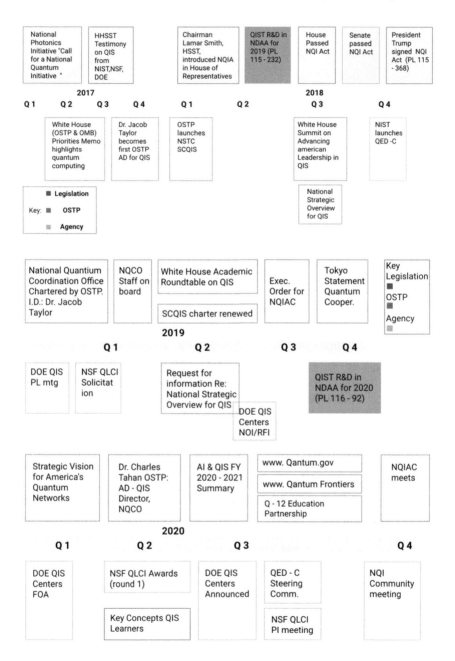

Figure 1.2 Prerequisites of the US National Quantum Initiative (2018).

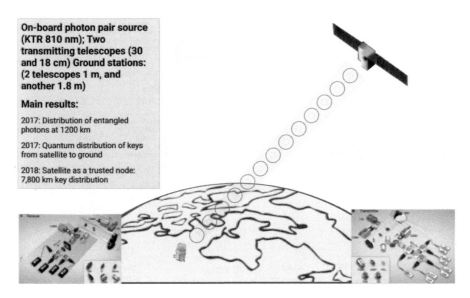

On-board photon pair source (KTR 810 nm); Two transmitting telescopes (30 and 18 cm) Ground stations: (2 telescopes 1 m, and another 1.8 m)

Main results:

2017: Distribution of entangled photons at 1200 km

2017: Quantum distribution of keys from satellite to ground

2018: Satellite as a trusted node: 7,800 km key distribution

Figure 1.3   Quantum Satellite Communications of China (Micius, 2016).

- National Science Foundation (NSF) in the amount of $250 million (50 million per year) for the creation and development of interdisciplinary research centers for exploratory research and training (Multidisciplinary Centers for Quantum Research and Education)[7];

- Coordination Office in the amount of $200 million (40 million per year) for project management in the field of quantum technologies.

During the discussion of budget items in the US House of Representatives, the US Department of Energy was additionally allocated $625 million (125 million per year) for the creation of five leading research centers (National Quantum Information Science Research Centers).[8] As a result, the total amount of funding for the implementation of the US National Quantum Initiative amounted to $1.275 billion USD on December 21, 2018; this budget was approved by US President Donald Trump.

The US National Science Foundation (NSF) has planned two strategic projects for the period 2019–2025. In the first project is developing a

---

[7] https://www.nsf.gov/mps/quantum/quantum_research_at_nsf.jsp
[8] https://www.energy.gov/articles/doe-announces-30-million-quantum-information-science-tackle-emerging-21st-century

practically useful quantum computer (Software-Tailored Architecture for Quantum, STAQ) co-design.[9] The main objectives of this project are:

- development of a promising architecture of a quantum computer with 64 or more qubits;

- ensuring the required stability and noise immunity of the functioning of quantum computers in real operating conditions;

- development of quantum algorithms, system, and application software for solving dual-use scientific and technical problems.

The second project *"Facilitating the Quantum Leap"* (Enabling Quantum Leap: Convergent Accelerated Discovery Foundries for Quantum Materials Science, Engineering, and Information, Q-AMASE-i)[10] was aimed at creating new samples of quantum materials. The total amount of funding for these projects amounted to $25 million USD.

The US Department of Energy has funded 85 promising projects in the field of quantum technologies for the period 2019–2024 for a total of $218 million USD, including the *Lawrence Berkeley National Laboratory (LBNL/Berkeley Lab)* project to create a special test laboratory (*Advanced Quantum Testbed, AQT*).[11] At the same time, the Lincoln Laboratory from the Massachusetts Institute of Technology (*MIT-Lincoln Laboratory, MIT-LL*) was involved in developing a program and testing methods for various architectures of quantum computers.[12]

Also in 2018, another important US bill was passed *"The Quantum Computing Research Act of 2018 (Quantum Computing Research Act of 2018),"*[13] which was aimed at supporting scientific and technical research in the interests of the US Department of Defense.

In 2019, the Deputy Secretary of Defense of the United States for Scientific Work (Under Secretary of Defense for Research and Engineering)[14]

---

[9] https://www.nsf.gov/awardsearch/showAward?AWD_ID=1818914#:~:text=The%20 Software%2DTailored%20Architecture%20for,advantage%20over%20current%20 computer%20technology

[10] https://www.nsf.gov/pubs/2018/nsf18578/nsf18578.htm#:~:text=The%20new%20 program%20of%20Enabling,of%20quantum%20materials%20and%20devices

[11] https://aqt.lbl.gov/

[12] https://www.ll.mit.edu/

[13] https://www.congress.gov/115/bills/s2998/BILLS-115s2998is.pdf

[14] https://www.cto.mil/

has prepared the *Prospective R&D Plan* (for the period 2019–2025) in the following areas:

- creation of new images of weapons and equipment based on quantum technologies (Q);

- development of promising models and methods for collecting and processing big data (Big Data) based on quantum technologies (Q), artificial intelligence (AI), and machine learning (ML) methods (national security data sets);

- development of quantum algorithms for solving military-technical problems of analysis and synthesis (including cryptanalysis);

- creation of trusted quantum communication systems, including the development of an appropriate component base and communication protocols;

- development of quantum computers with 100 or more logical qubits;

- development of mathematical and programming software for quantum computers;

- development of promising architectures of quantum systems and networks for performing quantum computing;

- development of models and methods of quantum cryptography, etc.

From 2019, the US defense budget in the R&D section provides annual funding for fundamental and applied research in the field of quantum technologies. For example, the ground forces (program element 0601102A) and the US Navy (program element 0601153N) receive $5 million each year for relevant research. It is interesting that within the framework of the defense budget under the article "Advanced Simulation and Computing,"[15] more than $700 million is reserved for the US Department of Energy annually, which significantly exceeds the Pentagon's "quantum" budget. This is due to the fundamental nature of the proposed exploratory research in the field of quantum technologies.

Note that the number of Interdisciplinary University Research Initiative (MURI) for the needs of the US Department of Defense has grown from 12 projects in 2016 to 60 projects in 2021. One of such projects is an interdisciplinary university project to create a prototype of a scalable quantum network

---

[15] https://www.lanl.gov/projects/advanced-simulation-computing /

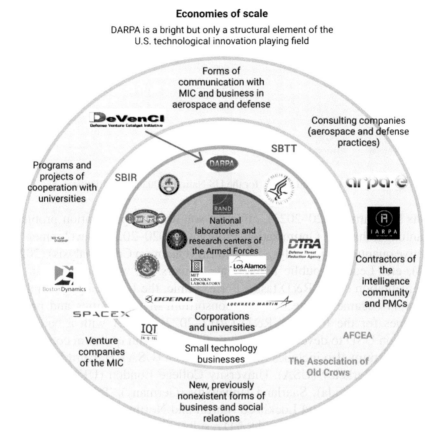

Figure 1.4 The role and place of DARPA and IARPA in the implementation of the US National Quantum Initiative (2018).

and quantum memory (Tri-Service Quantum Science and Engineering Program, QSEP).[16]

Additionally, the leading American Advanced Research Agencies for the Intelligence Community (IARPA)[17] and for the US Defense agencies (DARPA)[18] (Figure 1.4) have put a number of dual-use R&D, including R&D in order to overcome the limitations of known quantum systems (Logical

---

[16] https://research.uga.edu/team-pre-seeds/projects/quantum-science-and-engineering-program/

[17] https://www.iarpa.gov/

[18] https://www.darpa.mil/

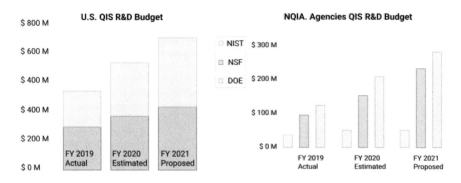

Figure 1.5   Budget line for the US National Quantum Initiative.

Qubits Program) (2020–2023); effective solution of optimization problems (Quantum Enhanced Optimization Program) (2020–2023); development of effective quantum cryptanalysis algorithms (Quantum Cryptanalysis) (2021–2024), etc. Leading public and private universities were involved in the implementation of the R&D tasks. For example, the University of Southern California became the head in the consortium of universities and private companies for the five-year R&D (2017–2022) IARPA with a budget of $45 million USD to develop the world's first 100-qubit quantum computer.[19] This consortium also includes: MIT-LL, Caltech (USA), Harvard University (USA), UC Berkeley (USA), University College London (UK), University of Waterloo (Canada), Saarland University (Germany), Tokyo Institute of Technology (Japan), and Lockheed Martin and Northrop Grumman (USA). The acceptance of the mentioned R&D results will be carried out by representatives of the NASA's Ames Research Center and Texas A&M University.[20]

In 2021, the budget of the National Quantum Initiative Supplement to the President's FY 2021 Budget was revised upwards[21] (Figure 1.5). The total budget for the implementation of the US National Quantum Initiative exceeded $2.5 billion USD. In 2022, the budget of the US National Quantum Initiative was also increased.[22]

At the same time, $50 million USD were directed to the development of the new quantum algorithms (including quantum cryptanalysis algorithms) in the interests of the intelligence community and the defense structures of the

---

[19] https://viterbischool.usc.edu/news/2017/06/usc-lead-iarpa-quantum-computing-project/
[20] https://viterbischool.usc.edu/news/2017/06/usc-lead-iarpa-quantum-computing-project/
[21] https://www.quantum.gov/wp-content/uploads/2021/01/NQI-Annual-Report-FY2021.pdf
[22] https://www.quantum.gov/wp-content/uploads/2021/12/NQI-Annual-Report-FY2022.pdf

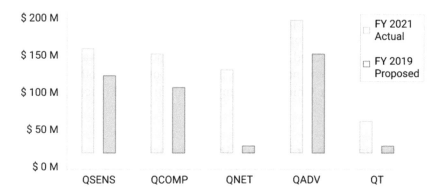

Figure 1.6 The priority of the development of quantum algorithms in the interests of the US Department of Defense.

United States and NATO (Figure 1.6) [1–4, 8, 10–13, 18–23, 25, 26, 30–37, 40, 42–54, 57, 65–70, 81–108, 169].

- Therefore, starting in 2018, research and development in the field of quantum technologies in the United States are under the close attention of government and military structures. A strategically important task has been set to retain technological leadership in this area in the medium and long term.

- Large public investments in the development of quantum technologies in the United States (more than $2.5 billion) are explained by the strategic importance of these technologies for ensuring national security, including in the information sphere.

- The implementation of this task is also facilitated by private investments from the largest American manufacturers and service providers in information technology, including *Amazon*,[23] *Google*,[24] *IBM*,[25] *Intel*,[26] and *Microsoft*.[27] Other companies, for example, *SpaceX*,[28] *Lockheed*

---

[23] https://aws.amazon.com/ru/quantum-solutions-lab /
[24] https://www.theverge.com/2021/5/19/22443453/google-quantum-computer-2029-decade-commercial-useful-qubits-quantum-transistor
[25] https://quantum-computing.ibm.com/lab
[26] https://www.intel.com/content/www/us/en/research/quantum-computing.html
[27] https://azure.microsoft.com/en-us/solutions/quantum-computing /
[28] https://seekingalpha.com/news/3645454-spacex-aiming-for-quantum-computing-breakthrough-morgan-stanley

Martin,[29] and *Boeing*[30] quantum technologies are already being applied in practice to solve specific technological problems. In total, the investments of private companies in the United States on quantum technologies approached $1 billion. At the same time, private investment continues to grow not only in the USA but also in other countries, for example, in China, Germany, Great Britain, France, Japan, and Singapore.[31,32]

1.2 The Available Scientific Groundwork

In quantum cryptology, consisting of quantum cryptography and cryptanalysis, the following main technologies are distinguished:

- quantum super-dense encoding of information using "entangled" and "hyper-entangled" particles (one quantum bit (qubit) can carry up to two ordinary bits), which increases the bandwidth of the quantum communication channel;

- coding methods and algorithms in quantum information transmission systems;

- quantum key distribution (QKD) and quantum encryption in fiber-optic communication channels and in open space;

- quantum hashing and quantum digital signature;

- quantum cryptanalysis.

The main stages of the formation of a scientific foundation for solving practical problems of cryptography and cryptanalysis are presented in Table 1.2 [4, 8–13, 21–27, 32–38, 42–46, 57, 61–68, 71–80, 82–93, 97–108].

---

[29] https://www.lockheedmartin.com/en-us/news/features/2017/quantum-computing-spot-checking-millions-lines-code.html

[30] https://boeing.mediaroom.com/2018-10-17-Boeing-Launches-New-Organization-to-Unleash-the-Power-of-Advanced-Computing-and-Networks-in-Aerospace

[31] https://finance.yahoo.com/news/10-biggest-quant-funds-world-233332516.html?guccounter=1&guce_referrer=aHR0cHM6Ly93d3cuZ29vZ2xlLmN-vbS8&guce_referrer_sig=AQAAAFrEQR902AUnjtjqeUzywqouflwv0lo_MmSEX7iq4zVu5YZYHcvQZHMAsaUEjAIrSxt9VNh9B7Wr1fWCXihGDnMzQ5EWr3mL3yHk1LKbS89i92PN1ydesNGqSm0UZaIUPtF4lnCG34J16dIRO8oGNIr00cgEHQ_YbwpoR6qA8lSy

[32] https://www.reuters.com/markets/deals/saudi-telecom-sets-up-new-entity-data-centres-cable-assets-2022-02-02/

Table 1.2   The main stages of the formation of a scientific foundation for solving practical problems of cryptography and cryptanalysis.

Discovery or hypothesis	The meaning of discovery or hypothesis	Year and author of the discovery
Geizenberg indeterminacy principle	One of the cornerstones of physical quantum mechanics is a consequence of the principle of corpuscular-wave dualism. It establishes a limit to the accuracy of simultaneous determination of a pair of quantum observables characterizing a system. In other words, the more accurate is a measurement of one characteristic of a particle, the less accurate is a measurement of the second one can be measured	Discovered in 1927 by the German theoretical physicist Werner Heisenberg (1901–1976), one of the founders of quantum mechanics, winner of the Nobel Prize in Physics (1932).
Einstein–Podolsky–Rosen paradox	According to Heisenberg's principle, it is not possible to accurately measure the coordinate of a particle and its momentum at the same time. Based on the assumption that the cause of uncertainty is that the measurement of one quantity introduces a fundamentally unrecoverable perturbation to the state and produces a distortion of the value of the other quantity, a hypothetical way was proposed by which the uncertainty ratio can be circumvented. It points to the incompleteness of quantum mechanics.	In 1935, one of the founders of quantum theory, Albert Einstein (1879–1955), together with the American physicist of Russian origin Boris Podolsky (1896–1966) and American–Israeli physicist Nathan Rosen (1909–1995) in the article "Can the quantum-mechanical description of physical reality complete?" outlined a thought experiment, which was later called the Einstein–Podolsky–Rosen paradox (EPR).

Table 1.2 Continued

Discovery or hypothesis	The meaning of discovery or hypothesis	Year and author of the discovery
Bell theorem	It shows that regardless of real presence in quantum-mechanical theory of some hidden parameters, influencing any physical characteristic of a quantum particle, it is possible to conduct a serial experiment, statistical results of which will confirm or refute presence of such hidden parameters in quantum-mechanical theory.	In 1964, the Irish physicist John Stuart Bell (1928–1990) formulated and proved the inequalities that later became known as Bell's theorem. As a result, the theoretical basis for experimental investigations of the EPR paradox was laid.
The birth of quantum information theory	Section of mathematics, studying general laws of information transmission, storage, and transformation in systems subject to laws of quantum mechanics.	Quantum theory of information as an independent scientific discipline was formed in 1990s. It is based on the basics of classical information theory by a famous mathematician Claude Elwood Shannon (1916–2001) and on potential noise resistance theory by an outstanding Soviet mathematician V. A. Kotelnikov (1908–2005).
Functional architecture and construction principles of a quantum computer	Today are known quantum computers D-Wave Systems, which, since 2007, has demonstrated a number of prototypes of adiabatic type, IBM, HP, Google, etc., as well as domestic samples Rosatom, VNIIA named Durov, etc.	The idea for a quantum computer belongs to the brilliant physicist, Nobel laureate Richard Feynman.
Shor's algorithm for factorization of integers that are the product of two prime odd numbers	It solves the problem in polynomial time and on polynomial number of qubits, while the best classical algorithms solve it in superpolynomial (subexponential) time. This means that as soon as a quantum computer with enough qubits is created, all modern cryptographies will be at risk of being compromised.	Developed in 1994 by the famous mathematician Peter Shor (born in 1959). In 2001, the efficiency of Shor's algorithm was demonstrated by a group of IBM specialists (number 15 was divided into multiples 3 and 5 by means of a quantum computer with 7 qubits).

		In 2016, a group of scientists from the Massachusetts Institute of Technology and the University of Innsbruck designed a quantum computer that implements a scalable version of the Shor algorithm proposed by Russian physicist Alexei Yurievich Kitaev (born in 1963), which reduces the number of qubits used to perform the operation.
Grover's algorithm	The algorithm uses the property of quantum interference to solve the problem of finding the value of a certain parameter on which a given function produces a certain result. It has been proven that a better result cannot be achieved within the framework of the quantum computing model (in more particular algorithms, such as Shor, this is possible).	Developed in 1996 by Indo-American mathematician Lov Kumar Grover (born in 1961)
Quantum error correction (QEC)	Protection of quantum computing from errors due to decoherence and other quantum noise. It is a quantum analogue of error correction in classical computer science.	The development of the theory of error-correcting quantum codes was started by Peter Shor in 1995 and then developed by many authors (M. Nielsen, I. Chang (2006), J. Preskill (2011), and others).
Criteria Di Vincenzo	Requirements that must be met to build a useful quantum computer	First described by the famous physicist DiVincenzo (Director of the Institute for Theoretical Nanoelectronics (Julich, Germany) in his article "Topics in Quantum Computing" (1996))

Numerical field sieve method (best known classic algorythm)

$$L_{clas} \approx exp\left(\left(\frac{64}{9}\right)^{\frac{1}{3}} n^{\frac{1}{3}}(ln(n))^{\frac{2}{3}}\right)$$

$$L_{quant} \approx n^2 \, ln(n) \, ln \, (ln(n))$$

n -number of binary digits

k - number of decimal places

n= k ln (10)

Shor algorithm (1994)

Classic exascale computer (10^{18} op/sec) vs. megahertz quantum computer (1 million op/sec).			
k – number of decimal digits	k = 250	k = 500	k = 1000
Labor intensity of classic algorithm	200 hours	5 million years	4×10^{17} years
Labor intensity of quantum algorithm	4 seconds	18 seconds	84 seconds

Figure 1.7   Estimation of the complexity of decomposing a large integer into prime factors.

In quantum cryptanalysis challenges, Shor's algorithm provides *exponential acceleration* of solving factorization problems, discrete logarithm problem (DLP), and elliptic curve discrete logarithm problems (ECDLP), widely used in cryptographic applications in cyberspace [1, 2, 17, 30, 33, 48, 81, 85, 106, 168]. Therefore, the well-known safest protocols TLS, SSH, IPsec, etc., rely on Diffie–Hellman key agreements (which depend on the strength of DLP or ECDLP), digital signatures (DSA, ECDSA or RSA-PSS), or public key encryption (El Gamal or RSA-OAEP). Thus, Shor's algorithm potentially violates all these algorithms, and with them, all the mechanisms of public key cryptography deployed in cyberspace (Figure 1.7).

On the other hand, to implement Shor's algorithm for decomposing a 2048-bit number, it will take more than 4000 stable qubits and billions of logic gates. Since the duration of such a calculation will be much longer than the time during which the qubits can remain stable (coherence time), other methods are required to maintain the information in the qubit. These methods, such as quantum error correction, are not yet feasible with the current capabilities of quantum computers. Consequently, even the most optimistic forecasts estimate a period of 5–10 years before the first demonstration of the Shor algorithm on a 2048-bit number.

The main quantum algorithms for solving cryptanalysis problems are presented in Table 1.3.

In general, all known quantum algorithms can be divided into two groups: providing *exponential gain* (for example, Shor's algorithm) and

Table 1.3 Basic quantum algorithms for solving cryptanalysis problems.

Full enumeration of keys of encryption algorithms	Grover's algorithm
Slide attack, discrimination method for CBC-MAZ, PMAC, GMAC, GCM, OCB modes, Feistel networks, and connected keys	Saimon's algorithm
Determination of the key of the Evan–Mansour scheme, FX – constructions, generalized Feistel networks	Combination of Grover's and Simon's algorithms
Matching "Meet-in-the-Middle" method	Random walks, a combination of Grover's and Simon's algorithm
Factorization and discrete logarithm	Shor's algorithm and Ecker's algorithm
Search for linear and difference ratios, key recovery by difference ratio	Bernstein–Wazirani, Simon, and Grover algorithm
Special methods	Grover's algorithm
Collision search and multicollisions	Random walks, Grover, and others
Linear simultaneous equation solutions, AES algebraic attack, Trivium, SHA-3, and MPKC	Harrow, Hassidim, and Lloyd

providing *quadratic gain* (for example, Grover's algorithm) [8, 18, 21, 33, 85, 94, 98, 106]. Due to the fact that the class of problems solved by quantum algorithms in polynomial time has not yet been significantly expanded, much attention is paid to cryptanalysis, based on the Shor algorithm (Figure 1.8) and other polynomial algorithms in order to identify the generality and the most important properties of these algorithms, as well as the corresponding tasks that achieve polynomial.

For example, Table 1.4 shows the current results on the factorization of numbers used as a public key in the most common RSA public key cryptosystem [15, 27–29, 42–47, 96]. The results of factorization achieved at the same time on classical computers are also presented for comparison.

Figure 1.9 shows graphs of extrapolating functions, constructed from the second and third columns of this table (on the *X*-axis – the year and on the *Y*-axis – the number of bits in RSA numbers factorized by a quantum computer (blue) and a classical computer (orange)). If current trends continue, by 2024, quantum computers will surpass classical RSA cryptanalysis tasks, and by 2025, they will be able to effectively crack RSA with the minimum recommended key length of 2048 bits by international standards.

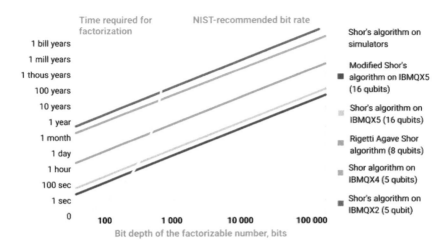

Figure 1.8 The relevance of the software-technical implementation of the Shor quantum algorithm for opening asymmetric encryption schemes.

Table 1.4 The main current results of factorization of numbers used as a public key in the RSA public key cryptosystem.

Year	Number (Q-computer)	Number (classical computer)
2012	143 (8 bit)	RSA-768 (768 bit)
2014	56,135 (16 bit)	-//-
2016	200,099 (18 bit)	-//-
2019	291,311 (18 bit)	RSA-240 (795 bit)
2020	1,099,551,473,989 (41 bit)	RSA-250 (829 bit)

Today, it can be argued that a number of modern algorithms in the field of algebraic geometry and algebraic number theory can be transformed into effective quantum algorithms. For example, the above-mentioned decomposition into prime factors of an integer can be performed exponentially faster than a classical one by a quantum computer. In terms of cryptographic applications, the studies on the evaluation of the complexity of the quantum *algorithm of the discrete logarithm of Shor* for the case of a group of points of an elliptic curve defined over a finite simple field [85, 106].

Many potential applications have a *quantum search algorithm*. Therefore, it can be used to find statistics (for example, the smallest element) in an unordered data set faster than on a classical computer. It can be used to speed up algorithms for solving some problems of the *NP* class – the ones for which a better algorithm than a direct search is unknown. Finally, its

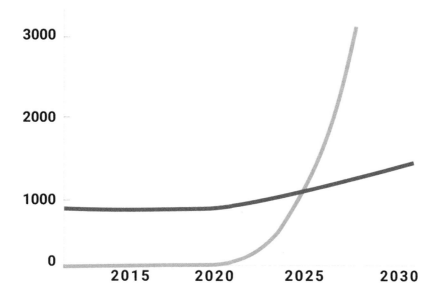

Figure 1.9 Extrapolation of RSA number factorization capabilities.

application makes it possible to speed up the key search for such cryptosystems as the widely known *DES* algorithm [31, 33, 42-45, 80].

The quantum Fourier transformation also has many interesting applications. With its help, you can solve the problems of calculating the discrete logarithm and factorization. This, in turn, allows "cracking" many of the most popular cryptosystems, including *RSA*, using a quantum computer.

Thus, *Grover's algorithm* is a search algorithm in an unsorted list that can be applied to many types of computational problems [3, 18, 33, 98]. The downside of this algorithm is that it offers more limited acceleration than, for example, *Shor's algorithm*. The results of this algorithm are not expected to be as impressive as other algorithms, but, nevertheless, they are also important for some applications.

The *quantum enumeration algorithm* is also interesting. This algorithm is a combination of quantum search and Fourier transformation, and it can be used to estimate the number of solutions to the search problem faster than possible in the case of using a classical computer [31, 33, 42–45, 80].

Note that only specific algorithms are subject to the quantum threat and not encryption in general. According to the reports of the American National Institute of Standards (NIST) of the crypto algorithms used in the USA and

NATO countries, *AES, SHA-2, SHA-3, RSA, ECDSA, ECDH, and DSA are subject to quantum threat.* And even in such a situation, the prospect of decrypting the intercepted data by experts is estimated for years. Experts say that there is a one-in-seven probability that the algorithm with the public key will be decrypted by 2025 and fifty-fifty that by 2030.

Other promising areas of research in the field of quantum cryptography are [24, 40, 41, 49–53, 80, 114, 115, 125–165]:

• quantum encryption;

• quantum authentication;

• quantum intractability (non-malleability);

• quantum fully homomorphic encryption;

• secure multi-sided quantum computing;

• functional quantum encryption;

• quantum machine learning;

• quantum generation of random numbers, etc.

Quantum computers (Table 1.5) allow performing the calculations at completely different speeds than modern computing technology, which makes the task of decrypting encrypted text quite real. For data requiring confidentiality for a period of 10 years or more, the issue of choosing the right cryptography is most acute and quantum computers can become a very real threat to such data, which we need to prepare for now.

In terms of quantum computing, all cryptography can be conditionally divided into *quantum-secure and quantum-insecure*. The *first* category includes many symmetric algorithms (including *AES* and *GOST R 34.12-2015*) but with at least twice the length of the key (which length will be sufficient is still unknown). However, crypto algorithms, based on the complexity of factorization of integers (for example, *RSA*) or discrete logarithm (for example, *El Gamal* or elliptic curves) are not quantum-safe (Table 1.6). These include modern asymmetric cryptographic algorithms. They use integer factorization tasks to generate public and private keys, which are difficult to overcome with current computing power.

Also, advances in quantum computing and quantum cryptanalysis may become significant for the security of blockchain platforms (Table 1.7), which are widely used in the world. For example, Bitcoin uses cryptographic algorithms to create a pair of public and private keys and an address that is obtained using hashing operations and a checksum of the public key.

Table 1.5 The most common models of quantum computers, 2021.

Company	Type	Technology	Now	Next goal
D-Wave	Annealing	Superconducting	2048	5000
Fujitsu	Digital Annealer	Classical	1024	8192
Google	Gate	Superconducting	72	TBD
IBM	Gate	Superconducting	50	TBD
Intel	Gate	Superconducting	49	TBD
University of Wisconsin	Gate	Neutral atoms	49	TBD
Intel	Gate	Spin	26	TBD
IQOQI	Gate	Ion trap	20	TBD
Rigetti	Gate	Superconducting	19	128
IonQ	Gate	Ion trap	11	79
USTC(China)	Gate	Superconducting	10	20
NTT/Japan NII	Qtm Neural Network	Photonic	2048	>20,000
University of Maryland/NIST	Quantum Simulator	Ion trap	53	TBD
Harvard/MIT	Quantum Simulator	Rydberg atoms	51	TBD
Huawei-HiQ Cloud	Software simulator	Classical	42-169	N/A
Alibaba/Univ. Michigan	Software simulator	Classical	144	N/A
USTC/Origin QC	Software simulator	Classical	64	N/A
University of Melbourne	Software simulator	Classical	60	N/A
IBM Research	Software simulator	Classical	56	N/A
ETH Zurich	Software simulator	Classical	45	N/A
Intel-qHipster	Software simulator	Classical	43	N/A
Atos	Software simulator	Classical	41	N/A
Microsoft-Azure	Software simulator	Classical	40	N/A
Rigetti-Forest	Software simulator	Classical	36	N/A
Microsoft-PC	Software simulator	Classical	30	N/A
iARPA QEO	Annealing	Superconducting	N/A	100
NSF STAQ Pro	Gate	Ion trap	N/A	>64
Silicon	Gate	Spin	N/A	10
CEA-Leti/INAC	Gate	Spin	N/A	100

Table 1.6   Estimates of the cryptographic strength of the most common crypto algorithms in the USA and EU countries.

Cryptoscheme	Key size, bit	Effective durability, bit	Required number of logical qubits	Required number of physical qubits	Time estimation
AES	128	128	2953	4.61×10^6	2.61×10^{12} years
	192	192	4449	1.68×10^7	1.97×10^{22} years
	256	256	6681	3.36×10^7	2.29×10^{32} years
RSA	1024	80	2290	2.56×10^6	3.58 hours
	2048	112	4338	6.2×10^6	28.63 hours
	4096	128	8434	1.47×10^7	229 hours
ECDLP	256	128	2330	3.21×10^6	10.5 hours
(NIST P-256	386	192	3484	5.01×10^6	37.67 hours
NIST P-386	512	256	4719	7.81×10^6	95 hours
NIST P-521)					
SHA256	N/A	72	2403	2.23×10^6	1.8×10^4 years

Table 1.7   List of potentially vulnerable blockchain systems.

Blockchain	Subgroup finding algorithm (Shor's)	Amplitude Amplification (Grover's)
Bitcoin	X	–
Ethereum	X	–
Litecoin	X	–
Monero	X	V
ZCash	X	–

Disclosure of the address alone is not a big risk. However, disclosure of the address and the public key used in the transaction is potentially dangerous because if there is sufficient progress in quantum computing, it will allow obtaining a private key.

Therefore, the number of countries, mainly the USA and the European Union, already plan to switch to stable quantum cryptography.[33] The mentioned NIST is now developing the quantum cryptography standards, and the NSA recommends its suppliers to implement SHA-384 instead of SHA-256.

In 2017, NIST organized an open competition[34] to create new post-quantum standards for asymmetric encryption (*public key encryption*) and digital signatures (*digital signatures*). Sixty-nine development teams from all over the world took part in the competition. On July 22, 2020, seven main candidates, four for asymmetric encryption and three for digital signature, made it to the final of the mentioned competition.[35]

The main candidates for new post-quantum standards for public key encryption/KEMs are:

- *Classic McEliece* – based on error correcting codes. The basic design of the scheme was proposed back in 1979 and has been well studied. It has small ciphertext sizes, but a very large key size. Because of this, it has the same problems as Rainbow and is recommended for use only for specific tasks.

- *CRYSTALS-KYBER* – on lattices. Cryptanalysis is reduced to solving the Module-LWE problem. The Fujisaki–Okamoto transformation is used to ensure resistance to attacks with adaptively selected ciphertexts. It has good performance and security, but NIST also reminds that Module-LWE is a relatively little-studied problem and requires more detailed cryptanalysis.

- *NTRU* – on lattices. The NTRUEncryt scheme, proposed more than 20 years ago, is taken as a basis. The problem of NTRU, unlike Module-LWE (and other modifications), has been very well studied, which is a very important factor.

- *SABER* – on lattices. Cryptanalysis diluted into an MLWR problem (Module-LWE, where rounding by a smaller module is used instead of

[33] https://nvlpubs.nist.gov/nistpubs/specialpublications/nist.sp.800-175b.pdf
[34] https://csrc.nist.gov/Projects/post-quantum-cryptography/post-quantum-cryptography-standardization/Call-for-Proposals
[35] https://csrc.nist.gov/News/2020/pqc-third-round-candidate-announcement

addition with an error vector). The Fujisaki–Okamoto transformation is used, as in CRYSTALS-KYBER.

At the same time, NIST stated that only one of the lattice circuits (CRYSTALS-KYBER, NTRU, and SABER) will be standardized.

The main candidates for the new post-quantum digital signature standard (Digital Signatures) are:

CRYSTALS-DILITHIUM – on lattices. The Fiat-Shamir circuit with interruptions is taken as a basis. Cryptanalysis is reduced to solving the Module-LWE and Module-SIS problems. It has good performance and can be effectively implemented on low-resource devices. NIST asked the authors to add a set of system-wide parameters for level-5 security.

FALCON – on lattices. But the GPV framework is taken as a basis. Cryptanalysis is reduced to the SIS problem on NTRU lattices. The main disadvantage of this scheme is a complex software and hardware implementation. The scheme uses calculations over floating-point numbers, which greatly complicates both the analysis of resistance to attacks through third-party channels, and implementation for low-resource devices.

Rainbow is based on multivariate transformations. The UOV scheme is taken as a basis. The main advantage is the size of the digital signature. But due to the large size of the key, it is recommended to use this scheme only for specific tasks where the size of the keys is not critical.

According to *NIST*, one of the *CRYSTALS-DILITHIUM and FALCON* schemes will be standardized. The *Rainbow* cryptosystem will be recommended for more specific tasks.

Eight alternative candidates for new post-quantum standards were also selected, *five* candidates for public key encryption/KEMs – BIKE, FrodoKEM, HQC, NTRU Prime, and SIKE, and *three* candidates for digital signatures – GeMSS, Picnic, and SPHINCS+.

Thus, NIST experts identified *seven main and eight alternative algorithms* out of 69 candidate algorithms submitted by development groups from different countries, including international ones, which could potentially be standardized. Based on the experience of similar contests held by NIST earlier on the choice of a block cipher (AES) and hashing function (SHA-3), the process of standardization of quantum-stable algorithms may be completed by 2023.

Thus, post-quantum cryptography involves the introduction of new encryption algorithms (Figures 1.10–1.15 and Table 1.8), which are difficult to crack by both classical and quantum computers. These can be both new and previously known algorithms, the use of which was limited due to the

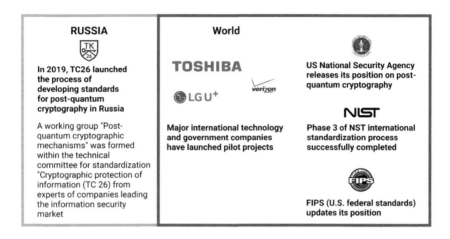

Figure 1.10   The first pilot solutions of post-quantum cryptography.

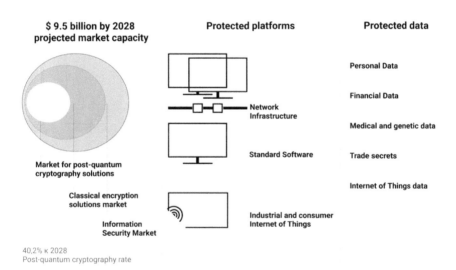

Figure 1.11   Evaluation of the post-quantum cryptography market.

increased resource intensity of calculations. Here, post-quantum cryptography is the answer to quantum challenges. The main efforts in this area are focused on the tasks of synthesizing cryptographic algorithms and protocols resistant to the capabilities of quantum computers. At the same time, there are four main areas of research:

• cryptography on integer lattices;

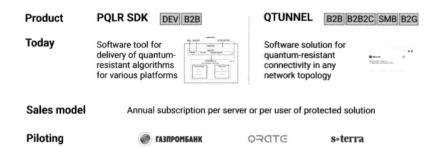

Figure 1.12   Possible solutions to post-quantum cryptography, Qapp.tech.

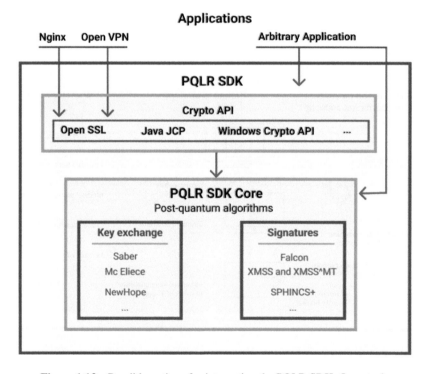

Figure 1.13   Possible options for integrating the PQLR SDK, Qapp.tech.

- Merkle's electronic signature scheme;
- quantum electronic signature scheme;
- authentication of quantum information.

It should be noted that most modern publications are devoted to the creation of cryptographic systems with a public key and electronic signature

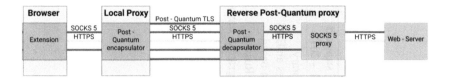

Figure 1.14 How Qtunnel and Qapp.tech work.

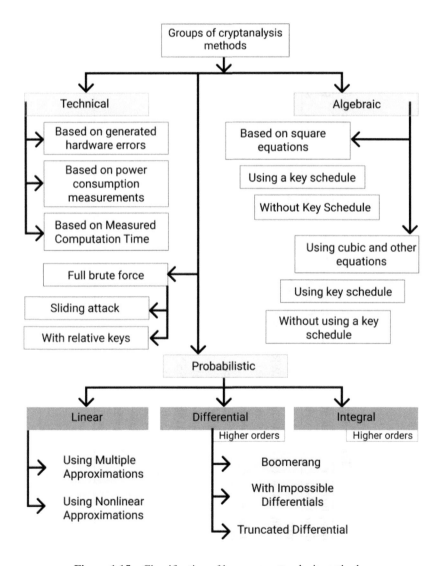

Figure 1.15 Classification of known cryptanalysis methods.

Table 1.8   PQLR SDK – a library of quantum-stable algorithms integrated with OpenSSL and Qapp.tech.

Cross-platform and portability	Quantum resistant algorithms inside	Integration with OpenSSL	Ease of operation	Reliability and security	GOST support P34.11 – 2012
Linux On x86 –64, ARM v7	**Saber** (Module – LWR based key exchange)	**OpenSSL** 1.0.2	The library is written in C	Theoretical validation	Our library includes an EDS version based on the Russian
Windows 2012+, on x86 –64	**Falcon** (Lattice-based)	1.1.0 1.1.1	**No dependencies** The code is well documented	Implementation testing	cryptographic **hash function GOST** P34.11 – 2012
Android ARM v7	MC Ellece (Code-based)	**TLS** 1.3		Updates are released 1–2 times a month	**"Stribot"**
X86 ARM	**XMSS/XMSS^MT** (Hash-based)	1.2 KEM			
	SPHINCS+ (Hash-based)	Digital signatures			
	NewHope (Lattice-based)				

schemes. At the same time, the post-quantum protocols of interactive authentication, voting, electronic payments, etc., have not been sufficiently studied.

The emergence and rapid expansion of the research, united by the concept of "post-quantum cryptography" [144–165], testifies to the serious attitude of the cryptographic world to the problems that the implementation of quantum algorithms entails and makes it advisable to continue research on both quantum cryptanalysis and quantum cryptosynthesis. Also, an equally important issue from the point of view of ensuring information security is the development of the architecture and functionality of classical computers that ensure the operation of quantum computers. The fact is that the modern fleet of quantum computers is small, and individual prototypes of quantum computers are quite expensive (more than \$15 million). At the same time, modeling of quantum algorithms on quantum circuits is available on simulators using appropriate libraries and software packages. This makes it possible to investigate the necessary quantum algorithms and then transfer the simulation results to real quantum computers. There are also quantum algorithms in which the so-called "oracle" can be calculated in advance on a classical computer and then use it to solve more complex problems in a quantum model. At the same time, the main problem of modeling a quantum algorithm on a classical computer is that only data sets of limited dimensions can be used for work. The difficulty of modeling medium and large quantum circuits on classical computers is due to the fact that the number of complex numbers required to describe a quantum circuit increases exponentially with increasing system size, and not linearly, as for classical systems.

It should be noted that currently most quantum systems are closed. Therefore, the issues of ensuring information security at the stages of modeling and programming quantum algorithms are still theoretical issues. Also, it is necessary to take into account the features of the quantum key distribution (the collapse of the wave function after measuring its state, the inability to determine the wave function by other means, measuring the wave amplitude (probability), which significantly complicate debugging quantum programs after the fact to detect and neutralize possible vulnerabilities). Also, classical monitoring and logging operations of computing systems are significantly limited and/or even impossible here. Here, simulators partially eliminate this drawback, but the limited capabilities of a classic computer do not allow a full simulation.

1.3 Limiting Possibilities of Cryptanalysis Methods

- In cryptanalysis, the following three groups of methods are better known today: linear, differential, and integral cryptanalysis (Figure 1.15) [15, 22, 27–29, 42–48, 68–70, 80, 83, 118].

The operation principle of probabilistic methods of linear, differential, and integral cryptanalysis is constructing some statistical cyclic pattern of the encryption block under study (BS), reflecting one of the sides of the algorithm behavior (nonlinearity, differential homogeneity, etc.) with the subsequent extension of this pattern to as many rounds as possible – that is, the construction of some statistical model of the entire BS. The main disadvantage of these methods is the exponential dependence of the attack complexity on the number of cycles; so the number of resources required for its implementation quickly becomes practically inaccessible.

Algebraic methods of cryptanalysis are also used; they are considered promising in terms of implementing crypto attacks. Theoretically, they determine the secret key by analyzing one or two plaintext–ciphertext pairs. The essence of these methods is constructing a super-defined sparse system of nonlinear (square) equations describing the behavior of the algorithm, the solution of which gives the secret key used in encryption. The principal feature of these methods is that their complexity subexponentially increases together with the number of rounds, and this allows cryptanalysis of ciphers without reducing the number of rounds, as it was often done in classical probabilistic methods, and this increases the practical applicability of these methods.

Note that the methods of quantum cryptanalysis (Figure 1.16) are just beginning to be introduced into the practice of cryptanalysis. It is essential that on a quantum computer, it is fundamentally possible to solve complex mathematical problems with acceptable complexity and reliability. At the same time, the acceleration of the computational process in the operation of quantum devices is explained by the property of quantum parallelism. It is a fact that an elementary step in quantum computing is a unitary operation on an n-qubit superposition of a register of n-qubits. In this case, parallel processing of all 2^n possible states is performed at once. For a classic computer, such an operation requires 2^n steps.

1	- Frequency analysis
2	- Full search of keys
3	- Key generator analysis
4	- Solving factorization and discrete logarithm problems
5	- The "Meeting-in-the-middle" method

6	- Difference analysis
7	- Linear analysis
8	- Collision method
9	- Analysis by side channels
10	- Quantum analysis

A quantum computing system including 1000 efficiently used qubits is equivalent to using $2^n = 2^{1000} = 10^{301}$ bits in a classical computing system. For comparison, it should be noted that the number of elementary particles (nucleons) in the Universe is "only" about 10^{78}. Thus, a quantum register consisting of *1000* qubits, effectively used for calculations, is sufficient to solve practically significant problems.

In general, all known quantum algorithms can be divided into two groups: providing exponential gain (for example, Shor's algorithm) and providing quadratic gain (for example, Grover's algorithm). Due to the fact that the class of problems solved by quantum algorithms in polynomial time has not yet been significantly expanded, much attention is paid to cryptanalysis, based on the Shor algorithm and other polynomial algorithms in order to identify the generality and the most important properties of these algorithms, as well as the corresponding tasks that achieve polynomial (Table 1.9).

The systematization of Shor-type algorithms for algebra problems can be based on the fact that Shor's algorithm contains a fundamental core and an environment that reduces the original problem to this core. In Shor's

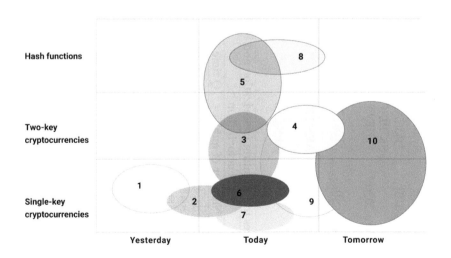

Figure 1.16 The role and place of quantum cryptanalysis methods.

Table 1.9   Evaluation of cryptographic strength of encryption algorithms.

Bits of security	Symmetric key algorithms	FFC (DSA, D-H, and MQV)	IFC (RSA)	ECC (ECDSA)
80 (before 2010)	2TDEA SKIPJACK	$L = 1024$ $N = 160$	$k = 1024$	$f = 160{-}223$
112 (before 2030)	3TDEA	$L = 2048$ $N = 224$	$k = 2048$	$f = 224{-}255$
128 (after 2030)	AES-128	$L = 3072$ $N = 256$	$k = 3072$	$f = 256{-}383$
192	AES-192	$L = 7680$ $N = 384$	$k = 7680$	$f = 384{-}511$
256	AES-256	$L = 15.360$ $N = 512$	$k = 15{,}360$	$f = 512+$

Resources for quantum factorization and ECDLP

Factorization			ECDLP			
n	Number of qubits	Q time	n	Number of qubit	Q time	Classic time
512	1024	$0.54*10^9$	110	700	$0.5*10^9$	$6.4*10^{16}$
1024	2048	$4.3*10^9$	163	1000	$1.6*10^9$	$3.0*10^{24}$
2048	4096	$34*10^9$	224	1300	$4.0*10^9$	$9.2*10^{33}$
3072	6114	$120*10^9$	256	1500	$6.0*10^9$	$6.0*10^{38}$
15360	30720	$1.5*10^{13}$	512	2800	$50*10^9$	$2.1*10^{77}$

Resources for quantum solution of the symmetric cryptosystem key search problem

k	Number of qubits	Q time	Classic time
56	56	$2.1*10^8$	$7.2*10^{16}$
80	80	$8.6*10^{11}$	$1.2*10^{24}$
112	112	$5.7*10^{16}$	$5.2*10^{33}$
128	128	$1.4*10^{19}$	$3.4*10^{38}$
168	168	$1.5*10^{25}$	$3.7*10^{50}$
256	256	$2.7*10^{38}$	$1.2*10^{77}$

algorithm, such a core is an algorithm for finding the period relative to exponentiation, namely, finding for the given mutually prime natural numbers a and q the smallest positive t such that a $t = 1 \pmod q$. Since the problem of finding the period is a special case of the hidden subgroup problem, much attention is paid by modern researchers to the study of the features of quantum algorithms for solving this problem, as well as the related graph isomorphism problem.

As a result of the analysis of the Shor and Simon algorithms, which can be reduced to the problem of a hidden subgroup, it is possible to identify their important common parts and differences. So, these algorithms use the idea of moving from a group G to some dual object, acting with it and moving back. At the same time, they use quantum *Fourier* transformation on the group *G*. The main core in these algorithms is a quantum subroutine, which, according to a given mapping of an Abelian group into a finite set, builds a special probability distribution on the group of characters of the original group. The analysis showed that three variants of quantum algorithms for the hidden subgroup problem are currently known. Two of them find the order of the maximal cyclic subgroup in the hidden factor group. The third finds the hidden subgroup itself.

Interesting results are obtained by considering the features of quantum algorithms containing various integral transformations. It is shown that some principles of constructing classical fast orthogonal transformations are useful for them. Today, recurrent structures, based on quantum gates, are known for quantum algorithms that implement the following orthogonal transformations (*Fourier*, *Walsh–Hadamard*, *Hartley*, as well as the *Wavelet and Slant transformations*).

All these transformations require for their implementation no more than $O(n^2)$ operations on a quantum computer with a quantum register of n length. The researchers also identified a number of algebra problems in which the application of the quantum *Fourier* transformation gives a significant acceleration. There are the shift problem, the hidden adjacent class problem, the character shifts problem of finite fields. The features of solutions related to the hidden subgroup problem when the initial group is not Abelian are considered [22, 42–45, 47].

In terms of cryptographic applications, the studies on the evaluation of the complexity of the quantum algorithm of the discrete logarithm of Shor for the case of a group of points of an elliptic curve defined over a finite simple field.

Today, it can be argued that a number of modern algorithms in algebraic geometry and algebraic number theory can be transformed into effective quantum algorithms. For example, quantum algorithms, based on the arithmetic properties of elliptic and hyperelliptic curves over finite fields, were considered. During the analysis of the discrete logarithm problem in *Jacobi* groups of hyperelliptic curves, a way was proposed to improve the factorization algorithm using *Jacobi* sums due to the use of a subexponential labor-intensive algorithm *Lenstra* at the stage of preliminary calculations. These results served as the basis for the assumption that iterative algorithms using elliptic integrals can also have effective quantum implementations. Recently, an analysis of the features of the implementation of iterative algorithms using elliptic integrals and the arithmetic-geometric mean method has been carried out. As a result, an effective method for constructing iterative algorithms using complete elliptic integrals was obtained for calculating the values of various algebraic functions, theta functions, and modular equations [42–45, 47].

Note that the effectiveness of quantum cryptanalysis algorithms largely depends on the level of study of the issues of creating modern *quantum computing systems* in the following areas:

- standard quantum computing systems, where the execution of computational algorithms is carried out using a universal set of quantum logic gates;

- quantum computing operations on ions and neutral atoms in traps; quantum computers on molecular clusters, quantum computing devices on *nv*-centers in diamonds; solid-state qubits on quantum dots and computing devices based on them;

- quantum computing devices based on superconducting structures (charge, phase, and hybrid qubits on contacts *josephson*);

- Non-standard quantum computing systems, where the execution of computational algorithms is carried out without a universal set of quantum logic gates): computers implementing unidirectional (*one-way*) quantum computing; topological quantum computers; adiabatic quantum processors.

1.4 The Quantum Threat of Blockchain

Quantum computing poses a certain threat (Figures 1.17 and 1.18) to many cryptographic protocols in force today. According to available forecasts and expectations, a quantum computer capable of cracking the RSA2048 cryptographic scheme will be built by 2030. Blockchain technologies rely on

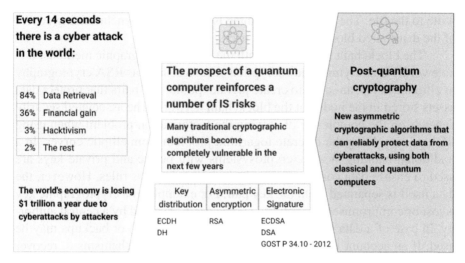

Figure 1.17   Risks of a quantum threat to blockchain systems.

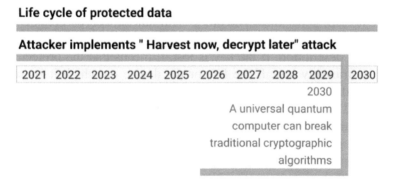

Figure 1.18 Data with a long life-cycle is more vulnerable (data interception now, delayed data hacking).

cryptographic protocols for many of their core routines. Only some of these protocols are open to quantum attacks.

Blockchain network construction technologies are one of the most popular technologies along with Big Data. Blockchain is a system of distributed registries, where data storage devices are separate and do not connect to a common server. These registries provide the ability to store an ever-increasing list of records ordered in a certain way, which are called blocks; each includes a timestamp and a link to the previous block. Data is protected and its integrity is guaranteed via encryption. The user's access to changing part of the blockchain is provided by encrypted keys; without them, it is impossible to write to the file. The integrity guarantee is achieved by synchronizing copies of the distributed blockchain for all users.

The blockchain is protected with the use of cryptographic methods. It is noteworthy that asymmetric encryption schemes, such as RSA cryptography or elliptic curves, are used to create private–public key pairs that protect data assets stored in the nodes of the blockchain network. The associated security depends on the complexity of solving the factorization problem when using RSA or on solving the discrete logarithm problem from elliptic curves. In a traditional banking system, cryptosystems with public and private keys are used to ensure data confidentiality, integrity, and access rules. However, the data itself is separated from the key pair. For example, if a cryptographic key is lost or compromised, its validity can be easily revoked by a central authority. In case of a data leak, the servers may be shut down or backups may be used. If an account is compromised, there are often mechanisms to recover that account for the rightful owner. On the contrary, there is no central authority in the blockchain system to manage user access keys. The owner of the resource is, by definition, the one who has the private encryption keys, while there are no offline backups. The blockchain object, a cryptographic system permanently located on the network, is considered a resource, or at least its authoritative description. If the key is lost, it means that the protected data asset is irretrievably lost. If the key or the device on which it is stored is compromised, or contains a vulnerability, then the data asset may be irretrievably stolen. Thus, in blockchain technologies, protected resources cannot be easily separated from the used encryption system. This makes blockchain technologies particularly vulnerable to attacks using a quantum computer.

It is impossible to predict the progress and development of future technologies with absolute accuracy. Nevertheless, it is possible to extrapolate current and past trends in the development of quantum technologies, including all important components such as the number of qubits, gate accuracy, error correction, and fault tolerance. By doing this, we can unequivocally conclude that by 2030, quantum technology is likely to be sufficiently developed to effectively crack RSA2048. This conclusion was the basis for the fact that the US National Institute of Standards and Technology (NIST) began the process of standardization and deployment of quantum-secure public key cryptography. Given the strong connection between data and cryptosystems in blockchain technologies, the potential vulnerability of these cryptosystems to quantum attacks, the emergence of capable quantum computers is likely in the medium term.

According to forecasts, the blockchain and distributed ledger technology (DLT) market will be estimated at $7.59 billion by 2024. Industries with

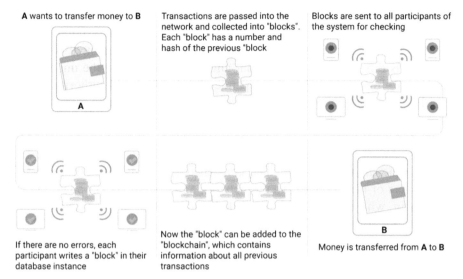

A wants to transfer money to **B**

Transactions are passed into the network and collected into "blocks". Each "block" has a number and hash of the previous "block

Blocks are sent to all participants of the system for checking

If there are no errors, each participant writes a "block" in their database instance

Now the "block" can be added to the "blockchain", which contains information about all previous transactions

Money is transferred from **A** to **B**

Figure 1.19   A typical scheme of the functioning of the blockchain.

strong use cases include finance, logistics, and legal fields. At the same time, many large global corporations join and integrate the technology: IBM, J.P. Morgan, Amazon, and Facebook are also announcing their own Libra cryptocurrency. The technology of building such networks eliminates the need for a trusted third party to ensure the transfer of data and assets. Blockchain networks are managed by independent nodes that must reach a consensus before updating the registry with newly verified transactions. There are many mechanisms that allow the network to reach consensus, the most popular is proof-of-work (PoW). This consensus mechanism and the underlying cryptographic methods make blockchain technologies vulnerable to cryptographic attacks using a quantum computer.

As a rule, the blockchain networks work by connecting blocks in chronological order (Figure 1.19). These blocks are groups of information transactions or cryptocurrencies that nodes transmit to the network. This forms an immutable series of information or a chain. Each block in the chain will contain a group of transactions and their information that has been announced on the network. This is usually done by transferring tokens (cryptocurrencies). These tokens have an intrinsic value and do not just contain information about this value, such as a bank account balance. However, unlike traditional currencies, they are not controlled by the central bank. Tokens are distributed among miners, which are the nodes, and form a group consensus and perform work on the network as a reward for good work. This work mainly consists of creating blocks in the chain, as well as verifying that the transactions are correctly formed and mathematically fair in the network, that is, not to create or destroy tokens and not to spend more than the user transferring tokens can afford. It is this group consensus that allows a network and the underlying economy to function fairly and independently of any central authority.

Blockchain technologies can be simplified to two components: a consensus protocol and a transaction mechanism. The transaction mechanism is how the authors transfer tokens and information – it requires providing a digital signature to confirm that they own the public and private keys used to create the digital signature. The consensus mechanism determines how the verifiers or mining nodes in the network agree on the next update of the blockchain, which transactions are added, and whether the transactions and the block are cryptographically and structurally valid.

PoW is the most commonly used consensus mechanism in blockchain technologies. It requires the miner to prove that he has made some effort, spending computing resources to create a new block. This mechanism was adopted by Bitcoin, forcing the miner to do some work when compiling transactions into a block, that is, to spend computational and financial resources on solving the problem. This prompts the miner to generate a valid block containing only valid transactions. This work is also easily verified by any node connected to the network. This expended energy ensures that the costs are associated with the creation of the block. Negligent or malicious miners who have spent energy on completing the PoW algorithm but have created a bad block (that includes at least one transaction that, while being included in the chain, will create an incorrect state, for example, expenses over the user's balance) will be detected by other nodes in the network. The block will be invalid, and other miners will not consider it as part of the main chain, as a result of which the miner will be in a worse financial position since he will not receive a reward for mining. This guarantees the accuracy of the information contained in the block, which is considered by the network as the head of the current longest chain (the block to which miners will try to add the next block in the chain).

The complexity of this PoW determines how quickly each block is added to the chain: if the complexity of the problem increases, then miners will need more time to solve the problem, since more work will be required to be done by mining nodes. Determining the ownership of assets in the blockchain network is comparatively more difficult compared to centrally controlled networks and financial exchanges. The owner of some tokens must be able to demonstrate that he has the ability and authority to spend tokens. In a centralized system, this is controlled by a central authority; in decentralized systems, cryptographic methods such as electronic signature schemes must be used to demonstrate ownership.

Bitcoin, first described in an article by Satoshi Nakamoto, is the most popular and the first real blockchain technology. This 2008 document paved the way for the development of the distributed registry technology space. It is based on cryptographic schemes that allow peers in the network to verify transactions in a non-trusting environment and store them in a cryptographically secure and immutable registry. These cryptographic methods are protected from attack on a classical computer, but can be used by a sufficiently powerful quantum computer. Bitcoin uses Hashcash as a POW mechanism. Hashcash was originally developed as a denial-of-service measure for email systems. This was done by requiring a potential sender to spend time solving a computationally complex problem before he could send an email. As implemented in Bitcoin, Hashcash requires a potential miner to calculate the SHA-256 hash value for the header plus some random number so that the hash value is less than a predetermined number. This number is a regulated parameter in the Bitcoin network. The smaller the number, the higher the computational complexity of the task.

Using the Hashcash mechanism as a PoW has two common effects. First, with the current parameter of high complexity, miners are interested in using specialized equipment, such as ASIC miners, or joining mining pools where work and rewards are distributed among different users. More importantly, PoW discourages attempts to add bad blocks to the network. These blocks have a very high probability of being rejected by the network due to error correction and therefore provide very high wasted losses for a potential miner. The Bitcoin transaction engine uses the ECDSA signature scheme (Figure 1.20) to confirm the authority and ownership of the tokens, as well as irrefutable evidence that the tokens were spent and that the transaction was not tampered with after the transaction was signed. The elliptical curve that Bitcoin uses for its ECDSA is called secp256-k1.

Bitcoin and its underlying cryptographic schemes are vulnerable to possible quantum attacks. One of these attacks uses Grover's search algorithm to perform SW significantly faster than classic miners. The attacker will seek to generate as many PoW as the rest of the network combined, effectively imposing consensus on any block that the attacker wishes (such an attack can be attributed to 51% attacks). Current ASIC miners are capable of performing approximately 18 TH/S. This, combined with the current size of Bitcoin networks, makes a 51% quantum attack currently unworkable.

However, the most destructive attack on the Bitcoin blockchain is related to its ECDSA scheme, namely, on transactions that have been announced on

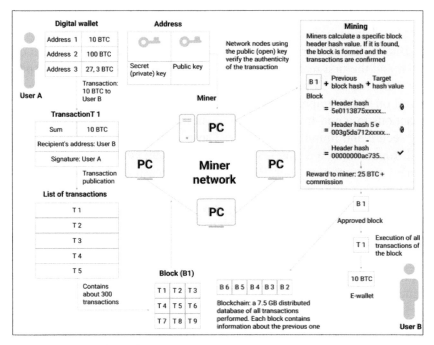

Figure 1.20   The diagram of Bitcoin blockchain.

the network and have not yet been added to the blockchain. The complexity of ECDSA depends on the complexity of the discrete logarithm problem of an elliptic curve. This problem can be solved in polynomial time. It should also be borne in mind that Bitcoin wallets, as a rule, do not reuse the same key pairs. Bitcoin transactions send the entire UTXO (withdrawal of unspent transactions). In the simplest form of a Bitcoin transaction, one UTXO will be spent on the input, and there will be two at the output. A new UTXO of the amount transferred to the corresponding account is created. If the input UTXO is greater than the output UTXO, a second UTXO is created as a change, which will be returned to the original user. This account to which the change is sent will usually be controlled by a newly generated public and private key pair. This means that an attack designed to gain access to the user's entire wallet, although possible on the Bitcoin network, is less likely due to the general security mechanism of changing the public–private key pair after each transaction.

An effective quantum attack will be to search for the private key when the public key is revealed after the broadcast of the signed transaction to the network. This allows an attacker to sign a new transaction using a private key, posing as the key owner. As long as a "quantum attacker" can guarantee that his transaction will be placed on the blockchain before a genuine transaction, he can essentially steal the transaction and forward the newly created unspent transaction output (UTXO) to any account he chooses. It can be calculated that a quantum computer with 485,550 qubits and a clock frequency of 10 GHz can solve the problem using the Shor algorithm in 30 minutes. At the same time, the average waiting time for transactions in the pool of transactions currently awaiting integration into a block in Bitcoin often exceeds 30 minutes. This makes this type of attack quite feasible. At the beginning of the Bitcoin implementation, Bitcoin users could receive payments directly to their public key (P2RK) and not to the hash of the public key, which is usually known as the user's billing address. This may have implications for older Bitcoin accounts. An example of this is the first ever Bitcoin transaction between Hal Feeney and Satoshi Nakamoto in the 170th block of the Bitcoin blockchain. This transaction form is common in early Coinbase transactions (a common platform that buys, sells, and stores cryptocurrency) used to reward Bitcoin miners. This means that some of the original accounts may have revealed their public key in the early stages of Bitcoin blockchain development. Thus, these accounts are extremely vulnerable to quantum attacks using the Shor algorithm. Unlike the ECDSA signature scheme attack, there is no time limit for performing this type of attack. As soon as a sufficiently large quantum computer appears, a quantum attacker can easily calculate the private keys of these accounts, sign new transactions on behalf of these users, and clear these accounts of all their funds.

The quantum attack threat has generated many solutions, one of which is a Bitcoin post-quantum project. This project was a hard fork (a change in the cryptocurrency protocol that is incompatible with previous versions) of the Bitcoin network with a block height of 555,000 (mined on December 22, 2018) This project uses a quantum secure digital signature scheme as well as the implementation of the Proof-of-Work mechanism using the birthday paradox. However, since this project is a fork, it does not provide any real advantages in terms of security compared to the original Bitcoin version of the chain.

A more successful example is the company quantum-resistant ledger (QRL), which appeared in 2016. In order to complicate the determination of the relationship between the public and private keys of users, they proposed to use the Winternitz one-time signature algorithm and expand it using the Merkle tree structure (XMSS - extended Merkle signature scheme).

IOTA is also a good example of how blockchain is resistant to quantum computers. According to its creators, the coin is able to effectively resist "51% attacks" involving quantum devices, thanks to the use of ternary calculations instead of binary ones, with which almost all computers work today. But here lies one of the main problems of the project because, now, IOTA is working on modern equipment, based on binary calculations, which means its code requires much more power to store the entire amount of data, resulting in bugs in Curl (IOTA hash functions).

Thus, research on the resistance of blockchain technology to quantum attacks is very relevant. Here, the most common vulnerability open to attack will be transactions that have been announced on the network but have not yet been added to the block. The most vulnerable are those accounts that revealed their public key in the early days of the Bitcoin network. Finally, the Bitcoin consensus mechanism demonstrates vulnerability to attacks based on Grover's algorithm. However, since Grover's algorithm provides only a quadratic advantage, advances in classical computer technology are likely to protect Bitcoin from this type of attack much earlier than from attacks based on Shor's algorithm. Note that since a provably secure mechanism for reaching consensus has not yet been created and most block currencies are Bitcoin "forks" with rare exceptions, they have almost the same vulnerabilities as Bitcoin.

1.5 Requirements for Quantum Cryptanalysis

As a rule, currently, the implementation of quantum algorithms on quantum circuits is carried out (modeled) (Tables 1.10–1.12 and Figure 1.21) using the following three main classes of tools (software packages).

An analysis of the capabilities of the known quantum emulators showed the following.

The *first class* includes the mathematical packages *Maple and Mathematica* general purpose, as well as libraries of *LIP, CLN, LiDIA, GMP, NTL*, etc., functions for working with arbitrary-precision arithmetic. The *second class* includes quantum computing emulators: *Quantum Development Kit (MS QDK), Quantum Computing Playground, JQuantum, QuEST, Quantum Programming Studio, Q-Kit*, etc. The *third class* contains software platforms for working with hybrid computing systems, based on prototypes of real quantum computers and emulators on classical computers: *QISKit for IBM Q* (up to 20 qubits), *Forest (pyQuil) for Rigetti* (up to 8 qubits), *ProjectQ for ETH Zurich* (up to 16 qubits), etc. We will conduct a comparative analysis of the functionality of the mentioned software packages to develop possible functional and technical requirements for promising software complexes of quantum cryptanalysis.

Table 1.10 Known integer factorization methods.

Factorization problem solution	
Method's name	**Complexity**
Ferm	$T(N) = O\left(N\frac{1}{3}\right)$
Lenster	$T = O(e^{\sqrt{2ln\,p\,ln\,ln\,p}})$
Dikson	$T = O(L(n)^2)$
Quadratic sieve	$T = O(\exp((1+o(1))\sqrt{n\log n\log N}))$
Numeric fieldsieve method	$T(N) = O(n\,log\,n\,log\,N)$
Shor's method	$T = O(log_3\,M)$
Discrete logarithm problem solution	
Method's name	**Complexity**
Adleman	$T = O(c^{ln\,p^{\frac{1}{2}}})$
COS	$T = O(\exp((1+o(1))\log p\log\log p)\frac{1}{2}))$
Numerical field sieve	$T(N) = O(n\,log\,n\,log\,N)$
Shor	$T = O(log_3\,M)$

Table 1.11 Results of comparison of mathematical software packages for modeling quantum algorithms on quantum circuits.

Estimation criteria	Solution						
	Mathematica	**LIP**	**CLN**	**LiDIA**	**GMP**	**NTL**	**CRYPTO**
Computational efficiency	–	–	–	–	+	+	+
Ability to build in Windows OS	+	+	+	–	–	+	+
Availability of algorithms for sparse matrices	–	–	–	+	+	–	+
Availability of algorithms for factorial base, sieve and multiplier decomposition	–	–	–	–	–	–	–
Convenience of positive interface	+	–	–	–	–	–	–

Table 1.12 Results of comparison of quantum computing emulators.

	QDK	QCP	JQuantum	QuEST	QPS	Quantum-Kit
Supported platforms	Windows, macOS, and Linux	Web	Windows	Windows, macOS, and Linux	Web	Windows, macOS, and Linux
Source code	(+)	(+)	(+)	(+)	(+)	(−)
Graphical application or library	Q Library#	Web application	Graphical application	Library for C++	Web application	Graphical application
Number of logical qubits	32	22	15	29	24	30
Number of gates implemented	17	21	16	29	30	21
The ability to create your own gates	(+)	(+)	(−)	(+)	(+)	(+)
Наличие внутреннего языка программирования	(+)	(+)	(+)	(+)	(+)	(−)
Documentation	(+)	(−)	(+)	(+)	(+)	(−)

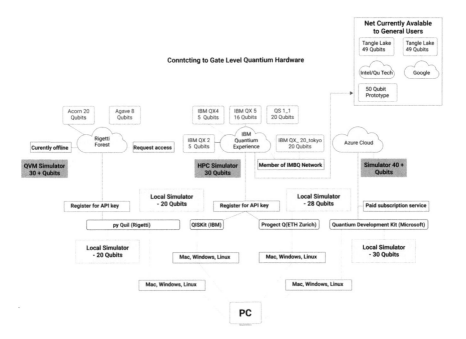

Figure 1.21 Existing ways to connect a personal computer to demonstration prototypes of real quantum computers.

First class. The mathematical packages *Maple [20] and Mathematica [21]* are characterized by the ease of use and programming of the quantum algorithms of Shor, Grover, Deutsch, etc., and also do not have built-in restrictions on the bitness of operands. However, they are platform-dependent and are characterized by low efficiency of performing number-theoretic operations. Increased efficiency will require connecting the built-in tools of a low-level programming language to develop special functions required for quantum analysis. Note that the numeric types of the programming languages C and C++ have a limited number of bits: *long* is 32 bits; *long long* is 64 bits; *double* is 53-bit mantissa; 11 bits is exponent; *long double*: depending on the language implementation, it can be defined as a *double* or *extended double*: 64 bits – mantissa; 15 – bit exponent [22].

And in the implementation of languages on the platform, .NET does not have the extended double type: it is only available implicitly when performing intermediate calculations (for example, where multiplication gives a result that goes beyond the range of double values, but subsequent division returns the intermediate result back to this range). In addition, there is a built-in 128-bit decimal data type that represents small numbers with a bit depth of up to 96 bits (in accordance with the size of the mantissa), but it is implemented in emulation mode since there is no hardware support for this type today [23].

The *Java* programming language supports the ability to work with long numbers and has portability, but its disadvantage is the low efficiency of the implementation Shor and Grover quantum algorithms, etc.

There are also a number of specialized libraries in the public domain, namely *LIP*, *CLN*, *LiDIA*, *GMP*, and *NTL*, for working with arbitrary-precise arithmetic. One of the first libraries (Long Integer Package, LIP) [24] was developed in the ANSIC language by *Arjen K. Lenstroy* and *Paul Leyland.* With good portability in various operating environments, the mentioned library is characterized by insufficient efficiency for the implementation of Shor and Grover quantum algorithms. In addition, it lacks support for the implementation of high-level number-theoretic algorithms.

The *CLN* (*class library for numbers*) library [25] models a number of elementary arithmetic, logical, and transcendental functions. The authors of *CLN* are *Bruno Haible and Richard Kreckel. CLN* contains a large set of classes implemented in C++, in particular, classes to support operations with integers, rational and complex numbers, floating point numbers, and modular arithmetic. The *CLN* library was conceived as a universal one, which led to limitations of applicability for solving highly specialized problems of quantum cryptanalysis.

The *LiDIA* library of number-theoretic algorithms [26] has been developed by *Thomas Papanikolaou (Technical University of Darmstadt)* in the *C++ programming language.* The *LiDIA* library supports other packages for working with integers (*GMP*, *CLN*, and *LIP*) and is characterized by a fairly high efficiency of implementing data types with increased accuracy, as well as implementations of quantum algorithms with high time complexity. The disadvantages of the *LiDIA* library include the inability to build and use in the MS Windows operating environment, which somewhat limits the use of this library in cryptanalysis practice.

The *GMP library (GNU multiple precision arithmetic library)* [27] was developed by *Torbjord Granland* and is characterized by increased performance. Some of the functions of this library were written in a programming language *C*, partially on *Assembler*. The GMP library is compatible with the *MS Windows* operating environment. The disadvantage of *GMP* is the lack of algorithms for the formation of a factor base, factorization, and a number of others necessary for quantum cryptanalysis.

Library for doing number theory [28] was developed by Victor Shoup in C++ for modeling number-theoretic algorithms. The NTL library is compatible with the *GMP* library and has a developed API interface that allows cryptanalysts to develop their own cryptanalysis algorithms. As a result, the *NTL* library places increased demands on cryptanalysts in terms of programming skills.

Demonstration prototype of the software package *"Tools for cryptanalysis of asymmetric ciphers" (CRYPTO)* was developed by *A. A. Savelyeva (HSE)* [14, 15] in 2013 and is one of the first domestic software packages for solving problems of cryptanalysis of asymmetric ciphers. The named software package includes a *library, a constructor with appropriate* cryptanalysis primitives, and an *analyst application* for organizing access to factorization and discrete logarithm algorithms. At the same time, the *NTL library was used to perform operations with long numbers.* The CRYPTO complex was developed in the C++ programming language and contains components that implement the following basic functions: discrete logarithm; factorization of integers; checking numbers for simplicity; calculating Bezu coefficients; performing basic operations on matrices in residue rings and finite fields; solving systems of linear equations in residue rings and finite fields; restoring the general solution of a system of linear equations in a residue ring by solving systems of linear equations in finite fields using the Chinese remainder theorem.

The CRYPTO software package is characterized by a developed functionality for a demonstration prototype (used for the study of crypto attacks), as well as the compactness of the code (approximately 600 KB).

The second class of software packages is represented by quantum computing emulators *Quantum Development Kit, Quantum Computing Playground, JQuantum, QuEST, Quantum Programming Studio*, and *Q-Kit*. Technical documentation for these and other possible emulators (more than 50 are known) is presented on the specialized quantum computing portal *Quantiki*.[36]

Quantum Development Kit (QDK) was developed by *Microsoft* to learn the basics of quantum programming in MS Q#. At the same time, the *QDK is integrated into the Microsoft Visual Studio (VS) development environment and* supports the *Python, Q#,* and *C#* programming languages. Since QDK does not have its own graphical shell, programs can be written in *VS (or VS code)* environments, or in *Notebook Jupyter, for example,* in *Python (in this case,* the functions of the Q# library are involved). The *QDK* technical documentation includes a number of Quantum Katas tutorials, including a Q# programming manual [15].

---

[36] https://www.quantiki.org /

The advantages of QDK include:

- possibility of modeling quantum algorithms in the MS Q# programming language;
- sufficiently developed library of programs in the Q language#;
- support for working with open-source software;
- ability to compile, debug, and profile programs;
- ability to evaluate and control computing resources;
- support for working in the MS Azure cloud (20 or more qubits);
- advanced program verification and testing capabilities.

The advantages of QDK include:

- working with MS Azure is not supported from Russia;
- errors are observed when working with Jupyter.

Quantum Computing Playground (QCP) was developed by *WebGL Chrome* for research purposes. The emulator includes a QScript scripting *language*, a *debugger*, and an *IDE graphical web interface*. The emulator implements a graphical way of observing the states of qubits in 2D or 3D, where the points describe the superposition of qubits, and their color or the height of the bands describe the amplitude and phase of a given superposition.
The advantages of the *QCP* emulator include:

- possibility of modeling quantum algorithms in QScript *language*;
- open-source support;
- advanced program debugging functionality;
- cross-platform support.

  The disadvantages of the *QCP* emulator include:

- high requirements for memory and computing resources in general;
- Limited set of implementations of quantum algorithms;
- incompleteness of the *Qcp* technical documentation.

JQuantum is a Java program (requires a Java virtual machine) for modeling quantum algorithms (support for up to 15 qubits).
The advantages of *JQuantum* include:

- user-friendly graphical interface;

- it runs as an applet from the browser or as an executable jar file on the desktop;

- advanced library of quantum algorithms;

- source code is publicly available;

- support for well-known java frameworks and libraries since java version 5;

- *Kotlin* programming language support from the Russian company *JetBrains* (java code conversion to Kotlin and back is available).

The disadvantages of *JQuantum* include:

- there is no optimization of the program's operating time comparable to theoretical quantum computers;

- limited possibilities for changing quantum circuits (partial or even full initialization of circuit gates is required);

- limited set of gates for representing quantum circuits.

QuEST is one of the first GPU simulators of universal quantum circuits with open source (a hybrid of *OpenMP and MPI*).
The advantages of *QuEST* include:

- does not require large computational resources for modeling quantum algorithms (support for up to 20 qubits);

- source code is publicly available;

- cross-platform is supported;

- organization of calculations on several processor cores;

- ability to transfer calculations to graphics processors.

The disadvantages of *QuEST* include:

- limited possibilities of graphical representation of the quantum circuit;

- incompleteness of the QCP technical documentation.

Quantum Programming Studio (QPS) is a web application for modeling quantum algorithms and running programs in emulators or on quantum computers.
The advantages of the *QPS* emulator include:

- availability for computing devices with Internet access;

- ability to run the program on a quantum computer;

- visibility of algorithm models on quantum circuits;

- source code is publicly available;

- ability to export code to other programming languages.

The disadvantages of the *QPS* emulator include:

- lack of the possibility of autonomous operation;

- limitations of modeling quantum circuits up to 20 qubits;

- relatively small number of implemented quantum algorithms.

Quantum-Kit (Q-Kit) is a graphical simulator for modeling quantum algorithms on a quantum circuit.
The advantages of the *Q-Kit* emulator include:

- user-friendly interface for modeling quantum circuits;

- cross-platform support;

- visual representation of various primitives of the quantum circuit;

- ability to create original quantum circuits.

The disadvantages of the *Q-Kit* emulator include:

- limitations of modeling quantum circuits up to 20 qubits;

- lack of a built-in programming language.

Table 1.12 presents the results of comparison of the considered quantum computing emulators:

- QPS, JQuantum, and QCP are suitable for initial acquaintance with quantum computing;

- Q-kit, JQuantum, and QPS are suitable for modeling complex quantum algorithms and studying their properties;

- QDK, QuEST, and JQuantum are more suitable for creating original models of quantum algorithms based on advanced embedded programming languages, as well as functional tools for debugging programs.

The **third class** of software packages includes software platforms for connecting to demonstration prototypes of real quantum computers (Figure 1.21) and modeling quantum cryptanalysis algorithms on quantum circuits: QISKit for IBM Q (up to 20 qubits), Forest (pyQuil) for Rigetti (up to 8 qubits), ProjectQ for ETH Zurich (up to 16 qubits), etc.

The QISKit software platform for the IBM Q quantum computer.
The advantages of the mentioned platform include:

- High availability of the IBM quantum computer (up to 16 qubits maximum and 20 qubits for members of the IBM Q Network community). Programs are sent directly to the job queue to run.

- Relatively good reproduction quality of a single-qubit gate with an accuracy of more than 99.5% for all qubits (accuracy = 1 – error). Multicubit accuracy is higher than 94.9% for all pairs of qubits in the topology; the reading error is in the range of 6%–12.4%.

- Developed libraries for modeling quantum algorithms on real quantum circuits and gates.

- Large amount of educational material and examples of models of quantum algorithms.

- Availability of functionally developed simulators: local_qasm_simulator, local_state_vector_simulator, ibmq_qasm_simulator, local_unitary_simulator, and local_clifford_simulator.

The disadvantages of the QISKit platform are related to the known limitations of IBM Q quantum computers. For example, for IBMQX5 (16 qubits), the minimum coherence time (T2) is 31 ± 5 microseconds on the 0th qubit, and the maximum is 89 ± 17 microseconds on the 15th qubit. A single-bit gate needs 80 nanoseconds for execution and +10 nanoseconds for depreciation after each pulse. CNOT gates need about two to four times more, starting from 170 nanoseconds for cx q [6] and q [7] up to 348 nanoseconds for cx q [3] and q [14].

The distinctive features of QISKit quantum simulators are the following. The unitary simulator implements basic (unitary) matrix multiplication and is severely limited by RAM. The vector state simulator does not store the complete unitary matrix, but only the state vector and one or more qubit gates are loaded. Using a local unitary simulator, a circuit with 10 qubits and a depth of 10 is simulated in 23.55 seconds. Adding another qubit increases the time by about ten times – 239.97 seconds, and at 12 qubits, the simulator exceeds the waiting time after 1000 seconds (about 17 minutes). This simulator quickly achieves long simulation times and memory limitations, since for n qubits, a $2n \times 2n$ unitary matrix must be stored in memory. The vector state simulator is significantly superior to the unitary simulator. Simulation of a quantum circuit of 25 qubits takes place in 3 minutes. All circuits up to 20 qubits with a depth of up to 30 are simulated in less than 5 seconds.

PyQuil software platform for Rigetti quantum computer (up to 8 qubits):
The advantages of the mentioned platform include:

- developed libraries for modeling quantum algorithms;

- built-in quantum virtual machine (qvm) simulator to run in the cloud (api key required);

- possibility of modeling a quantum algorithm on a quantum circuit up to 23 qubits and a depth of 10 (with more than 23 qubits, qvm crashes);

- high-speed simulation of a quantum circuit (for a 16-qubit circuit and a depth of 10 in an average of 2.61 seconds).

The disadvantages of the PyQuil platform are related to the technical characteristics of the Rigetti quantum computer available today (Table 1.13).

ProjectQ platform for the ETH Zurich quantum computer (up to 16 qubits):
The advantages of the mentioned platform include:

- developed fermilib library with plug-ins for modeling quantum algorithms;

- compatibility with the openfermion open-source project for the development of quantum algorithm models;

- built-in productive simulator in C++ simulates a quantum circuit of up to 28 qubits in less than 10 minutes (569.71 seconds) with a circuit depth of 20;

Table 1.13   Evaluation of the accuracy of quantum operations.

Computer	1-Qubit gate fidelity	2-Qubit gate fidelity	Read out fidelity
IBM Q5 Tennerife	99.84%	95.98%	94.46%
IBM Q16 Melbourne	99.68%	92.84%	93.02%
IBM Q20 Poughkeepsie	99.89%	97.75%	TBD
IBM Q20 Tokyo	99.80%	97.16%	91.72%
IBM Q System One	99.96%	98.31%	TBD
Rigetti 16Q Aspen-1	97%	91%	93%
Rigetti 8 Q Agave	96.15%	87.00%	83.84%
Rigetti 19Q Acorn	98.63%	87.50%	93.30%
IonQ 11 Qubit	>99%	>98%	99.80%

- advanced quantum circuit draftsman (you can use tikz to create high-quality images in TEX);

- disadvantages of the project q platform for the ETH Zurich quantum computer (up to 16 qubits) include the following (Table 1.14). The project does not have its own quantum equipment (connection to an IBM Q quantum computer is provided.

Now, based on the analysis, we will formulate the main functional and technical requirements for promising software complexes of quantum cryptanalysis, in particular, the "Q-cryptanalysis" platform developed by the author of the monograph.

Functional requirements for the "Q-cryptanalysis" platform:

1. The platform should perform cryptanalysis of asymmetric encryption schemes (RSA or El Gamal) and digital signature (DSA, ECDSA, or RSA-PSS) by exponentially accelerating the solution of factorization problems, discrete logarithm (DLP), and discrete logarithm with elliptic curve (ECDLP). Therefore, the well-known protocols TLS, SSH, IPsec, etc., rely on Diffie–Hellman key agreements (which depend on the strength of DLP or ECDLP), digital signatures (DSA, ECDSA, or RSA-PSS), or public key encryption (El Gamal or RSA-OAEP).

2. Platform should be focused on working with users of various qualifications in the field of cryptanalysis (shift operator, administrator, application and system programmer, and cryptanalyst of the middle and highest categories).

3. Data preparation for cryptanalysis of asymmetric encryption schemes (RSA or El Gamal) and digital signature (DSA, ECDSA, or RSA-PSS) should be carried out by a separate module.

4. Data preparation for the conclusions of the cryptanalysis results of asymmetric encryption schemes (RSA or El Gamal) and digital signature (DSA, ECDSA, or RSA-PSS) and storage in special SQL and/or NoSQL databases of types should be carried out by a separate module.

5. Data preparation for cryptanalysis of asymmetric encryption schemes (RSA or El Gamal) and digital signature (DSA, ECDSA, or RSA-PSS) should be carried out by a separate module.

6. Platform should output information about the results of cryptanalysis of asymmetric encryption schemes (RSA or El Gamal) and digital signature (DSA, ECDSA, or RSA-PSS).

Table 1.14 Results of comparison of platforms for connection to quantum computers IBM Q (up to 20 qubits), Rigetti (up to 8 qubits), and ETH Zurich (up to 16 qubits).

Title Q-platforms	PyQuil	QISKit	ProjectQ	QDK
Developer	Rigetti	IBM	ETH Zurich	Microsoft
The first version of the Q platform	v0.0.2 on January 15, 2017	0.1 on March 7, 2017	v0.1.0 on January 3, 2017	0.1.1712.901 on January 4, 2018 (pre-release)
Available version of the Q platform	v1.9.0 on June 6, 2018	0.5.4 on June 11, 2018	v0.3.6 on February 6, 2018	0.2.1802.2202 on February 26, 2018 (pre-release)
Open-source software support	✓	✓	✓	✓
License	Apache-2.0	Apache-2.0	Apache-2.0	MIT
Documentation	Docs, tutorials (Grove)	Docs, tutorial notebooks, hardware	Docs, example programs, paper	Docs
OC Requirements	Mac, Windows, and Linux Python 3 and Anaconda (recommended)	Mac, Windows, and Linux Python 3.5+, Jupyter Notebooks (for tutorials), and Anaconda 3 (recommended)	Mac, Windows, and Linux Python 2 or 3	Mac, Windows, and Linux Visual Studio Code (strongly recommended)
Programming language	Python	Python	Python	Q#
Built-in Q programming language	Quil	OpenQASM	None/hybrid	Q#
Characteristics of the Q-computer available for connection	8 qubits	IBMQX2 (5 qubits), IBMQX4 (5 qubits), IBMQX5 (16 qubits), and QS1_1 (20 qubits)	No dedicated hardware, can connect to IBM backends	None
Simulator limitations	~20 qubits locally, 26 qubits with most API keys to QVM, 30+ w/private access	~25 qubits locally; 30 through cloud	~28 qubits locally	30 qubits locally; 40 through Azure cloud

- Platform should provide the ability to save the results of cryptanalysis of asymmetric encryption schemes (RSA or El Gamal) and digital signature (DSA, ECDSA, or RSA-PSS) for further analytical processing and use.

- Platform should be universal and have opportunities for further refinement and improvement.

Functional requirements for the "Q-cryptanalysis" platform:

1. Platform should run on classic von Neumann architecture computers and demonstration prototypes of the IBM Q quantum computer with 16 or more logical qubits.

2. Platform should be implemented on the basis of the following software architectures: monolith, two- and three-link client-SOA server, and microservice.

3. Platform must be independent of the specific implementation of cloud computing (Amazon Web Services, Microsoft Azure, Google App Engine, Rackspace, Force.com from Salesforce, Intuit Partner Platform, Facebook, IBM Cloud, VMware vCloud, Sharepoint Online, Red Hat OpenShift Container Platform, etc.).

4. Platform must support a single programming stack (Python, Go, Scala, C++, .Net, Data Science, AI, and ML)

5. Platform must run under the operating systems (OS) of the MS Windows and Linux family (Astra Linux).

6. Platform should support open-source software as well as well-known quantum algorithm modeling libraries and software packages with long arithmetic.

7. Functional API should be provided for the development and improvement of the software package in the future.

1.6 Verbal Statement of the Research Problem

Given: Asymmetric encryption schemes (RSA or El Gamal) and digital signatures (DSA, ECDSA, or RSA-PSS), as well as corresponding applications and protocols (TLS, SSH, and IPsec) requiring quantum cryptanalysis (Table 1.15).

It is necessary to: Increase the effectiveness of quantum cryptanalysis of asymmetric encryption and digital signature systems (Figure 1.22), taking

Table 1.15   Asymmetric encryption and digital signature schemes for opening by quantum cryptanalysis algorithms.

Standard	Networks and systems	Volume
Algorithm	Internet	~25%
RSA	Intranet	
With key length	IIoT/IoT	
1024	Satellite networks	
2048		
4096		
Algorithm	Internet	~35%
RSA-OAEP	Intranet	
	IIoT/IoT	
	Satellite networks	
Algorithm	Internet	~35%
El Gamal	Intranet	
Over a group of points of an elliptic curve	IIoT/IoT	
	Satellite networks	
ECDLP	Internet	
NIST P-256	Intranet	
NIST P-256	IIoT/IoT	
NIST P-256	Satellite networks	
Protocols	Internet	~98%
TLS, SSH, and IPSec	Intranet	
(Rely on Diffie–Hellman key conventions and depend on the persistence of the discrete algorithm (DLP) and the elliptic curve discrete logarithm problem (ECDLP)		
Digital signatures	Internet	~75%
DSA,	Intranet	
ECDSA, and		
RSA-PPS		

into account the durability of the DLP and the ECDLP, depending on the following:

- complexity of the cryptanalysis algorithm for asymmetric encryption and digital signature systems;

- available real computing resources (a quantum computer or a simulator on a classical computer, the number of logical and physical qubits, the depth levels of the simulated quantum circuit, the stability indicators of the quantum computer, and the performance characteristics of the computer as a whole);

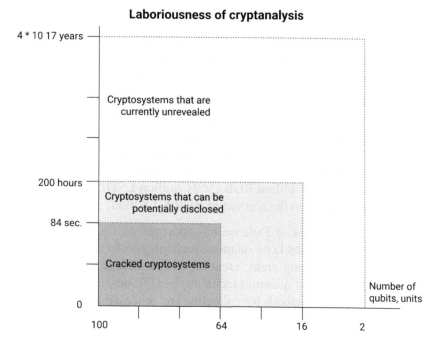

Figure 1.22 The area of guaranteed solution of the quantum cryptanalysis problem with the required performance.

• values of the probability of hacking the system of asymmetric encryption and digital signature.

Conclusions on Chapter 1

1. In most technological countries of the world, exploratory research is actively conducted in the field of artificial intelligence (AI), quantum technologies (Q), Big Data collection and processing (Big Data + ETL), and high and ultra-high performance machine computing (up to 10 Exaflops). In particular, in terms of quantum cryptanalysis to ensure the required cybersecurity of the digital economy.

2. For example, the US National Quantum Initiative (2018) has set the task of maintaining technological leadership in the field of quantum technologies in the medium and long term. For this purpose, starting in 2019, a series of (more than 80) dual-use R&D projects have been deployed

under the management of the NSA, the IERPA, and DARPA, the US National Science Foundation (NSF), the US Department of Energy, etc. At the same time, the US budget for the development of quantum technologies in 2021 exceeded $2.5 billion USD (for comparison, China's budget is $2.4 billion USD and Russia's budget is $691 million USD).

3. In 2019, Russia adopted the "Roadmap for the Development of Quantum Technologies" (QT). The main goal of the mentioned roadmap is to achieve in the medium- and long-term practically significant world-class scientific, technical, and practical results in the following areas. The total budget for the roadmap implementation (for the period 2019–2024) is 51.1 billion RUB ($691 million USD), including extra-budgetary funding in the amount of RUB 8.7 billion.

4. The US Department of Defense has approved and is implementing a plan for advanced R&D on quantum technologies for the period 2019–2024 in the following areas: creation of new images of weapons and equipment based on quantum technologies (Q); development of promising models and methods for collecting and processing Big Data, based on quantum technologies (Q), artificial intelligence (AI) and machine learning (ML) methods (national security data sets); development of quantum algorithms for solving military-technical analysis and synthesis tasks (including cryptanalysis tasks); creation of trusted quantum communication systems, including the development of appropriate component base and communication protocols; development of quantum computers (for 100 or more logical qubits); software development for quantum computers; development of promising architectures of quantum systems and networks for quantum computing; development of models and methods of quantum cryptography.

5. In quantum cryptography, an important role and place is given to solving problems of quantum cryptanalysis based on the promising quantum algorithms of Shor, Grover, Simon, etc. Shor's algorithm provides an exponential acceleration of solving factorization problems, discrete logarithm (DLP), and elliptic curve discrete logarithm problems (ECDLP). The mentioned tasks are widely used in TLS, SSH, or IPsec cryptographic applications of Internet/Intranet and IIoT/IoT networks, communication protocols based on Diffie–Hellman key agreements (depend on the strength of DLP or ECDLP), digital signature algorithms (DSA, ECDSA, or RSA-PSS), public key encryption algorithms (El Gamal or RSA-OAEP), etc. In other words, Shor's quantum algorithm

is potentially capable of violating these algorithms, and with them, all the mechanisms of public key cryptography deployed in cyberspace.

6. The conducted engineering and technical analysis of solving practical problems of cryptanalysis indicates the feasibility of developing promising quantum methods and algorithms for cryptanalysis of asymmetric encryption schemes (El Gamal or RSA-OAEP) and digital signatures (DSA, ECDSA, or RSA-PSS signatures), which are widely used in the United States and NATO countries. In particular, about the need to develop appropriate cryptanalysis software systems. Based on the conducted engineering and technical analysis, functional and technical requirements for the promising Q-cryptanalysis platform developed by the author of this monograph were developed. The verbal statement of the research problem is formulated.

2

Implementation of the Shor Algorithm on a Quantum Circuit

The applicability of Fourier transformations to determine the periodic structure of finite-length sequences is analyzed in the second chapter. The classical factorization problem is reformulated to solve it on modern quantum computers with 16 or more qubits. A modification of the basic Shor factorization algorithm is proposed for the possibility of its execution on a quantum computer. The complexity of the quantum factorization algorithm is estimated to determine the necessary and sufficient computing resources. An example of a possible implementation of the Shor factorization algorithm on a quantum circuit is presented. The estimation of the limiting capabilities of the quantum factorization algorithm for solving quantum cryptanalysis problems is carried out. The mathematical formulation of the work problem is given.

2.1 Applicability of Fourier transforms

When conducting classical and quantum computing, the *discrete Fourier transformation (DFT)* is used to determine the periodic structure of a sequence in the general case of complex values of finite length [42–48, 85–90]. The quantum factorization algorithm is a problem that requires finding out which periods of what length are present in the sequence [85]. In classical calculations, *DFT* is used when multiplying numbers by the Schonhage–*Strassen* method [8–10].

There *are classical, fast, and quantum Fourier transforms.*

Classical discrete Fourier transformation (DFT) sequences of values $h_0, h_1, \ldots, h_{N-1}, h_i \in C$, defined as [8–10, 37, 38, 77–80]

$$H_k = \sum_{n=0}^{N-1} e^{2\pi i k n / N} h_n.$$

The resulting set of complex values $H_0, H_1, \ldots, H_{N-1}$ is called the discrete spectrum of the original sequence, and the values themselves are called spectral coefficients. The greater the spectral coefficient H_i in its absolute value $|H_i|^2$, the greater the amplitude of the length periods in the sequence $N/(i+1)$. The direct DFT corresponds to the inverse transformation:

$$h_k = 1/N \sum_{n=0}^{N-1} e^{-2\pi i k n / N} H_n.$$

If we rewrite the DFT formula in the following form:

$$H_k = \sum_{n=0}^{N-1} W^{nk} h_n,$$

where $W = e^{2\pi i / N}$, it becomes clear that a string of spectral coefficients is H_k obtained by multiplying a string of values h_k by a matrix, whose elements are W^{nk}. The matrix has N dimensions; so the complexity of calculating *DFT* in this way is $O(N^2)$.

The fast Fourier transformation is defined as follows [8–12]. The *DFT* calculation can be done by $O(N \log N)$ multiplications. This transformation is called the *fast Fourier transform (FFT)*. *FFT* is based on the *Danielson–Lanczos* lemma, according to which the Fourier transform of even N size can be represented as the sum of two Fourier transforms of size $N/2$.

$$H_k = \sum_{n=0}^{N-1} e^{\frac{2\pi i k n}{N}} h_n = \sum_{n=0}^{\frac{N}{2}-1} e^{\frac{2\pi i k (2n)}{N}} h_{2n} = \sum_{n=0}^{\frac{N}{2}-1} e^{\frac{2\pi i k (2n+1)}{N}} h_{2n+1} =$$

$$= \sum_{n=0}^{N/2-1} e^{2\pi i k n / \left(\frac{N}{2}\right)} h_{2n} + \sum_{n=0}^{N/2-1} e^{2\pi i k / N} e^{2\pi i k n / \left(\frac{N}{2}\right)} h_{2n+1} = H^0 + W^k H^1.$$

The H^0 is the Fourier transform of even elements, and H^1 is the Fourier transform of odd elements original sequence. Each of these transformations is calculated for $(N/2)^2$ multiplications, and more N multiplications give additional multipliers W^k. It turns out that the original transformation, which requires N^2 multiplications, is simpler as a result of the decomposition:

$$2\left(\frac{N}{2}\right)^2 + N < N^2, N > 2.$$

If the size of the original sequence is a degree of 2, $N = 2^m$, then the sequential application of the lemma *Danielson–Lanczos* will lead to Fourier transformations of unit size, which are simply the values of the original sequence:

$$H_k^{010...10} = h_n.$$

Since each application of the lemma is a check of the lower bits of the indices of values, then reading the string from 010...10 from right to left, we get the binary index of the n value of the h_n original sequence corresponding to this unit Fourier transformation.

This method of finding the values of unit Fourier transformations performs a complete transformation as follows. First, the values of the original sequence are rearranged, when the binary index of the value is replaced by its reverse reading. Then according to the *Danielson–Lanczos* lemma, Fourier transformations of size 2, 4, and so on are sequentially calculated until a complete Fourier transformation of size N [8–12] is obtained. The process of calculating the *FFT* of size 4 is presented in the form of a graph in Figure 2.1.

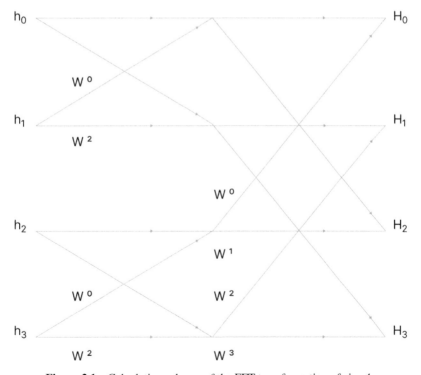

Figure 2.1 Calculation scheme of the FFT transformation of size 4.

Thus, the *FFT* of the N size is calculated in log$N$ steps, N multiplications are performed at each step. Rearranging the values of the original sequence requires N operations. As a result, the total complexity of the transformation carried out in this way is $O(N \log N)$. The considered algorithm is called time thinning. There is also a frequency thinning algorithm that has the same complexity.

The *Quantum Fourier transformation (QFT)* [8–10] transforms the state of the quantum register $|a\rangle$, where $a \in \mathbb{Z}, 0 \leq a < q$ for some q, into the following state:

$$\frac{1}{q^{1/2}} \sum_{c=0}^{q-1} |c e^{2\pi i a c / q}.$$

Thus, the action of *QFT* is described by using a unitary matrix, the value of which with the (a,c) index is equal to $\dfrac{1}{q^{1/2}} e^{2\pi i a c / q}$.

Let us fix the notation for this matrix A_q. The factorization algorithm uses a matrix A_q for q of exponential size. In this case, *QFT* can be performed in polynomial time if q is a power of 2 (in fact, according to the *FFT* principle) and also if q belongs to a special class of smooth numbers with small prime factors.

The construction A_q for $q = 2^l$, independently proposed for the first time, is considered below by *Coppersmith* [90–93] *and Deutch* [94, 95]. It will require two types of quantum gates. The first is the Hadamard gate acting on j, the qubit of the quantum register

$$R_j = \frac{1}{\sqrt{2}} \begin{vmatrix} 1 & 1 \\ 1 & -1 \end{vmatrix}.$$

The second gate acts on qubits with numbers j *and* k, $j < k$ and is defined as

$$S_j = \begin{vmatrix} 1 & 0 & 0 & 0 \\ 0 & 1 & 0 & 0 \\ 0 & 0 & 1 & 0 \\ 0 & 0 & 0 & e^{i\frac{\pi}{2^{k-j}}} \end{vmatrix}.$$

The *QFT* calculation is performed by applying the valves in the following order (from left to right):

$$R_{l-1} S_{l-2,l-1} R_{l-2} S_{l-3,l-1} S_{l-3,l-2} R_{l-3} \ldots R_1 S_{0,l-1} S_{0,l-2} \ldots S_{0,2} S_{0,1} R_0,$$

where the R_j valves are applied in reverse order from R_{l-1} to R_0, and between each R_j, R_{j+1}, the valves $S_{j,k}$ *are applied* for all $k > j$. As a result of these operations, we will get the following state:

$$\frac{1}{q^{1/2}} \sum_b e^{2\pi iac/q} |b\rangle$$

where b is the binary representation of c written in reverse order. Thus, for a *QFT* with $q = 2^l$ size, the $l(l-1)/2$ is required, that is, $O(l^2)$ quantum gates.

In order to show that the above operation is indeed a quantum Fourier transformation, consider the amplitude of the transition from $|a\rangle = |a_{l-1}...a_0\rangle$ to $|b\rangle = |b_{l-1}...b_0\rangle$.

As a result of multiplying the matrices, the R coefficients of $\frac{1}{\sqrt{2}}$ will give a multiplier $\frac{1}{\sqrt{q}}$, and, therefore, it remains to determine how the phase $2\pi iac/q$ in the $e^{(2\pi iac/q)}$ multiplier is obtained. Each multiplication by the Hadamard matrix R_j adds to the phase π if a_j and b_j bits are both equal to 1, and leaves the phase unchanged in the remaining cases. Indeed, in the case of $a_j = b_j = 1$ happens, the multiplication by $-1 = \cos \pi + i * \sin \pi = e^{i\pi}$. Further, each multiplication by the matrix $S_{j,k}$ increases the phase by $\pi/2^{k-j}$ only with $a_j = b_k = 1$. Therefore, when switching from $|a\rangle$ to $|b\rangle$, the phase has the following form:

$$\sum_{0 \le j<l} \pi a_j b_j + \sum_{0 \le j<k<l} \frac{\pi}{2^{k-j}} a_j b_k.$$

Since in this expression the first sum is a special case of the second at $j = k$, it can be rewritten as follows:

$$\sum_{0 \le j<k<l} \frac{\pi}{2^{k-j}} a_j b_k,$$

and since c is an inverted binary representation of b, we get

$$\sum_{0 \le j<k<l} \frac{\pi}{2^{k-j}} a_{jl-1-k}.$$

Replacing the sum k by $l - k - 1$, we write it as follows:

$$\sum_{0 \le j+k<l} 2\pi \frac{2^j 2^k}{2^l} a_{jk}.$$

Finally, if we extend the summation range by all j and k smaller than l, then the $j + k \ge l$ expression $(2^j 2^k)/2^l$ will take an integer value, and adding to the phase of terms that are multiples of 2π does not change the multiplier value. Hence, we get

$$\sum_{j,k=0}^{l-1} 2\pi \frac{2^j 2^k}{2^l} a_j c_k = \frac{2\pi}{2^l} \sum_{j=0}^{l-1} 2^j a_j \sum_{k=0}^{l-1} 2^k c_k = \frac{2\pi ac}{q}.$$

This expression is the phase for the amplitude of the transition from $|a\rangle$ to $|b\rangle$.

So, *QFT* reduces to a sequence of $O(l^2)$ quantum gates if $q = 2^l$. However, this requires valves with small phases, which, in practice, can be difficult to implement with any accuracy. *Coppersmith* showed [8–10, 90–93] that it is possible to exclude such gates and obtain an approximate Fourier transformation, the accuracy of which will be sufficient for the probability of success of Shore's quantum algorithm to remain acceptable. At the same time, the number of valves required for *QFT* is reduced to $O(l \log l)$.

2.2 Reformulation of the Factorization Problem

Consider Shor's algorithm for factorization of natural numbers [85]. Here, n is some factorizable number. There are currently two main subexponential methods for factorizing numbers on a classical computer:

- quadratic sieve method (proposed by K. Pomerans in 1981);

- numerical field sieve method (the first version, the so-called *SNFS – special number field sieve*, appeared in 1988 in the work by *Pollard*).

Denote the function expressing the subexponential complexity of the algorithm as follows:

$$L_n[\gamma; c] = e^{(c+o(1))(\log n)^\gamma (\log \log n)^{1-\gamma}},$$

where $0 < \gamma < 1$ and $c = \mathrm{const}$, $c > 0$.

In these notations, the heuristic estimation of the complexity of the improved quadratic number sieve (QNS) will be written as L_n [1/2; 1]. The heuristic estimate of the complexity of the general number field sieve algorithm *is* L_n [1/3; c] at some constant c. Thus, asymptotically, *GNFS* is faster than *QNS* (1/3 instead of 1/2). However, due to the fact that in *GNFS* $c > 1$, in practice, *QNS* begins to yield to *GNFS* only on numbers $n > 10^{110}$. *GNFS* is, by far, the asymptotically fastest known number factorization algorithm for a classical computer.

In contrast to these subexponential (but still not polynomial) classical algorithms, the quantum number factorization algorithm proposed by Peter Shore in 1994 [9] requires only

$$O((\log n\,)^2 \log \log n \log \log \log n)$$

steps on a quantum computer, i.e., the factorization problem is solved on a quantum computer in polynomial time. This algorithm also requires polynomial $\log n$ time post-processing on a classical computer (searching for the approximation of a fraction through chain fractions, Euclid's algorithm for finding the nodes of two numbers), which is necessary to obtain a specific prime factor of the factorizable number n from the output of the quantum algorithm. In principle, these calculations can also be performed on a quantum computer, and they are proposed to be done on a classical computer only so as not to build a quantum gate circuit for these tasks that arise at the stage of subsequent processing.

We reformulate the factorization problem into a form more convenient for solving on a quantum computer. Then we describe Shor's quantum algorithm for factorization of numbers and show some probabilistic characteristics of the algorithm output.

To find a nontrivial divisor of the number n, it is proposed to find the multiplicative order of some random x element of the ring, Z/nZ, i.e., the smallest natural r such that $xr \equiv 1 \pmod{n}$. Then, assuming that r is even, we get

$$x^r - 1 \equiv 0 \pmod{n},$$

$$(x^{\frac{r}{2}} - 1)\left(x^{\frac{r}{2}} + 1\right) \equiv 0 \pmod{n},$$

$$\left(x^{\frac{r}{2}} - 1\right) \neq 0 \pmod{n},$$

because r is the x order. Thus, if x is a nonzero and non-unit element Z/nZ, $x^{\frac{r}{2}} \neq -1 \pmod{n}$, and r is even, that $gcd\left(x^{\frac{r}{2}} - 1, n\right)$ is, a nontrivial divisor n.

The following statement can be proved: when applying this procedure to a random and equally probable, $a\ x \pmod{n}$ nontrivial divisor n is obtained with a probability of at least $1 - \frac{1}{2^{k-1}}$, where k is the number of different odd prime divisors n, if is odd, $k > 1$, i.e., n is not a power of a prime number.

The proof is based on the Chinese remainder theorem and the basic theorem of arithmetic. If the n is a degree of a prime number, you can use well-known efficient algorithms to find this prime number [10, 12, 14, 15].

We now describe an algorithm for finding the multiplicative order of an r element x (mod n). This algorithm uses two quantum registers, which contain integers represented in binary form. For the algorithm, a certain amount of additional workspace will also be needed, the contents of which are set to 0 after each subprocedure of the algorithm.

When describing the algorithm, this additional workspace will not appear.

Let n be a number for factorization, and let q be some number from the interval $[n^2; 2n^2)$, which is a power of 2, i.e., $q = 2^S$ for some natural s. Let also x be a random element of Z/nZ, the order of which will be determined by the algorithm described below. Parameters n, q, and x are not included in the description of the states of the quantum register, because they do not change during the operation of the algorithm and can be embedded in the structure of the array of quantum gates. More strictly, two registers are needed for the algorithm to work: one corresponding to the length in bits of the binary representation of a number n^2 (the first register) and the other to numbers n (the second register).

Shor's algorithm implemented on a quantum circuit:

Step 0 (preparation). Start the algorithm by bringing all qubits of quantum registers to the zero state:

$$\psi_0 = |0\rangle |0\rangle.$$

Step 1 (Hadamard valve). Apply the Hadamard gate to each qubit of the first register:

$$\psi_1 = \frac{1}{q^{1/2}} \sum_{a=0}^{q-1} |a\rangle |0\rangle,$$

which translates the register into an equally probable superposition of all possible states, i.e., each qubit of the first register is in the state described by the following expression:

$$\frac{1}{\sqrt{2}} \left(|0\rangle + |1\rangle \right).$$

Step 2 (Exponentiation). Calculate the value x^a (mod n) in the second register by taking the exponent from the first register. This transformation will leave the quantum computer in the following state:

$$\psi_2 = \frac{1}{q^{1/2}} \sum_{a=0}^{q-1} |a\rangle |x^a (\bmod n)\rangle.$$

Step 3 (Quantum Fourier transform). Perform a quantum Fourier transforma-tion on the first register. $|a\rangle$ in the first register will be displayed in

$$\frac{1}{q^{1/2}} \sum_{c=0}^{q-1} \exp(2\pi iac)|c\rangle.$$

Then the general state of the quantum computer will be written as follows:

$$\Psi_3 = \frac{1}{q} \sum_{a=0}^{q-1} \sum_{c=0}^{q-1} \exp(2\pi iac)|c\rangle|x^a \,(mod\,n)\rangle.$$

Step 4 (State monitoring). Measure the state of the registers of a quantum computer:

$$|c\rangle|x^k\,(mod\,n)\rangle,$$

where you can accept $0 \le k < r$ and complete the algorithm.

Next, it is necessary to interpret the measurement results and isolate the r element from the results of the multiplicative order x, which will be described in the next subsection.

2.3 Shor Algorithm Modification

Let us show how the probability of observing a particular state of $|c\rangle|x^k\,(mod\,n)\rangle$ is estimated when measuring at the last step of the algorithm [8–12]. Summing up all possible ways to achieve the specified state during measurement, we get the following probability:

$$\left|\frac{1}{q} \sum_{a:x^a \equiv x^k} \exp(2\pi iac\,/\,q)\right|^2,$$

where the sum is taken over all such a, where $0 \le a < q$, that $x^a \equiv x^k$ (mod n). Since the multiplicative order of x is r, this sum is taken over all a satisfying $a \equiv k$ (mod r). Assuming $a = k + br$, we write down the probability:

$$\left|\frac{1}{q} \sum_{b=0}^{[(q-k-1)/r]} exp\big(2\pi i(br+k)c\,/\,q\big)\right|^2.$$

Since b runs through values from 0 to $[(q - k - 1)/r]$, then

$$a_{max} = br + k = \left[\frac{q-k-1}{r}\right]r + k = (q-k-1)+k = q-1,$$

that is, *a* runs through all possible values from the interval from 0 to $q - 1$. Let us take the constant out from under the sign of the sum and square it:

$$\left| exp\left(2\pi ikc \,/\, q\right)\frac{1}{q} \sum_{b=0}^{[(q-k-1)/r]} exp\left(2\pi ibrc \,/\, q\right) \right|^2 =$$

$$= \left| exp\left(2\pi ikc \,/\, q\right) \right|^2 \left| \frac{1}{q} \sum_{b=0}^{[(q-k-1)/r]} exp\left(2\pi ibrc \,/\, q\right) \right|^2 =$$

$$= \left| \frac{1}{q} \sum_{b=0}^{[(q-k-1)/r]} exp\left(2\pi ibrc \,/\, q\right) \right|^2 .$$

In this formula, you can interpret the number *rc* as a deduction of $\{rc\}_q$, congruent *rc* (mod *q*), in the interval $(-q/2; q/2]$. Moving from the sum to the integral (see [8–10]), we can find the probability of obtaining a value during measurements $|c\rangle |x^k \,(mod\, n)\rangle$. For sufficiently large *n*, this probability is equal to

$$Pr\left\{ |c\rangle |x^k (mod\, n)\rangle : \frac{-r}{2} \le \{rc\}_q \le \frac{r}{2} \right\} \ge \frac{1}{3r^2}.$$

Thus, it is assumed that there exists *d* such that

$$\frac{-r}{2} \le rc - dq \le \frac{r}{2}.$$

The mentioned inequality in modular form looks like this:

$$\left| rc - dq \right| \le \frac{r}{2}, \left| \frac{c}{q} - \frac{d}{r} \right| \le \frac{1}{2q}$$

Because $q > n^2$, then there is at most one fraction d/r, $r < n$ satisfying the last inequality. In this expression, *c* and *q* are known. It is required to find *r, d* -parameter. At the same time, $c/qd/r$ are quite close to each other.

The fraction d/r can be found with c/q in polynomial time (since only division is used) by approximation of c/q through chain fractions. In a number of approximations of c/q, we will consider only those fractions whose denominator is smaller than *n*, because we need to find an approximation with a denominator $r < n$ that is unknown in advance.

Among these fractions, the nearest one will give us *r* in the denominator if $(d, r) = 1$. Let us count the number of $|c\rangle |x^k \,(mod\, n)\rangle$ states that can be found in the r described way. When calculating, we take into account the following factors:

- The number of different x^k.

Since r is the order of x, then there is r number of distinct x^k.

$$\Pr\left\{c \big| x^k \,(mod\, n): \frac{-r}{2} \le \{rc\}_q \le \frac{r}{2}\right\}.$$

This probability is estimated as $\ge \dfrac{1}{3r^2}$.

- Quantity $d \in Z/nZ$: $(d,r) = 1$, $d < r$.

There are such deductions modulo $r\phi$ (r), where ϕ is the Euler function.

Then there are $r\phi(r)$ various states of a quantum computer of the form: $|c\rangle|x^k$ (mod n)$\rangle$ which would provide a search r according to the described scheme. However, each of these states occurs with $\ge \dfrac{1}{3r^2}$ probability. Therefore, the probability of getting values with properties that find when measuring the state of registers r is

$$r\phi(r)\frac{1}{3r^2} = \frac{\phi(r)}{3r}.$$

There is a theorem [8–12] that estimates the value of this probability from below:

$$\frac{\phi(r)}{3r} > \frac{\delta}{\log \log r},$$

where δ is some constant. Repeating the algorithm $O(\log \log r) = O(\log \log n)$ once, we get a fairly high probability of a positive solution.

Let us now consider in more detail how the second step of the quantum factorization algorithm is performed, which is its most time-consuming part. At the input of the step, the quantum registers are in a state $|a\rangle |0\rangle$ that needs to be converted to $|a\rangle |x^a$ (mod n)$\rangle$ at the output, where a, x, and n are l-bit numbers and x and n are the array parameters of the gates.

When working with l-bit numbers, the classical binary algorithm requires $O(l)$ squaring and multiplication modulo. There are more efficient general exponentiation algorithms that improve the constant, but also require $O(l)$ in squaring and multiplication. If multiplications in a binary algorithm are performed according to the *Schonhage–Strassen algorithm*

[8–12, 42–48], asymptotically the fastest among the known ones and having complexity $O(l \log l \log \log l)$, the total complexity of exponentiation is O $(l^2 \log l \log \log l)$. However, the Schonhage–Strassen algorithm is good at constructing arrays of gates for long numbers. For small values, l the fastest classical arrays of gates are built according to the usual "school" column multiplication algorithm, which has $O(l^2)$ complexity, which leads to a total $O(l^3)$ complexity.

The calculation using the binary exponentiation algorithm reversible is to be implemented on quantum gates, since all physical transformations of a quantum system are reversible and elementary quantum gates are described by unitary matrices. Any irreversible calculation can be performed using a set of one- or two-bit gates; to perform reversible transformations other than linear Boolean operations, at least one reversible three-bit gate is required. As a consequence, turning the calculation into reversible requires the expenditure of a certain number of additional bits [10]. In [91–95], a general method is given for turning an arbitrary calculation with polynomial complexity into a reversible one, and an estimate of the additional time and memory costs that arise in this regard. Here, we present a method for constructing a reversible array of gates for exponentiation modulo using the "school" multiplication algorithm.

The main cycle of the algorithm is described by the following pseudocode, which converts a pair of values $(a,1)$ into $(a,x^a \ (mod \ n))$:

Power: $= 1$
for $i = 0$ *to* $l - 1$
     if $(a\_i == 1)$ *then*
            power: $= power *x\hat{\ }(2\hat{\ }i) \ (mod \ n)$
     endif
endfor

Here a_i denotes the ith bit a. The degrees x^{2^i} can be pre-calculated in a classical way and embedded in the structure of an array of quantum gates. The procedure that converts b the input to $bc \ (mod \ n)$ the output is required to execute the fourth line of the pseudocode of the main loop; this calculation can be reversible if $(c,n) = 1$, and such a condition is sufficient for the factorization algorithm.

The calculation consists of two steps. The first step takes b at input and gives a pair of values $(b,bc \ (mod \ n))$ at the output, performing multiplication by sequential addition modulo n, which corresponds to the following pseudocode:

```
result:= 0
for i = 0 to l – 1
        if (b_i == 1) then
                result: = result + (2^i)c (mod n)
        endif
endfor
```

Since the values of c are parameters of an array of gates, $2^i c$ can be classically pre-computed and embedded in the array. The second step converts the output of the first step to bc (mod n) so that the calculation is reversible. Since $(c,n) = 1$, then there exists c^{-1}, $cc^{-1} \equiv 1$ (mod n). Therefore, by multiplying by c^{-1}, it is possible to perform a reversible transformation from bc (mod n) to $(bc$ (mod $n)$, bcc^{-1} (mod $n)) = (bc$ (mod $n)$, $b)$, and applying it in reverse order to the output of the first step, reset b. The pseudocode for the second step looks like this:

```
for i = 0 to l – 1
        if (result_i == 1) then
                b: = b – (2^i)c^(–1) (mod n)
        endif
endfor
```

The above algorithm has $O(l^3)$ *complexity*, uses $O(l^2)$ quantum gates, and is made reversible at the cost of additional $O(l)$ qubits. Exponentiation modulo performing multiplication by the *Schonhage–Strassen* algorithm is calculated in $O(l^2 \log l \log \log l)$ time and uses $O(l \log l \log \log l)$ quantum gates but is made reversible using $O(l \log l \log \log l)$ qubits.

2.4 Estimating the Quantum Resources Needed

Performing two basic quantum operations is required to implement the described Shor algorithm [85]:

- exponentiation;

- quantum discrete Fourier transformation.

Let l be the number of bits in the binary representation of the factorizable number n. The asymptotically best multiplication algorithm for arrays of gates is the *Schonhage–Strassen* algorithm (see, for example, [8–12]). Its quantum version builds an array of quantum gates for exponentiation modulo volume $O(l \log l \log \log l)$, solving the problem in time $O(l^2 \log l \log \log l)$.

The elementary school method of multiplication by a "column" of complexity $O(l^2)$ leads to an array of quantum volume gates $O(l)$ that solves the problem in $O(l^3)$ steps.

The quantum discrete Fourier transformation in accordance with the quantum version of the classical *Cooley–Tukey* idea of the fast Fourier transformation requires $O(l^2)$ quantum gates (or $O(l \log l)$, if an approximate *QFT* is calculated) [8–12]. Shor showed [85] that his algorithm solves the factorization problem with probability $1 - \in$ for N runs of the basic algorithm:

$$N \geq \frac{1\log 1/\in}{\alpha\beta}l^2,$$

where α *and* β are independent constants relative to n. In [96], the estimate N is refined for the case of two simple factors. If $n = pq$, and q and are simple, then:

$$N \geq \frac{2\log 1/\in}{\alpha(1-\dfrac{1}{3}*\dfrac{2+2^{2\tau'}}{2^{\tau p}+\tau q})}l$$

where $p-1= 2^{\tau p}\sigma_p$, $q-1= 2^{\tau q}\sigma_q$ and $\tau' = \min\left(\tau_p,\tau_q\right)$, *and* σ_p *and* σ_q are such odd numbers that τ_p, $\tau_q \geq 1$. Based on these difficulties of exponentiation and Fourier transformation, the quantum running time of the basic Shor factorization algorithm (one iteration of the general algorithm) is $O(l^2 \log l \log \log l)$ [85].

Let us estimate the amount of quantum resources needed to solve some asymmetric cryptographic problems using derivatives of the Shor algorithm, with different parameters of these problems, and compare them with the complexity of solving the iterative problem when searching for the key of a symmetric cryptosystem. For example, for successful (in polynomial quantum time) cryptanalysis of the *RSA* cryptosystem, the length of the module used is 2048 bits; using the described quantum Shore factorization algorithm, it is necessary to build a quantum computer consisting of two quantum registers with a total length of about 4096 qubits. At the same time, about 34×10^9 quantum operations are required. To solve the ECDLP problem equivalent to it in the classical sense, 1300 qubits and 4×10^9 quantum operations are required. Table 2.1 provides further comparative data reflecting the amount of quantum resources needed to solve the factorization problem and the discrete logarithm in a group of points on an elliptic curve. This table, based on data from [8], is taken from [10] (in terms of quantum computing) and supplemented with its own data on classical complexity calculated by the $\sqrt{\pi 2^n}$

Table 2.1   Resources for quantum problem solving – factorization and discrete logarithm problems.

	Factorization			ECDLP		
	Number of qubits	Sq. time	n	Number of qubits	Sq. time	Cl. time
n	2n	4n³		f(n)	360n³	
512	1024	$0.54 \cdot 10^9$	110	700	$0.5 \cdot 10^9$	$6.39 \cdot 10^{16}$
1024	2048	$4.3 \cdot 10^9$	160	1000	$1.6 \cdot 10^9$	$3.03 \cdot 10^{24}$
2048	4096	$34 \cdot 10^9$	224	1300	$4.0 \cdot 10^9$	$9.20 \cdot 10^{33}$
3072	6114	$120 \cdot 10^9$	256	1500	$6.0 \cdot 10^9$	$9.20 \cdot 10^{33}$
15,360	30,720	$1.5 \cdot 10^{13}$	512	2800	$50 \cdot 10^{13}$	$2.05 \cdot 10^{77}$

formula, where n is the length in bits of the binary order representation of the point group of the corresponding elliptic curve.

The following value of $f(n)$ is accepted in this table:

$$f(n) = 5n + 8\sqrt{n} + 2\log_2 n + \in$$

where $\in$ = 10. The number of qubits and quantum steps for factorization corresponds to the modification of the *Beauregard* circuit [85–90] for the Shore algorithm. In each row of Table 2.1, the lengths of the asymmetric key are given, which determine the complexity of the factorization and discrete logarithm problem in a group of points on an elliptic curve, which require approximately the same number of operations on a classical computer. This complexity is shown in the last row of Table 2.1.

The table also shows that for the classically equivalent factorization and ECDLP problems, the following statement holds: the *quantum solution of the ECDLP problem* requires less resource (both qubit and quantum time) than the solution of the factorization problem; the gap in the required resources increases with increasing classical complexity.

However, the main obstacle in building a quantum computer capable of solving real asymmetric cryptanalytic problems is the difficulty of creating a quantum register of sufficiently large dimension and acceptable quality. Hence follows the natural method of protecting classical methods from the threat of quantum algorithms: assuming that at the moment it is technically possible to build a quantum register of length k qubits, it is proposed to use asymmetric algorithms based on *DLP* or factorization with $a > k/2$ bit length key, and based on *ECDLP* with $a > k/5$ *bit* length key. This parameter (the length of the quantum register) is key because it determines the fundamental

Table 2.2 Resources for quantum problem solution finding the key of a symmetric cryptosystem.

	Number of qubits	Sq. time	Av. time
k	k	$(\pi/4)\sqrt{2^k}$	
57	57	$2.8 \cdot 10^8$	$6.39 \cdot 10^{16}$
82	82	$1.93 \cdot 10^{12}$	$3.03 \cdot 10^{24}$
113	113	$1.06 \cdot 10^{17}$	$9.20 \cdot 10^{33}$
129	129	$2.76 \cdot 10^{19}$	$6.03 \cdot 10^{38}$
258	258	$5.03 \cdot 10^{38}$	$2.05 \cdot 10^{77}$

possibility of solving the problem in quantum polynomial time. We should divide the general problem into several subtasks that require fewer qubits, solved in polynomial quantum time to get a more complete picture of the possibilities of quantum cryptanalysis of these asymmetric algorithms.

In Table 2.2, you can find the corresponding classical complexities from Table 2.1 of the k length of the symmetric cryptosystem key, required to solve the problem by the *Grover's* algorithm of number of qubits, as well as the number of quantum steps. It is assumed that the vector of Boolean functions corresponding to symmetric cryptographic transformation is calculated in one quantum step, which in general does not correspond to reality. This assumption corresponds to a simplification of the key search problem and leads to quantum complexity, which can be considered as a lower (not always achievable) limit of durability. The classical complexity given in the table is called average since it corresponds to the average time of searching for a key on a classical computer.

If the quantum step is ever comparable in time with the classical one, and if we assume the presence of a quantum register of qubit length, where k is the length of the symmetric key, then it will be enough to increase the key length of the symmetric crypto algorithm by 2 times to obtain an equivalent complexity of solving the iterative problem.

Note that at the same time, the absolutely Shannon-resistant cipher remains absolutely stable, because it is not solved by brute force on a classic computer. In symmetric ciphers, it is possible to use shorter quantum registers to solve iterative problems arising in the process of cryptanalysis due, for example, to the decomposition of the original problem [27–29, 82].

2.5 Example Implementation of Shor's Algorithm

Using the example of solving the problem of finding the exponent (multiplicative order) of a simple integer modulo by another simple integer, we show the main features of modeling and engineering implementation of the quantum Shor algorithm [85–95].

Suppose there is a quantum memory register in which input data and intermediate results of calculations are stored and implemented as a set of quantum bits or qubits. Each qubit is a quantum system that has two different states, conventionally denoted as $|0\rangle$ and $|1\rangle$, where the symbol $|a\rangle$ corresponds to the standard designation of states in quantum mechanics. Unlike the classical bit, which can only be in one of the fixed states 0 or 1, a qubit as a quantum system can be in an arbitrary superposition of states $|0\rangle + |1\rangle$, where α and β are complex numbers satisfying the condition $|\alpha|^2 + |\beta|^2 = 1$. Thus, in the general case, the qubit state is a vector in a two-dimensional complex space, in which the states $|0\rangle$ $|1\rangle$ form an orthonormal basis and are called the states of the computational basis. Accordingly, the state of the memory register, containing n qubits is determined by a vector in a multidimensional complex space, the basis vectors of which are determined by the following relation:

$$|a_{n-1}\rangle \otimes |a_{n-2}\rangle \otimes ... \otimes |a_0\rangle \equiv |a_{n-1}\rangle |a_{n-2}\rangle ... |a_0\rangle \equiv a_{n-1}a_{n-2}...a_0\rangle,$$

where $a_j = 0,1 (j = 0,1,...,n-1)$, and the $\otimes$ symbol denotes the tensor product of vectors $|a_j\rangle$. Since any combination of zeros and ones of the form $(a_{n-1} a_{n-2} ... a_0)$ corresponds to the binary representation of some n-bit number k from the range $0 \le k < 2^n$, a shorter form of notation is usually used for basis vectors $|k\rangle_n$, where the index n determines the number of qubits in the register. Using the basic states of the $|0\rangle$ and the $|1\rangle$ qubit, the standard vector representation:

$$|0\rangle = \begin{pmatrix} 1 \\ 0 \end{pmatrix}, |1\rangle = \begin{pmatrix} 0 \\ 1 \end{pmatrix},$$

and definition, an arbitrary basis vector $|k\rangle_n$ can be represented as a column with the $(k + 1)$ component equal to 1, and all other components equal to zero:

$$|0\rangle_n = \begin{pmatrix} 1 \\ 0 \\ 0 \\ \vdots \\ 0 \end{pmatrix}, |1\rangle_n = \begin{pmatrix} 0 \\ 1 \\ 0 \\ \vdots \\ 0 \end{pmatrix}, ..., |2^n - 1\rangle_n = \begin{pmatrix} 0 \\ 0 \\ \vdots \\ 0 \\ 1 \end{pmatrix}.$$

Thus, the state of a memory register containing n qubits is a vector in a 2^n-dimensional complex space, which can be represented as a superposition

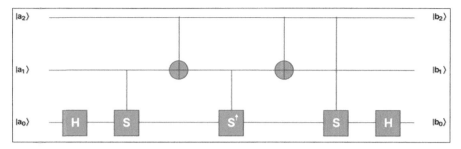

Figure 2.2 An example of a quantum circuit on three qubits.

of basis vectors. In general, the corresponding expression contains 2^n complex numbers whose values are limited by only one condition – the normalization. Consequently, the amount of memory required to write these numbers increases exponentially with the increase in the number of qubits, which imposes natural limitations on the possibility of modeling quantum computing using a classical computer.

When using the quantum circuit model, it is assumed that the quantum memory register can be prepared in the required initial state and then transformed so that after measuring the final state of the qubits, the desired result is obtained with high probability. In this case, transformations or calculations, as in the case of classical calculations, can be implemented in the form of a sequence of quantum logic gates acting on individual qubits or groups of qubits and depicted in the form of a diagram, which is called a quantum circuit. As an example, Figure 2.2 shows a quantum circuit on three qubits. The initial state of the memory register is depicted as a column of qubits $|a_2>$, $|a_1>$, $|a_0>$ on the left side of the diagram. Moving from left to right along the lines coming from the qubits reflects their evolution over time and interaction with each other by means of single-qubit and multi-qubit gates, for which standard values are used. As a result, the memory register is transferred to some final state, represented by the column $b_2>$, $|b_1>$, $|b_0>$ on the right side of the circuit, which can be measured. Since the change in the state of any quantum system in time is determined by the corresponding unitary evolution operator, and the state of the memory register is described by a vector in a 2^n-dimensional complex space, a unitary $2^n \times 2^n$ matrix can be mapped to each quantum scheme, which performs the transformation of the initial state of the register into the final one. Thus, the main task of the classical quantum computing simulator is to determine the $2^n \times 2^n$ unitary matrix corresponding to the quantum scheme on n qubits and predict the probabilities of various final states of the memory register according to a given initial state.

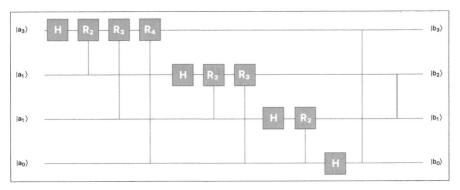

Figure 2.3 Four-qubit quantum Fourier transformation.

Consider a possible quantum scheme for calculating the Fourier transformation. The quantum Fourier transformation is the basis of many interesting and efficient quantum algorithms [8–12, 48]. In an orthonormal basis, this transformation is defined as a linear operator U_{FT} acting on the basis states by the following formula:

$$U_{FT} \,|\, x \rangle_n = \frac{1}{2^n} \sum_{y=0}^{2^n-1} \exp\left(2\pi i \frac{xy}{2^n} \right) |\, y \rangle_n .$$

For the transformation, there is a quantum circuit that computes it efficiently. Such a scheme includes quantum gates of only three types, namely the Hadamard gate (H), the controlled phase shift gate (R_k), and the SWAP gate, which exchanges the states of two qubits. As an example, Figure 2.3 shows a quantum scheme for calculating the Fourier transformation on four qubits. With an increase in the number of n qubits, the overall structure of the circuit is preserved, and the number of logical elements necessary for the implementation of the algorithm increases as $O(n^2)$. Note, however, that the best-known classical algorithms for calculating the discrete Fourier transformation of a 2^n component vector, such as the fast Fourier transformation (FFT), use $O(n \cdot 2^n)$ elements [8–10, 85–90]. Thus, performing the Fourier transformation on a classical computer requires exponentially more operations than solving the same problem on a quantum computer. When simulating the quantum Fourier transform on a classical computer, the computation time also increases exponentially with an increase in the number of qubits, regardless of the type of simulator. For example, 1024 × 1024, it takes about 70 seconds to calculate a unitary matrix of dimension corresponding to a 10-qubit quantum Fourier transformation on a personal computer with 4 GB RAM and a 2 GHz dual-core processor. At the same time, the addition of 1 qubit leads to an increase in the calculation time by about 4 times.

Now consider two mutually prime integers b and N_0, and $b > N_0$. Remember that the exponent of a number b modulo N_0 is the smallest positive integer r satisfying equality $b^r \pmod{N_0} = 1$.

The task of finding the indicator is to find the number r for the given numbers b and N_0. It is believed that this is a very difficult task for a classical computer in the sense that the algorithm solving it is unknown, the number of operations of which grows polynomial with the growth of n_0, where n_0 is the number of bits needed to write the number N_0.

Note that the function $f(x) = b^x \pmod{N_0}$ is periodic, and its period is equal to the exponent r. In this regard, it may seem that the task of finding a function period is not difficult. However, the $f(x)$ function is defined only for integers, and its values change rather randomly on the segment $x \in [0, r]$. Therefore, no information can be extracted from the value of the function at an arbitrary point about its possible value at a point $(x + 1)$. Figure 2.4 shows an example of such a function, which shows that it is extremely difficult to even estimate the value of the period according to the schedule, although it is 993. If we are talking about the numbers b and N_0 containing 100 or 200 digits, then the problem of finding the period becomes unsolvable on any classical computer, since the calculation time exceeds all reasonable limits [8–12, 42–48].

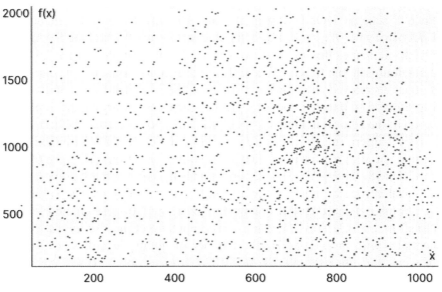

Figure 2.4 Function values.

2.6 Features of the Implementation of the Shor Algorithm

In 1994, P. Shor proposed an efficient quantum algorithm [85] for finding an exponent whose number of operations grows as $O(n^2 \log n \log \log n)$, where n is the number of qubits. Let us consider the model of Shor's quantum algorithm based on a quantum circuit in more detail.

Suppose there are two memory registers, the first of which contains n qubits and is called an input register, and the second contains n_0 qubits and is called an output register. The input register is used to write the argument x of the function $f(x) = b^x \pmod{N_0}$, and the output register is used to write the values of this function. The size n_0 of the output register is equal to the number of bits required to set the number N_0, since the function values $f(x)$ do not exceed $(N_0 - 1)$. The number of qubits n of the input register must be at least twice as large as n_0 in order for the accuracy of calculating the period r to be sufficiently high (see [2]). In the initial state, the qubits of the input register are set to the state $|o>$, and the qubits of the output register are set to the state $|1>$. It should be noted that to calculate the values of the function $f(x) = b^x \pmod{N_0}$, there is an effective quantum algorithm for calculating the values of the function (see [1]), which we will not discuss here, and we will denote the corresponding module on the quantum circuit by a controlled element U_f (Figure 2.4).

One of the important features of a quantum computer is the possibility of bringing its memory register into a state that is a superposition of all states of the computational basis with the same coefficients. For this, it is sufficient to apply a Hadamard valve to each qubit of the register in the $|o>$ state. In the diagram shown in Figure 2.5, the corresponding operation, indicated by a symbol $H^{\otimes n}$), is applied to the input register and puts it into the following state:

$$|0\rangle_n \rightarrow \frac{1}{2^{n/2}} \sum_{j=0}^{2^{n/2}-1} |j\rangle_n.$$

Thus, all possible values of the argument x arrive at the input of the controlled U_f, which performs the calculation of the function $f(x) = b^x \pmod{N_0}$ at the same time. The resulting quantum state of the registers contains information about all possible values of the function $f(x)$ and is determined by the following formula:

$$|0\rangle_n |1\rangle_{n_0} \rightarrow \frac{1}{2^{n/2}} \sum_{j=0}^{2^{n/2}-1} |j\rangle_n |1\rangle_{n_0} \rightarrow \frac{1}{2^{n/2}} \sum_{j=0}^{2^{n/2}-1} |j\rangle_n |f(j)\rangle_{n_0} =$$

$$= \frac{1}{2^{n/2}} \sum_{j=0}^{2^{n/2}-1} |j\rangle_n |b^j \bmod N_0\rangle_{n_0}.$$

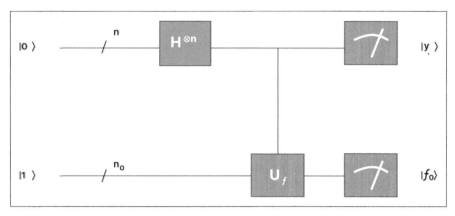

Figure 2.5   Quantum scheme for calculating the function.

This possibility of calculating all the values of a function in one call to the corresponding procedure U_f is called quantum parallelism and is one of the sources of the computing power of a quantum computer [85–90].

Note that the coefficients for all states on the right side of the sum are the same. Therefore, when measuring the state $|y>_n$ input register, we get one of the integers j from the interval $\lfloor 0, 2^n - 1 \rfloor$. However, the states of the input and output registers U_f are connected after assessing the procedure. In accordance with the Born rule, during the measurement of the input register, the output register will switch to the appropriate state $|b^j \bmod N_0 >_{n_0})$, and its subsequent measurement will give a number $(b^j \bmod N_0)$ with a probability of 1. In this case, information about the values of the function $f(x)$ with other values of the argument will be lost, and it will not be possible to determine the period of the function.

If you start measuring from the output register, you get one of the possible values of the function $f(x) = b^x \pmod{N_0}$, for example, f_0. Since this function is periodic with a period r, $[0,2^n-1]$, there are several integers x on the interval for which the function takes the same value f_0. Denoting by x_0 the smallest of these numbers $(0 \le x_0 < r)$, and by m the smallest integer satisfy-

ing the $x_0 + mr \ge 2^n$ inequality, it is easy to see that $m = \left[\dfrac{2^n}{r}\right]$ or $m = \left[\dfrac{2^n}{r}\right]+1$

depending on the value x_0, where $[a]$ denotes the integer part of the number a. As a result, the registers will go into a quantum state:

$$\frac{1}{\sqrt{m}} \sum_{k=0}^{m-1} | x_0 + kr \rangle_n \, | f(x_0) \rangle_{n_0}.$$

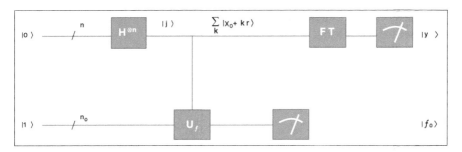

Figure 2.6 Quantum scheme for the algorithm of finding the order.

This state contains information about the r period of the $f(x)$ function, but measuring the input register will give with equal probabilities only one of their numbers of the $x_0 + kr$ form, which is also not enough to determine the period, since all three parameters x_0, k, and r are unknown. Repeating the calculations, we will again get a state with a different value x_0, since the probability of getting the same f_0 when measuring the output register is very small.

In order to avoid the dependence of the measurement result on the value x_0, we apply a quantum Fourier transformation to the input register in the state, and then we make the measurement. Thus, the complete quantum scheme, implemented using a quantum algorithm for finding the order, will take the form shown in Figure 2.6. Note that after measuring the output register, its state $|f_0\rangle$ remains unchanged; so next we will consider only the state of the input register.

As a result of the application of the quantum Fourier transformation, the state of the input register takes the following form:

$$\frac{1}{\sqrt{m}}\sum_{k=0}^{m-1}|x_0+kr\rangle_n \to \frac{1}{\sqrt{m}}\sum_{k=0}^{m-1}\frac{1}{2^{n/2}}\sum_{y=0}^{2^n-1}\exp\left(2\pi i\frac{(x_0+kr)y}{2^n}\right)|y\rangle_n =$$

$$= \sum_{y=0}^{2^n-1}\exp\left(2\pi i\frac{x_0 y}{2^n}\right)\left[\frac{1}{2^{n/2}\sqrt{m}}\sum_{k=0}^{m-1}\exp\left(2\pi i\frac{kry}{2^n}\right)\right]|y\rangle_n.$$

As you can see, the number x_0 is contained only in the phase multiplier on the right side and does not affect the measurement result, since the exponent modulus of a purely imaginary argument is 1. The probability of obtaining an arbitrary value of y from the interval $[0,2^n-1]$ as a result of measuring the input register is equal to the square of the modulus of the corresponding multiplier at $|y>_n$, enclosed in square brackets on the right side, and can be represented as follows:

$$p(y) = \frac{1}{2^n m} \left| \sum_{k=0}^{m-1} \exp\left(2\pi i \frac{kry}{2^n}\right) \right|^2 = \frac{1}{2^n m} \frac{\sin^2\left(\dfrac{\pi y m}{2^n / r}\right)}{\sin^2\left(\dfrac{\pi y}{2^n / r}\right)}.$$

If the desired period can be represented in the $r = 2^l$ form, where l is an integer, then the $m = \left[\dfrac{2^n}{r}\right] = 2^{n-l}$ formula takes the following form:

$$p(y) = \frac{1}{2^n m} \left| \sum_{k=0}^{m-1} \exp\left(2\pi i \frac{kry}{2^n}\right) \right|^2 = \frac{1}{r} \delta_{y,2^{n-l}j}, (j = 0,1,\dots,r-1).$$

Therefore, as a result of measurements of the input register, one of their numbers will be obtained with equal probability:

$$y = 2^{n-1}j = \frac{2^n}{r}j. \text{ Then } r = \frac{2^n}{y}j \text{ and,}$$

by checking the condition $b^r \pmod{N_0} = 1$ for different values of j with the help of a conventional computer, you can easily find the period of r. However, the probability that the period has the form $r = 2^l$ is extremely small and usually the ratio $2^n/r$ turns out to be a rational number.

Analysis of the function on the right side of the expression for probability shows that when the condition $r \ll 2^n$ is met, which is achieved by increasing the number of qubits in the input register compared to a given number of qubits n_0 in the output register, this function will take maximum values when:

$$y = y_j = \left[\frac{2^n}{r}\right]j, (j = 0,1,\dots,r-1).$$

Therefore, measuring the input register will result in one of the values with a high probability. Then, calculating the ratio $y_j/2^n$, we obtain an approximation of a rational number j/r with an accuracy determined by the inequality:

$$\left|\frac{y_j}{2^n} - \frac{j}{r}\right| = \frac{j}{r}\left|\frac{[2^n/r]}{2^n/r} - 1\right| \le \frac{j}{r}\frac{1/2}{2^n/r} = \frac{j}{2^{n+1}} < \frac{r}{2^{n+1}}.$$

Since the period of the $f(x) = b^x \pmod{N_0}$ function for the given numbers b and N_0 is fixed, the increase in the number of qubits n in the input register, it finds a rational number j/r with high accuracy, and its denominator is equal to the desired period.

As an example, consider the case $N_0 = 13$, $b = 7$. 4 bits are enough to write a N_0 number, i.e., $n_0 = 4$. Let the input register contain $n = 10$ qubits. Since the period r cannot exceed N_0, the ratio $y_j/2^n$ approximates a rational number j/r with accuracy:

$$\frac{r}{2^{n+1}} \sim \frac{2^{n_0}}{2^{n+1}} = \frac{1}{2^7} \approx 0.01.$$

We calculate the values of the $f(x) = b^x \pmod{N_0}$ function for all integers $x \in [0, 2^n-1]$, and then randomly select one of the values, simulating the process of measuring the output register to simulate a quantum algorithm for finding the order. We get, for example, $f_0 = 9$, and on the interval $[0, 2^n-1]$, there are $m = 85$ values of the number x for which the function $f(x)$ takes the same value f_0. Consequently, the state of registers contains a superposition of 85 basic states, which is easily found

Next, we calculate a unitary matrix that performs a quantum Fourier transformation on 10 qubits and use it to transfer the found state to the final state. Calculating the squares of the modules of the coefficients at $|y>_n$, we find the probabilities of obtaining different values of y when measuring the input register (Figure 2.7).

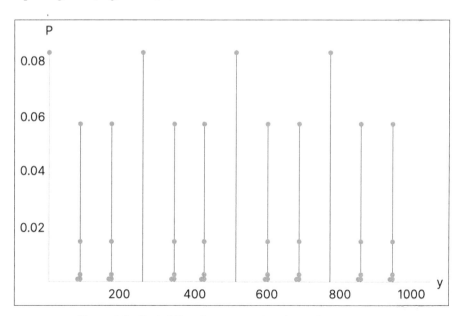

Figure 2.7 Probability distribution of getting different y values.

As you can see, $p = 0.083$; four numbers correspond to the maximum probability: $0, 256, 512,$ and 768. Suppose that as a result of measuring the input register, we got one of them, for example, $y = 256$. Then $\frac{j}{r} = \left[\frac{y}{2^n}\right] = \frac{256}{1024} = \frac{1}{4}$, which means that the desired period is an integer multiple of 4. A simple check shows that the required period is 12, i.e., $7^{12} \pmod{l3} = 3$.

Note that there are still a number of y values, for example, 85, 171, 341, 427, 597, 683, 853, and 939, the probability of obtaining which as a result of measurements of the input register $p = 0.057$, i.e., is quite high. Let us say, for example, we got a number $y = 597$. Then with an accuracy of 0.01, we find a rational number $\frac{j}{r} = \left[\frac{y}{2^n}\right] = 7/12$ whose denominator immediately gives the desired period. The remaining seven values of y given above give the same value of the period r.

Similarly, we make sure that there are eight more values of y, namely, 86, 170, 342, 426, 598, 682, 854, and 938, each of which can be obtained with probability $p = 0.014$ also result in an $r = 12$ period. Thus, the total probability of obtaining one of the above 20 numbers and finding the correct value of the period r exceeds 0.9, i.e., it is very high, even if we exclude the number $y = 0$, the receipt of which as a result of measurements does not lead to finding the period. In the case of $y = 0$, as well as when other y values are obtained as a result of measurements, the probability of which is small, the calculations should be repeated [85–95].

Note that modern classical cryptographic systems mean algorithms of *symmetric and asymmetric cryptography*, the security of which is based on the complexity of solving certain classes of problems on classical computers (*brute force, factorization, and discrete logarithm lie in the complexity class NPP in terms of key length in bits*), in contrast to quantum cryptography, the durability of which is based on the laws of quantum physics. *Symmetric cryptographic algorithms*, divided into stream and block, have the same nature in the sense, based on the complexity of the brute force problem noted above. *Asymmetric cryptoalgorithms* are based on the complexity of computing a discrete logarithm in finite groups defined over various algebraic constructions or on the complexity of decomposing a natural number into simple factors.

It should be noted that asymmetric cryptosystem based on the difficulty of computing discrete logarithms in a multiplicative group of simple fields F^*_p (*El Gamal, DSA, GOST P34.10-94*, etc.), discrete logarithms in the group of points on an elliptic curve (*ECDSA, ECGDSA, elliptic analogue of the El Gamal, GOST P34.10-2001*, etc.) and the factorization of numbers (*scheme authentication and electronic signature of the Fiat-Shamir, RSA*, etc.) are vulnerable to quantum cryptanalysis.

2.7 The Mathematical Task Definition

Initial data:
1. The structure of the asymmetric encryption scheme (*RSA* or *El Gamal*) and/or digital signature (*DSA, ECDSA,* or *RSA-PSS*).

2. Applications and/or protocols (*TLS, SSH,* and *IPsec*).

A set of restrictions corresponding to the capabilities of a cryptanalyst:
1. restrictions on the W-value of the complexity index of the cryptanalysis algorithm (*in sec.*) of the asymmetric encryption scheme (*RSA* or *El Gamal*) and/or digital signature (*DSA, ECDSA,* or *RSA-PSS*);

2. restrictions on N-time and computing resources for conducting a cryptographic attack (the permissible time period for a cryptographic attack, the type of computer – a quantum computer or a simulator on a classical computer, the number of logical and physical qubits, the number of depth levels of the simulated quantum circuit, the values of the stability indicators of the functioning of the quantum computer in the conditions of coherence, the values of the performance indicators of the computer in general, etc.);

3. restrictions on the value of P-probability of a successful cryptographic attack on the asymmetric encryption scheme (*RSA* or *El Gamal*) and/or digital signature (*DSA, ECDSA,* or *RSA-PSS*).

As a result of cryptanalysis, it is required to find:
1. A numerical complex assessment characterizing the resistance of the asymmetric encryption scheme (*RSA* or *El Gamal*) and/or digital signature (*DSA, ECDSA,* or *RSA-PSS*) to quantum cryptanalysis algorithms (successful cryptanalysis means restoring the secret encryption key or being able to decrypt a message without initial knowledge of the secret key).

2. $F_{\Sigma} = \Sigma_{i=1}^{s} f_i(W, N, P_{def}), F_{\Sigma} \geq F_{def}$, where F_{def} – reference value,

3. $f_i(W, N, P_{def}) = \begin{cases} 0, \forall W, N : P_{W,N} < P_{def} \\ 1, P_{W,N} \geq P_{def} \\ \dfrac{P_{def}}{\left(1 + \dfrac{W'}{W}\right)\left(1 + \dfrac{N'}{N}\right)}, P_{W,N} < P_{def}, \exists W', N' : P_{W',N'} \geq P_{def} \end{cases}.$

Table 2.3   Characteristics of cryptosystem durability.

For evaluation of cryptosystem components	For evaluation of components in general
Stimulates	Possible
Does not affect	Difficult
Makes it difficult	Significantly hindered
Makes it impossible	Impossible

4.   A detailed characteristic of the resistance of asymmetric encryption schemes (*RSA* or *El Gamal*) and/or digital signature (*DSA, ECDSA,* or *RSA-PSS*) to quantum cryptanalysis algorithms in the form of Table 2.3 containing fuzzy estimates from a given set.

Explanations: Most of the known cryptosystems of classical cryptography are vulnerable to attacks using a quantum computer. These vulnerabilities are expressed for each specific cryptosystem to varying degrees. Let n express the key length in bits. Then for symmetric cryptosystems (not a perfect cipher), quantum progress in cryptanalysis by total brute force is expressed as, $|K|^{1/2} = 2^{n/2}$, i.e., as the square root of the power of the key space.

This is due to *Grover's search* algorithm. On a classic computer, a bulkhead problem is solved in an average of $\dfrac{|K|}{2} = 2^{n-1}$ steps.

The discrete logarithm and factorization problems have asymptotic complexity when solving $O(n^2 \log n \log \log n)$ quantum steps on a quantum computer.

On a classical computer using the best-known algorithm – the numerical field sieve algorithm – the asymptotic complexity is: $O\left(e^{cn^{1/3}\log^{2/3}n}\right)$, where c is some constant.

The polynomial ECDLP solution on a quantum computer is also behind $O(n^2 \log n \log \log n)$ quantum steps, where n is the bit length of the representation of the elements of the base field over which the elliptic curve is defined. At the same time, this complexity has a significantly higher coefficient than the complexity of factorization of the corresponding number, assuming that the problems under consideration have the same complexity of solving on a classical computer. There is no subexponential algorithm for the discrete logarithm problem in a group of points of a general elliptic curve on a classical computer, which means that the complexity of solving this problem is equivalent to the complexity of *Pollard's p-method*, i.e., $\sqrt{\pi 2^n}$ classical operations.

Conclusions on Chapter 2

1. The analysis of probabilistic characteristics of quantum Fourier and Shore transformations indicates a significant quantum acceleration of solving cryptanalysis problems of asymmetric encryption schemes (*RSA* or *El Gamal*) and digital signature (*DSA, ECDSA,* or *RSA-PSS*) based on factorization of natural numbers and discrete logarithm in finite groups of various mathematical nature.

2. An example of solving the factorization and discrete logarithm in a quantum computing model has shown that it is possible to transfer these problems from a non-polynomial complexity class to a polynomial class. This is essential to increase the probability of opening asymmetric encryption and digital signature systems, as well as cryptographic primitives in applications and protocols (TLS, SSH, and IPsec), which have become widespread in the United States and the European Union.

3. The evaluation of the complexity of the quantum Shore factorization algorithm, taking into account the stability of the discrete algorithm (DLP) and the discrete algorithm with an elliptic curve (ECDLP), determines the necessary and sufficient conditions for the successful solution of cryptanalysis problems. The mathematical formulation of the work problem is formulated.

4. The analysis of the limiting capabilities of the known models of the Shor factorization algorithm on a quantum circuit formulated functional and technical requirements for the developed quantum algorithms for cryptanalysis of asymmetric encryption schemes (*RSA* or *El Gamal*) and digital signature (*DSA, ECDSA,* or *RSA-PSS*).

3

Development of Quantum Cryptanalysis Algorithms

The stability of the modern cryptographic algorithms is evaluated to clarify the tasks of cryptanalysis of asymmetric encryption schemes (RSA or El Gamal) and digital signature (DSA, ECDSA, or RSA-PSS) based on factorization and discrete logarithm problems (DLP and ECDLP) in various algebraic structures in a quantum computing model. The necessary and sufficient conditions are determined for the effective solution of cryptanalysis problems of asymmetric encryption schemes (RSA or El Gamal) and digital signature (DSA, ECDSA, or RSA-PSS) in a quantum computing model. A basic quantum Shor factorization algorithm is proposed. A quantum Grover search algorithm is developed. A quantum algorithm for symmetric encryption key recovery based on the message text and ciphertext is developed. A quantum algorithm for cryptanalysis of the RSA asymmetric encryption system is developed. A quantum algorithm for cryptanalysis of the El Gamal system is developed.

3.1 Assessment of the Durability of Modern Cryptographic Algorithms to Clarify the Cryptanalysis Tasks of Asymmetric Encryption Schemes (RSA or El Gamal) and Digital Signature (DSA, ECDSA, or RSA-PSS) in a Quantum Computing Model

Today, most of the well-known algorithms of asymmetric encryption are based on factorization problems (for example, the well-known *RSA* cryptosystem) and discrete logarithm in various algebraic structures (*El Gamal* electronic signature scheme) [17, 18, 27–29, 33, 36, 40, 42–48, 68, 69, 72, 77–80].

The asymmetric ciphers' development was laid in the work *"New Directions in Modern Cryptography"* by Whitfield Diffie and Martin

97

Hellman, published in 1976 [96–108]. In 2002, *Hellman* proposed calling this algorithm "*Diffie–Hellman–Merkle*," recognizing the contribution of *Merkle* in the invention of public key cryptography method (*Merkle's* public key distribution was invented in 1974 and published in 1978). A similar scheme has been developed by Malcolm Williamson[1] in the *1970s* but was kept secret until 1997.

In 1977, the scientists Ronald Rivest, Adi Shamir, and Leonard Adleman from The Massachusetts Institute of Technology (MIT) developed an encryption algorithm based on the factorization problem. The system was named after the first letters of their surnames (RSA – *Rivest, Shamir, and Adleman*). A similar system has been developed by Clifford Cocks in 1973,[2] who worked at the Government Communications Center (GCHQ) but was kept secret until 1977.[3] *RSA* was the first algorithm suitable for both encryption and digital signature.

With the concept of *public key cryptography*, the problems of factorization of integers and discrete logarithm have become the object of the close study of all mathematicians worldwide. Significant progress has been observed in this area in recent years [42–48, 92–108]. For example, *in 1977*, an American cryptographer *Ronald Rivest* suggested that factoring a 125-bit number would take *40 quadrillion years*, but already in *1994*, a number consisting of *129* binary digits was factorized.

Currently, factorization and discrete logarithm algorithms no longer have *exponential but subexponential* time complexity. These are algorithms using a factor base. The first subexponential algorithm for computing a discrete logarithm in a simple field Z_p was proposed by *Leonard Adleman*. In practice, the *Adleman* algorithm proved to be insufficiently effective; *Don Coppersmith*, *Andrew Odlyzko*, and *Richard Schreppel* proposed their own version of the subexponential discrete logarithm algorithm – "*COS*" [42–48, 92–108].

A number of successful crypto attacks on systems, based on the complexity of discrete logarithm in finite fields, led to the fact that the Russian and American electronic signature (*EP*) standards, which were adopted in

---

[1] https://ru.wikipedia.org/wiki/%D0%90%D0%BD%D0%B3%D0%BB%D0%B8%D0%B9%D1%81%D0%BA%D0%B8%D0%B9_%D1%8F%D0%B7%D1%8B%D0%BA

[2] https://ru.wikipedia.org/w/index.php?title=%D0%9A%D0%BE%D0%BA%D1%81,_%D0%9A%D0%BB%D0%B8%D1%84%D1%84%D0%BE%D1%80%D0%B4&action=edit&redlink=1byCliffordCocks https://ru.wikipedia.org/wiki/%D0%90%D0%BD%D0%B3%D0%BB%D0%B8%D0%B9%D1%81%D0%BA%D0%B8%D0%B9_%D1%8F%D0%B7%D1%8B%D0%BA

[3] https://ru.wikipedia.org/wiki/GCHQhttps://ru.wikipedia.org/wiki/1977_%D0%B3%D0%BE%D0%B4

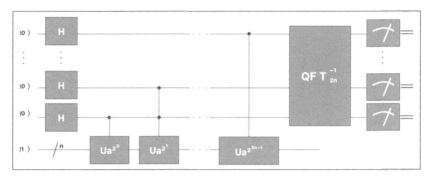

Figure 3.1   Shor's algorithm in the gate representation, 1994.

1994 and based on the *El Gamal scheme*, were updated in *2001* and trans-ferred to *elliptic curves*. At the same time, the EP schemes have remained the same, but elliptic numbers are now used as the numbers they operate with – solutions of the equation of *elliptic curves* over the specified finite fields. Research is being conducted to create algorithms that perform discrete logarithm on elliptic curves in the general case with at least *subexponential complexity* [92–108].

In 1994, *Peter Shor* discovered the so-called "*limited probability*" *factorization algorithm* [85, 92–108], which applies a quantum computer to factor a number in polynomial time from the dimension of the problem (Figure 3.1). According to a number of researchers [25–29, 48, 92–108], *Shor's algorithm* for factoring numbers is the **main achievement** in the field of quantum computing algorithms, and it clearly contributed to the creation and development of the first quantum computers [1–3, 8–10, 17, 18, 20–25, 29].

In general, all known crypto algorithms can be divided into symmetric and asymmetric (public key algorithms) [42–48]. A symmetric encryption algorithm (for example, *AES*, *RC6*, etc.) is considered sufficiently stable if no hacking methods faster than a full brute force are known for it. The complexity of a full search (for an attack with a known ciphertext) can be estimated as $O(2^k)$, where is the key length in bits. An American mathematician *L. Grover* proposed in 1996 his version of a cryptographic attack on symmetric ciphers (Figure 3.2). In 2002, with the help of an amateur distributed computing network distributed.net, the possibility of cracking a 64-bit key by brute force was demonstrated; now, the key length is 128 bits, and the maximum key length supported by most symmetric cryptographic algorithms is 256 bits.

There are cryptanalysis methods that work much faster than a full search for asymmetric crypto algorithms [85–108]. Because of this, asymmetric cryptographic algorithms have a much longer key length compared to

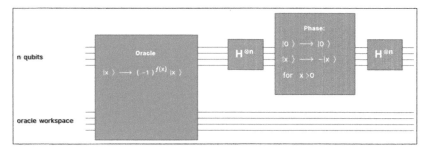

Figure 3.2   Grover's algorithm in the gate representation, 1996.

Table 3.1   Matching the length of symmetric keys and asymmetric ciphers with the same cryptographic strength.

Length of the symmetric cryptographic algorithm key	Key length of the RSA algorithm	Key length of the El Gamal algorithm over the elliptic curve group
80	1024	163
112	2048	224
128	3072	283
192	7680	409
256	15,360	571

symmetric ones (Table 3.1). Most often, the RSA algorithm is used, based on the computational complexity of the integer factorization problem, and the El Gamal algorithm, based on the computational complexity of the discrete logarithm problem. Moreover, versions of the El Gamal algorithm are used for various fields. In particular, the El Gamal algorithm over an elliptic curve group is of great importance [42–45].

It has been experimentally shown that the *numerical field sieve algorithm* proposed by *Oliver Shirokauer*, who $p > 10^{100}$ works more efficiently than the *COS* method. However, in a number of cases described in Tables 3.2 and 3.3, calculations on the quantum model show a significant advantage over calculations on the classical model.

3.2 Implementation of Cryptanalysis Algorithms

First, let us consider the features of modeling quantum cryptanalysis algorithms on a quantum scheme [48, 92–108]. We will show the differences between these algorithms and classical algorithms (the essence of the transformation of the well-known *"Church–Turing"* thesis into the

Table 3.2 Comparison of the complexity of the main tasks of cryptanalysis in classical and quantum models of computing.

	Classic model	Quantum model
Factorization of integers	$\exp[(1,923$ $+ o(1))(\log N)^{\frac{1}{3}}(\log\log N)^{\frac{2}{3}}$	Shor's method, $O(\log^2 N)$ operations
Discrete logarithm in a finite field	$\exp[(1,923$ $+ o(1))(\log P)^{\frac{1}{3}}(\log\log P)^{\frac{2}{3}}$	Shor's method, $O(\log^2 p)$ operations
Discrete logarithm on elliptic curves	$O\left(\sqrt{p}\right)$ operations on the curve	Shor's method, $O(\log^2 p)$ operations
Search for hash function collisions	$O(2^{n/2})$ hashing operations	Ambainis' method, $O(2^{n/3})$ operations
Search for a prototype	$O(2^n)$ hashing operations	Grover's method, $O(2^{n/2})$ operations

Table 3.3 Time gain for solving problems of quantum circuits on quantum computers.

Name of the task	Calculation time on a classic computer of the exaflop (10^{18} flop) performance		Calculation time on a quantum computer of megaflops (10^6) performance	
Decomposition of a natural number with the number of decimal places K into prime factors (factorization). Shor's algorithm	$K = 250$ $K = 500$ $K = 1000$	200 hours 10 million years $4 \cdot 10^{17}$ years	$K = 250$ $K = 500$ $K = 1000$	4 seconds 18 seconds 84 seconds
Calculating the discrete logarithm for numbers with the number of decimal places K	Acceleration is comparable to Shor's algorithm			
Quick search in a large database containing N elements. Grover's algorithm, acceleration in times	$N = 10^6$ $N = 10^9$ $N = 10^{15}$	10 c 3 hours 4 months	$N = 10^6$ $N = 10^9$ $N = 10^{15}$	10 ms 0.3 seconds 10 seconds
Finding a length substring in a length string . Ambainis' algorithm	Acceleration is comparable to Shor's algorithm			

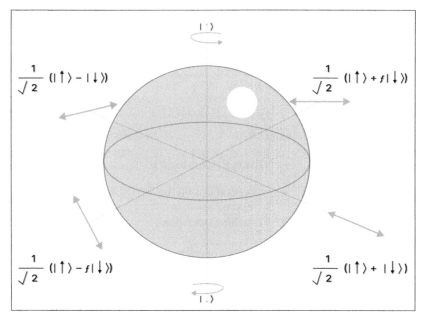

Figure 3.3   States of a qubit in the form of a Bloch sphere.

"*Church–Turing–Deutsch*" thesis) [85–92]. Then we will indicate a number of engineering problems [25–31, 33, 37, 38, 40, 42–57, 85–108] implementations of quantum cryptanalysis algorithms and analyze possible ways to resolve them.

The quantum analog of a bit (a quantum bit, or *qubit*) has quantum mechanical behavior features. Almost any quantum system (with at least two states) can act as a *qubit*. Its state space is a *Hilbert space* – a linear shell stretched over two (or more) basis vectors (in Dirac notation, quantum states are written as $|0\rangle$ and $|0\rangle$).

The general state of a quantum system with two states can be represented by a superposition of basic states $|\psi\rangle = \alpha|0\rangle + \beta|1\rangle$, with $|\alpha|^2 + |\beta|^2 = 1$ (Figure 3.3).

Note that a register composed of two L-level *qubits* can simultaneously store up to 2^L numbers in a *quantum superposition*. Therefore, if you replenish the register with additional *qubits*, the amount of information stored in the register will increase exponentially. For example, a 250-qubit register with atomic dimensions will be able to store more numbers than there are atoms in the known universe (10^{78}). Moreover, this is an understated estimate of the amount of quantum information contained in the quantum register, since the superposition vectors are in a continuously varying proportion – each with its

$$a\,|0\rangle + b\,|1\rangle \quad\boxed{X}\quad b\,|0\rangle + a\,|1\rangle$$

$$a\,|0\rangle + b\,|1\rangle \quad\boxed{Y}\quad -i\{b\,|0\rangle - a\,|1\rangle\}$$

$$a\,|0\rangle + b\,|1\rangle \quad\boxed{Z}\quad a\,|0\rangle - b\,|1\rangle$$

$$a\,|0\rangle + b\,|1\rangle \quad\boxed{H}\quad a\,\frac{|0\rangle + |1\rangle}{\sqrt{2}} + b\,\frac{|0\rangle - |1\rangle}{\sqrt{2}}$$

$$a\,|0\rangle + b\,|1\rangle \quad\boxed{S}\quad a\,|0\rangle + ib\,|1\rangle$$

$$a\,|0\rangle + b\,|1\rangle \quad\boxed{T}\quad a\,|0\rangle + e^{i\pi/4}b\,|1\rangle =$$
$$= e^{i\pi/8}\{e^{-i\pi/8}a\,|0\rangle + e^{i\pi/8}b\,|1\rangle\}$$

Figure 3.4 Example of basic one-bit gates.

own phase. Even in this case, if we measure the state of the register, we will get only one of those numbers. However, the exclusivity of quantum computing is that it is possible to carry out some nontrivial quantum computation using superposition – you can perform a series of mathematical operations, each of which operates with all stored data simultaneously (Figure 3.4).

The state of L qubit register can be represented by a 2^L-dimensional complex vector. The algorithm for a quantum computer must initialize this vector in some specified form (depending on the model of the quantum computer). At each algorithm step, this vector is modified by a unitary matrix, which is determined by the physics of the device. The matrix unitarity guarantees its reversibility (thus, each step is reversible). After the algorithm is completed, the 2^L-dimensional complex vector stored in the register must be read from the qubit register by quantum measurement. According to the laws of quantum mechanics, the result of this measurement will be a random string of L bits (and the measurement will destroy the final state). This random string can be used in calculating the function value because (according to the model) the probability distribution of the measured bit string is asymmetric toward the correct function value. The correct value can be determined with high probability by restarting the quantum computer and then measuring the output.

The quantum algorithm is performed by implementing a series of sequential unitary operations. Note that for this algorithm, the operations will always be performed in exactly the same order. There is no logical "IF, THEN" condition to vary the sequence, since there is no way to read the state of the qubit before the final measurement. But there are conditional operations implemented by the CNOT gate (Figure 3.5) [53, 54].

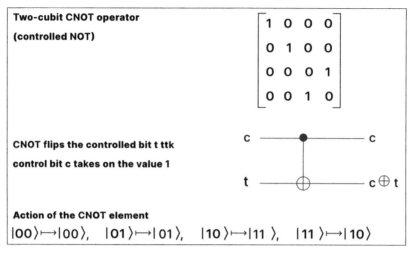

Figure 3.5   Application of the CNOT gate (operator).

According to D. Deutsch [94, 95], the following requirements are imposed on a quantum computer. A quantum computer is a set consisting of n qubits, for which the following operations are practically defined:

1.   Each qubit can be initialized in a known state (for example, a state $|0\rangle$).

2.   Each qubit can be measured in the basis $\{|0\rangle, |1\rangle\}$.

3.   A universal quantum gate (or a set of gates) can affect any limited subset of *qubits*.

4.   The state of the qubits does not change except through the above transformations.

This description does not affect certain technological aspects but contains the basic ideas of designing a quantum computer.

Note that the theoretical model of quantum computing is a network one and implies a consistent effect of *logical gates* on a set of *qubits*. *Logic gates* of a classical electronic computer are located on a circuit board separately from each other; in a quantum computer, logic gates are considered as interactions of several qubits occurring at a certain time. At the same time, qubits form a certain configuration in which there are fundamentally more options for interaction between elements than in a classical computer. It is possible to study other models of quantum computing, for example, the cellular automaton model [38, 48].

A universal quantum gate is the quantum equivalent of a classical *Boolean function* from a universal set and is a *gate* that, by acting on a *qubit* or their various combinations, can simulate the action of any other quantum gate. In 1985, D. Deutsch showed that fairly simple quantum gates can make up a universal set that will be sufficient to build a quantum computer. For example, a pair of one-bit gates $V(\theta,\varphi)$ and the two-qubit gate "CNOT," where $V(\theta,\varphi)$ is the gate of arbitrary rotation of one qubit:

$$V(\theta,\varphi) = \begin{pmatrix} \cos\left(\dfrac{\theta}{2}\right) & -ie^{-i\varphi}\sin\left(\dfrac{\theta}{2}\right) \\ -ie^{i\varphi}\sin\left(\dfrac{\theta}{2}\right) & \cos\left(\dfrac{\theta}{2}\right) \end{pmatrix};$$

and CNOT can be represented by a matrix

$$\text{CNOT} = \begin{pmatrix} 1 & 0 & 0 & 0 \\ 0 & 1 & 0 & 0 \\ 0 & 0 & 0 & 1 \\ 0 & 0 & 1 & 0 \end{pmatrix}$$

and can be considered as a universal set. Any unitary matrix of dimension $n \times n$ can be formed by combining two-qubit CNOT gates and rotation gates of one qubit. A description of such universal gates can be found in the work of D. Deutsch, S. Lloyd, D. P. di Vincenzo, and A. Barenzo [94–108].

A quantum algorithm is an algorithm that uses the quantum properties of an object for the calculation process. It is possible to formalize the description of quantum computing in terms of the classical computing model. For example, logical operations on computer memory bits by Turing classical calculations are replaced by unitary transformations acting on a fixed finite number of qubits.

In the study of quantum algorithms, it turns out to be interesting to find polynomial-time algorithms in problems for which classical polynomial algorithms for their solution are not known. According to researchers [29], quantum computers will be able to solve cryptanalysis problems much more efficiently than classical ones.

Thus, quantum computers are based on quantum registers, which consist of quantum bits (qubits). When measuring a quantum system, a quantum bit can have such a state that the measurement can show with some probability $|0\rangle$ and with some other probability can show $|1\rangle$.

A quantum register consisting of n quantum bits has dedicated states corresponding to n bit binary numbers from $|00K0\rangle$ to $|11K1\rangle$. The state of the quantum register is recorded as a linear combination of all these selected states:

$$\sum_{x=0}^{2^n-1} a_x |x\rangle.$$

In this case, the normalization condition is met:

$$\sum_{i=0}^{2^n-1}|a_i|^2 = 1 .$$

The a_x coefficients are complex numbers. They are called the amplitudes of the corresponding states $|x\rangle$.

The state of a system consisting of n quantum bits is described by a vector of unit length in a 2^n-dimensional complex unitary space (the scalar product of states $|a\rangle = |a_1\ Ka_n\rangle$ and $|b\rangle = |b_1\ Kb_n\rangle$ denoted as $\langle a|b\rangle$ and entered in the usual way: $\langle a|b\rangle = \Sigma a_i\ b_i$. A quantum registers of n length can represent different values of an n-bit word simultaneously.

It is necessary to make a measurement to extract information from the quantum register. At the same time, any set of quantum bits can be measured. In addition, since quantum states form Euclidean space, measurements can be carried out in various bases. However, the measurement leads to the transition of the system to the basic state corresponding to the measurement results.

A quantum computer can perform transformations over a quantum register. We will call a quantum transformation the mapping of a unitary space formed by a quantum system into itself. With quantum systems, only linear unitary transformations can be performed, and any linear unitary transformation is permissible. Due to linearity, quantum transformations are completely determined by their action on the basis vectors. Table 3.4 shows the main quantum gates.

The engineering problems of implementing quantum cryptanalysis algorithms include keeping computer elements in a relatively stable (coherent) state as well as protection against decoherence errors. The first problem is related to the fact that, in practice, the interaction of a quantum system with the outside world leads to a loss of coherence (otherwise, it is decoherence) and, consequently, to an emergency shutdown of the computer. This effect leads to a violation of the unitary nature (or, more precisely, reversibility) of quantum computing steps soon after the algorithm is launched, which will result in the inability to solve complex cryptanalysis problems.

The fact is that the fourth point of D. Deutsch's requirements for a quantum computer about the immutability of the state of a quantum system is, in principle, physically impracticable [94, 95]. In fact, there is no perfect quantum gate as well as a completely isolated system. It is possible to strive for the most accurate approximation of a real device to an ideal one, but, at present, this is not feasible. At the heart of such gates as XOR is the interaction of two initially separated qubits. But if qubits interact with each other, then they will inevitably interact with something else [20, 33, 38, 40]. In practice, it

Table 3.4 Basic elementary transformations (or quantum gates).

Name, designation, and brief description of quantum gate	Action on base states	Matrix
Identical transformation I	$\lvert 0\rangle \rightarrow \lvert 0\rangle$ $\lvert 1\rangle \rightarrow \lvert 1\rangle$	$\begin{pmatrix} 1 & 0 \\ 0 & 1 \end{pmatrix}$
Negation of X	$\lvert 0\rangle \rightarrow \lvert 0\rangle$ $\lvert 1\rangle \rightarrow \lvert 0\rangle$	$\begin{pmatrix} 0 & 1 \\ 1 & 0 \end{pmatrix}$
Phase shift Z	$\lvert 0\rangle \rightarrow \lvert 0\rangle$ $\lvert 1\rangle \rightarrow -\lvert 1\rangle$	$\begin{pmatrix} 1 & 0 \\ 0 & -1 \end{pmatrix}$
Phase shift Z by negating Y	$\lvert 0\rangle \rightarrow -\lvert 1\rangle$ $\lvert 1\rangle \rightarrow \lvert 0\rangle$	$\begin{pmatrix} 0 & 1 \\ -1 & 0 \end{pmatrix}$
Controlled-NOT CNOT. Adds the first modulo 2 to the second bit	$\lvert 00\rangle \rightarrow \lvert 00\rangle$ $\lvert 01\rangle \rightarrow \lvert 01\rangle$ $\lvert 10\rangle \rightarrow \lvert 11\rangle$ $\lvert 11\rangle \rightarrow \lvert 10\rangle$	$\begin{pmatrix} 1 & 0 & 0 & 0 \\ 0 & 1 & 0 & 0 \\ 0 & 0 & 0 & 1 \\ 0 & 0 & 1 & 0 \end{pmatrix}$
Controlled-controlled-NOT Tofolli valve. Adds to the third bit the product of the first two modulo 2	$\lvert 000\rangle \rightarrow \lvert 000\rangle$ $\lvert 001\rangle \rightarrow \lvert 001\rangle$ $\lvert 010\rangle \rightarrow \lvert 101\rangle$ $\lvert 011\rangle \rightarrow \lvert 010\rangle$ $\lvert 100\rangle \rightarrow \lvert 100\rangle$ $\lvert 101\rangle \rightarrow \lvert 101\rangle$ $\lvert 110\rangle \rightarrow \lvert 111\rangle$ $\lvert 111\rangle \rightarrow \lvert 110\rangle$	$\begin{pmatrix} 1 & 0 & 0 & 0 & 0 & 0 & 0 & 0 \\ 0 & 1 & 0 & 0 & 0 & 0 & 0 & 0 \\ 0 & 0 & 1 & 0 & 0 & 0 & 0 & 0 \\ 0 & 0 & 0 & 1 & 0 & 0 & 0 & 0 \\ 0 & 0 & 0 & 0 & 1 & 0 & 0 & 0 \\ 0 & 0 & 0 & 0 & 0 & 1 & 0 & 0 \\ 0 & 0 & 0 & 0 & 0 & 0 & 0 & 1 \\ 0 & 0 & 0 & 0 & 0 & 0 & 1 & 0 \end{pmatrix}$
Transformation Hadamard H	$\lvert 0\rangle \rightarrow \dfrac{1}{\sqrt{2}}\left(\lvert 0\rangle + \lvert 1\rangle\right)$ $\lvert 1\rangle \rightarrow \dfrac{1}{\sqrt{2}}\left(\lvert 0\rangle + \lvert 1\rangle\right)$	$\dfrac{1}{\sqrt{2}}\begin{pmatrix} 1 & 1 \\ 1 & -1 \end{pmatrix}$

turned out that constructing a quantum system in which the loss of coherence would occur less than once per million applications of the XOR gate turned out to be a rather difficult engineering task. According to the researchers, it remains to be seen whether the laws of physics find the lower limit of the rate of coherence loss. This problem was identified in the works of S. Haroche, J. M. Raymond, R. Landauer, Ts. Miguel, and A. Barenzo [20, 33, 92–108].

Thus, periodically projecting the state of the computer through carefully selected measurements is not sufficient. Therefore, for the required protection of quantum systems from decoherence errors and other quantum noise, methods of quantum error correction (QEC) have become widespread [20]. For quantum systems, they were first proposed and considered in the works of E. Stin and independently in the works of A. R. Kalderbank and P. Shor [85–108]. The scientists noted the importance of quantum error correction for noise-resistant quantum computing, not only to combat noise in stored quantum information but also to compensate the "noisy" quantum gates, as well as to compensate for imperfections of quantum measurement tools. Initially, it was not clear whether the network data should be perfect when using error correction methods. P. Shor showed [85] how to make error correction networks insensitive to errors within these networks. In other words, it turned out that such networks "with error correction" neutralize interference more than they create.

The discovery of the quantum error correction method approximately coincided with the appearance of the associated "gearing amplification" method, which also provides interference-free transmission of quantum states via a quantum channel with interference [20, 77–79]. The main idea of this method is that the sender forms a set of hooked pairs of qubits and then sends one qubit from each pair over a channel with interference to the receiver. The sender and receiver accumulate qubits and then perform a parity-controlled measurement: for example, the receiver performs an XOR ("exclusive – OR") operation for the received and the following qubits and then measures the resulting qubit. After the sender performs identical operations on their qubits, they compare the results. If the results match, then the states of more than half of the unmeasured qubits accidentally coincide with the required one: $|00\rangle + |11\rangle$. If the results do not match, the qubits are discarded. A detailed description of the method of "gearing reinforcement" is given in the work of Ch. Bennett [20] and significantly developed in the works of the Russian mathematician A. Holevo [77–79].

3.3 Implementation of the Shor Factorization Algorithm

Shor's algorithm is a quantum algorithm for factoring a number N for $O((\log N)^3)$ time and $O(\log N)$ resources [85]. The algorithm exposes the RSA key (a popular cryptographic method) to the danger of being easily hacked if it is run on a quantum computer large enough for this. Shor's algorithm can do this in polynomial time [1, 2, 48, 85–92, 95–108].

Like many of the quantum computer algorithms, Shor's algorithm is probabilistic: it gives the correct answer with any predetermined probability. This is achieved by repeatedly re-executing the algorithm. Since the proposed solution is verifiable in polynomial time, the algorithm can be modified to work in the expected polynomial time with zero error.

Shor's algorithm (Figure 3.6) was developed in 1994, but the classical part was developed before *J. L. Miller*. Seven years later, in 2001, Shor's quantum algorithm was demonstrated by a group at IBM, which carried out the factorization of the number 15 into 3 and 5 using a quantum computer with 7 qubits. In 2016, scientists at the Massachusetts Institute of Technology and the University of Innsbruck designed a quantum computer that implements a scalable version of the Shor algorithm proposed by a Russian physicist, *Alexey Kitaev* [85–92, 95–108]. This significantly reduced the number of qubits used to perform operations.

The task to be solved was to find the integer divisor of a p integer N in the interval between 1 and N.

Shor's algorithm consists of two parts:

1. reduction of the factorization problem to the order search problem, which can be solved on a classical computer;

2. execution of a quantum algorithm to solve the problem of finding the order.

The classical part of Shor's algorithm looks like this:

1. We select a random number $a < N$.

2. We calculate GCF (a,N) (the GCF is the largest common divisor). This can be done using Euclid's algorithm.

3. If GCF $(a,N) \neq 1$, then there is a nontrivial divisor N, and then the execution of the algorithm ends.

4. Otherwise, we use the period search routine (below) to find the r period of the following function: $f(x) = a^x \bmod N$, i.e., the smallest integer r for which $f(x + r) = f(x)$.

5. If r is odd, go back to step 1.

6. If $a^{r/2} \equiv -1 \bmod N$, go back to step 1.

7. The divisors of N are $\mathrm{GCF}\left(a^{\frac{r}{2}} \pm 1, N \right)$.

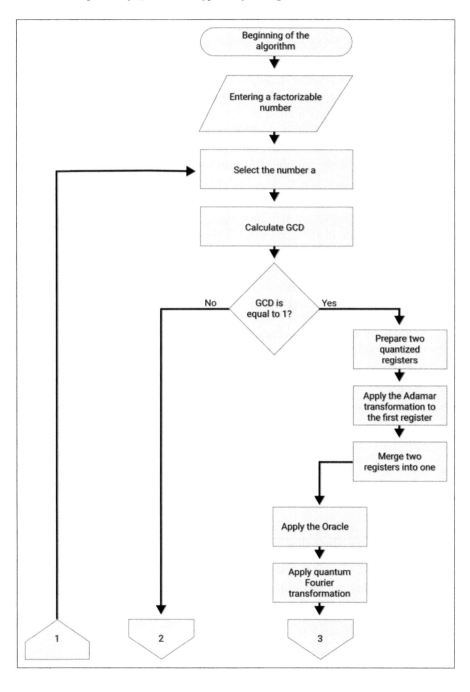

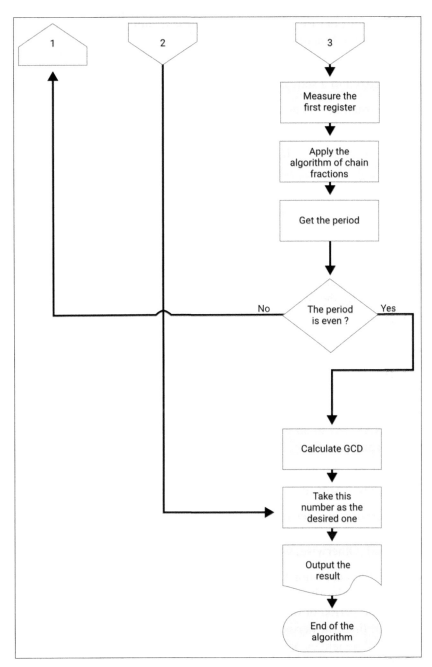

Figure 3.6 Diagram of the Shor factorization algorithm.

The quantum part of the Shor algorithm is a subroutine for searching for the period of the function:

1. A pair of initial and output qubit registers with $\log_2 N$ qubits are each initialized in a state $N^{-1/2} \sum_x |x\rangle |0\rangle$ where x runs from 0 to N−1.

2. Constructing $f(x)$ as a quantum function and applying it to the above state, we get

$$U_{QFT} |x\rangle = N^{-1/2} \sum_y e^{-2\pi i xy/N} |y\rangle.$$

3. This leaves us in the following state:

$$N^{-1} \sum_x \sum_y e^{-2\pi i xy/N} |y\rangle |f(x)\rangle.$$

4. Let us make a measurement. We will get some output y in the intro-ductory register and $f(x_0)$ in the output register. Since f is periodic, the probability of obtaining a certain pair during measurement of y and $f(x_0)$ is given by the following expression:

$$\left| N^{-1} \sum_{x: f(x)=f(x_0)} e^{-2\pi i xy/N} \right|^2 = \left| N^{-2} \sum_b e^{-2\pi i (x_0 + rb)y/N} \right|^2.$$

5. The analysis shows that this probability becomes higher, when yr/N becomes closer to the whole.

6. Convert yr/N to an irreducible fraction and find the denominator r^i that is a candidate for r.

7. Let us check whether $f(x) = f(x + r')$ is being executed. If yes, then the problem is solved.

8. Otherwise, we get more candidates for r, using values close to y, or multiples of r^i. If one of these candidates is suitable, the problem is solved. Otherwise, we return to step 1 of the subroutine.

Thus, the classical Shor factorization algorithm consists of two parts. The first part of the algorithm reduces the factorization problem to the problem of detecting the period of the function and can be implemented classically. The second part finds the period of the function using the inverse quantum Fourier transform (it generates quantum acceleration).

Therefore, in the first stage, there are divisors by period. Integers that are less than N and mutually prime with N form a finite multiplication group modulo N, which is usually denoted by $(Z/NZ)^x$. By the end of step 3, there is an integer a in this group. Since the group is finite, a must have a finite order r, the smallest positive integer such that $a^r \equiv 1 \bmod N$.

Suppose there is an opportunity to find r, and it is even. Then

$$a^r - 1 = \left(a^{\frac{r}{2}} - 1 \right)\left(a^{\frac{r}{2}} + 1 \right) \equiv 0 \bmod N, \Rightarrow N \,|(a^{r/2} - 1)\,(a^{r/2} + 1)\rangle$$ where r is the

smallest positive integer such that $a^r \equiv 1$; therefore, N is not a divisor $a^{r/2}-1$. If N is also not a divisor of $a^{r/2} + 1$, then N must have a nontrivial common divisor with each of $(a^{r/2}-1)$ и $(a^{r/2} +1)$, which leads us to factorization N. If N is the product of two primes, then this is the only possible factorization.

The second part of the algorithm is devoted to finding the period. Here, Shor's algorithm relies on the ability of a quantum computer to be in a super-position of states. The function is calculated at all points simultaneously in order to calculate the period of f function. Quantum mechanics does not allow access to this information directly. The measurement will result in only one of all possible values, destroying all the others. Therefore, it is necessary to transform the superposition into another state, which will return the cor-rect answer with a high probability. This is achieved by the inverse quantum Fourier transformation [48].

Shor had to solve the following three "implementation" problems, and all of them had to be implemented "quickly." This means that they can be implemented with a set of quantum gates that are polynomial in $\log N$ [85–92, 95–108]. So, it is necessary to do the following:

1. Create superpositions of states. This can be done by applying Hadamard gates to all qubits of the input register. Another approach would be to use the quantum Fourier transformation.

2. Apply function f as a quantum transformation. Shor used multiple squaring for his modular exponential transformation to achieve this. Note that this step is more difficult than the quantum Fourier transfor-mation, which requires auxiliary qubits and a significantly larger num-ber of gate triggers.

3. Perform the inverse quantum Fourier transformation. When using con-trolled rotation gates and Hadamard gates, Shor constructed a circuit for the quantum Fourier transformation, which uses only $O((\log N)^2)$ gates.

After all these transformations, the measurement will give an approximate value of the r period. For simplicity, let us assume that there exists such y that $\frac{yr}{N}$ is an integer. Then the probability to measure y is 1. We then notice that $e^{\frac{2\pi i b y r}{N}} = 1$ for all b integers. Therefore, the sum which square gives the probabil-ity to get when measured y will be equal to N/r, since b roughly takes values of

N/r and thus the probability is equal to $1/r^2$. There are such *yr* that *yr/N* is an integer, and also *r* probabilities for $f(x_0)$; so the sum of probabilities is 1 [85].

3.4 Implementation of the Grover's Search Algorithm

Consider Grover's algorithm, a quantum algorithm for fast search in an unordered database [3, 21, 30, 31, 98]. With the existing technical means, one of the fastest classical search algorithms is linear search, which requires $O[N]$ time. Grover's algorithm, using the capabilities of quantum computers, solves the problem of searching in *N* records for the desired time $O\left[\sqrt{N}\right]$ using $O[\log N]$ space. It is proved that it is the fastest quantum algorithm for searching in an unordered database and that there are no classical algorithms of the same efficiency. Grover's algorithm provides a quadratic increase in speed, while some other quantum algorithms, for example, the Shor factorization algorithm, give an exponential gain compared to the corresponding classical algorithms. Despite this, the quadratic increase is significant for sufficiently large values of *N* [3, 21, 29, 30, 31].

Although the main purpose of Grover's algorithm is considered to be a database search, it can be more accurately described as a "function reversal" algorithm. Technically speaking, having a function $y = f(x)$ that can be calculated using a quantum computer, Grover's algorithm calculates *x* knowing *y*. The search in the database corresponds to the call of a function that takes a certain value if the argument *x* corresponds to the desired record in the database. Grover's algorithm can also be used to find the median and the arithmetic mean of a number series. In addition, it can be used to solve *NP* complete problems by an exhaustive search among a variety of possible solutions. This can lead to a significant increase in speed compared to classical algorithms, although it does not provide a "polynomial solution" in general form [3, 21, 29, 30, 31].

Like most quantum computer algorithms, Grover's algorithm is probabilistic in the sense that it gives the correct answer with some probability (generally speaking, with any given in advance). The probability of an incorrect answer can be reduced by increasing the number of repetitions of the algorithm (an example of a deterministic quantum algorithm is the Deutsch–Joz algorithm [94, 95], which always gives the correct answer with fixed confidence). As an example, let us give Grover's algorithm, which searches for a single matching record.

Suppose there is an unordered database with *N* records. The algorithm requires a *N*-dimensional state space *H* that can be generated by $\log_2 N$ qubits. Let us number the database entries in this way: 0,1,2,... ,*N*–1.

Let us choose an observable Ω acting in H *with* N different eigenvalues, which are all known. Each of the eigenstates Ω encodes one of the records in the database in the way described below. Let us denote the eigenstates (using Dirac notation) as $|0\rangle$, $|1\rangle$,...,$|N{-}1\rangle$ as their corresponding eigenvalues $\{\lambda 0, \lambda 1,\dots, \lambda N{-}1\}$.

Consider a unitary operator U_ω that acts as a subroutine comparing database records by some search criterion. The algorithm does not specify how this subroutine works, but it should be a quantum subroutine that works with superpositions of states. Further, the operator U_ω must act only on its own state $|\omega\rangle$, which corresponds to the database record that falls under the search criterion. We will require that U_ω performs the following transformation: $U_\omega |\omega\rangle = - |\omega\rangle$ and $U_\omega |x\rangle = |x\rangle$ for every $x \neq \omega$. The goal is to identify the eigenstate $|\omega\rangle$ or, equivalently, the eigenvalue of ω, on which the operator acts U_ω.

Grover's algorithm (Figure 3.7) consists of the following steps [98]:

1. Initialize the system in the state $|s\rangle = \dfrac{1}{\sqrt{N}} \sum_x |x\rangle$.

2. Perform the following "Grover iterations" $r(N)$ times.

3. Function $r(N)$ is described below.

    a. Apply the U_ω operator.

    b. Apply the $U_s = 2|s\rangle\langle s|{-}1$ operator.

4. Let us take a Ω measurement. The result of the measurement will be λ_ω with a probability tending to 1 at $N \gg 1$. Knowing the value of λ_ω can be obtained the value of ω.

Our initial state is $|s\rangle = \dfrac{1}{\sqrt{N}} \sum_x |x\rangle$. Consider a plane spanned by vectors $|s\rangle$ and $|\omega\rangle$. Let $|\omega^s\rangle$ be a ket vector in this plane perpendicular to the $|\omega\rangle$ vector. Since $|\omega\rangle$ is one of the basis vectors, the overlap is equal to $\langle \omega|s\rangle = \dfrac{1}{\sqrt{N}}$. In geometric interpretation, between $|\omega\rangle$ and the $|s\rangle$ angle is $\pi/2{-}\theta$, where θ is determined from $\cos(2\pi - \theta) = \dfrac{1}{\sqrt{N}}$ and $\sin\theta = \dfrac{1}{\sqrt{N}}$. The operator U_ω acts as a reflection in a hyperplane orthogonal to $|\omega\rangle$; for vectors in a plane spanned by vectors $|s\rangle$ and $|\omega\rangle$, it acts as a reflection relative to a straight line defined by a $|\omega^s\rangle$ vector. The U_s operator is a reflection relative to a line defined by a $|s\rangle$ vector. Consequently, the state vector remains in the plane stretched over the vectors $|s\rangle$ and $|\omega\rangle$, after each action of the U_s operator and U_ω operator, and it can be directly verified

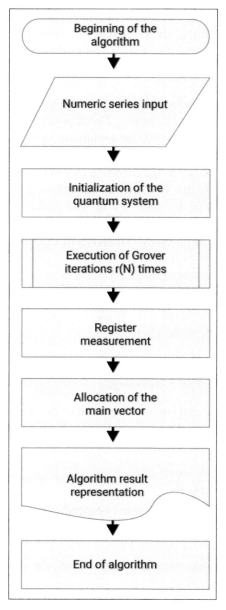

Figure 3.7 Diagram of Grover's quantum search algorithm.

that the $U_s U_\omega$ operator of each iterative step of the Grover algorithm rotates the state vector by an angle 2θ in the $|\omega\rangle$ direction [3, 20, 21, 29–31].

It is necessary to stop when the state vector passes close to the $|\omega\rangle$ vector; after that, the subsequent iterations rotate the state vector in the direction from $|\omega\rangle$, reducing the probability of getting the correct answer. The number of required iterations is equal to r. You need $\dfrac{\pi}{2} - \theta = 2\theta r$, $r = \dfrac{1}{4\left(\frac{\pi}{\theta}-2\right)}$ to combine the state vector exactly with $|\omega\rangle$ However, the number r must be an integer; so, in general, it can only be selected as the closest to $1/4(\pi/\theta - 2)$. The angle between $|\omega\rangle$ and the final state vector is equal $O(\theta)$; so the probability of getting an incorrect answer is equal to $O(1 - \cos^2 \theta) = O(\sin^2 \theta)$, $\theta \approx N^{-\frac{1}{2}}$, at $N \gg 1$. Therefore, $r \to \dfrac{\pi\sqrt{N}}{4}$. Moreover, the probability of getting an incorrect answer becomes $O(1/N)$ and tends to be zero for large N [3, 21, 29–31].

3.5 Development of an Algorithm for Recovering a Symmetric Encryption Key

Grover's algorithm is usually described as a search algorithm in an unordered array [98]. We modify Grover's algorithm into an algorithm for recovering the symmetric encryption key from the message text and ciphertext (Figure 3.8). When using a classic computer, this will require a complete search with complexity $O(2^m)$, where m is the length of the key. For a quantum computer, this complexity can be greatly reduced as follows.

Consider the function $y = f(k,x)$. This function encrypts the message x on the key k where $x, y \in Z_{2^n}$. Let the message–ciphertext pair be known: $x1$, $y1$. Consider the following function:

$$f(k) = \begin{cases} 1, if \mathbb{A}(k, x_1) = y_1 \\ 0, if \mathbb{A}(k, x_1) \neq y_1 \end{cases}.$$

Find the value of the argument at which this function is equal to 1.

We propose the following quantum algorithm for solving the problem.

Shor's algorithm implemented on a quantum circuit:
Step 1. Let us start the algorithm by bringing the quantum register to the state:

$$\frac{1}{\sqrt{2^m}} \sum_{t=0}^{2^m-1} |t\rangle.$$

Step 2. Calculating the function f from this register:

$$\frac{1}{\sqrt{2^m}} \sum_{x=0}^{2^m-1} |t|f(t)\rangle.$$

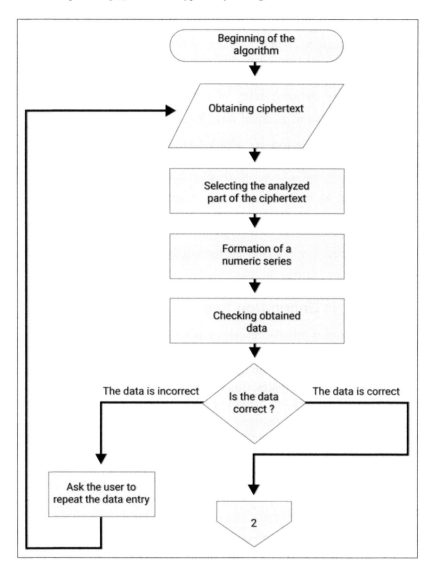

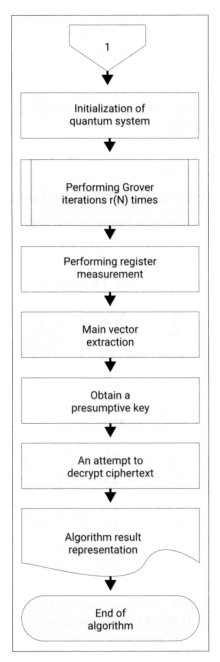

Figure 3.8 Quantum algorithm for symmetric encryption key recovery based on the message text and ciphertext has been developed.

Step 3. Repetition $\frac{\pi}{4}\sqrt{2^m}$ times of the procedure of increasing the ampli-tude of all t_i for which $f(t_i) = 1$ (the description of the procedure is given below).

Step 4. Measurement of the state of the register. The result will be equal to the desired key with probability 2^{-n}.

Step 5. Checking the result. In case of unreliability, the algorithm is executed again. The end of the algorithm.

The procedure for increasing the amplitude consists of two stages.

1. The change in an amplitude from a_j to is a_j for all t_i is such that $f(t_i) = 1$. This operation is a transformation Z over the last quantum bit of the register.

2. Inversion relative to the mean. This transformation can be written as follows:

$$\sum_i |t_i\rangle \rightarrow \sum_i \left(2a_{cp} - a_i\right)|t_i\rangle,$$

where a_{cp} is the average amplitude.
The inversion relative to the mean can be written as a matrix:

$$D = \begin{pmatrix} \frac{2}{N} - 1 & \frac{2}{N} & K & \frac{2}{N} \\ \frac{2}{N} & \frac{2}{N} - 1 & L & \frac{2}{N} \\ L & L & L & L \\ \frac{2}{N} & \frac{2}{N} & L & \frac{2}{N} - 1 \end{pmatrix}$$

L. Grover showed [98] that this transformation can be efficiently imple-mented on a quantum computer, and the complexity of the corresponding $O(2^{n/2})$ *algorithm*. Thus, the advent of quantum computers will reduce the effective key length by half. This suggests that symmetric ciphers with a key length of at least *256* bits should already be used.

In addition, a similar algorithm can be used to crack hash functions, and, therefore, hash functions with a block length of at least *256* bits should be used.

3.6 Development of an Algorithm for Cryptanalysis of the RSA Asymmetric Encryption System

The stability of the RSA asymmetric encryption system is based on the super-polynomial computational complexity of factorization of natural numbers. However, there is a quantum algorithm whose complexity is polynomial.

Let us set the problem as follows: for a natural N number having exactly two prime divisors, find these divisors. Note that for some a number, its order modulo N is such that it is $a^r = 1 \mod N$ even. Then we will write the expression $a^r = 1 \mod N$ in the following form:

$$\left(a^{r/2} - 1\right)\left(a^{r/2} + 1\right) = 0 \mod N$$

Thus, knowing r, we can efficiently find the divisors of a number N. Note that the order r is actually the period of the function $a^x \mod N$.

There is the following quantum algorithm (Figure 3.9) to find the period of the function. Consider the periodic function $f(x)$. The domain of definition and the domain of values of this function are sets of integers, with $0 \le x \le 2^n-1$ and $0 \le f(x) \le 2^m-1$. A quantum register consisting of $n + m$ quantum bits is required to find the period of this function. Let us bring it to the following state:

$$\frac{1}{\sqrt{2^n}} \sum_{x=0}^{2^n-1} |x,0\rangle.$$

Now, we calculate the function f so that we get the state:

$$\frac{1}{\sqrt{2^n}} \sum_{x=0}^{2^n-1} |x, f(x)\rangle.$$

Let us measure the last m quantum bits, i.e., the quantum bits related to $f(x)$. Then the quantum register will switch to the state:

$$\sum_{x:f(x)=u} |x,u\rangle.$$

Let us carry out the quantum Fourier transformation (the algorithm is given below); as a result, we get the state:

$$\sum_{j} c_j \left| j\frac{2^n}{r}\right\rangle,$$

where c_j are equal to zero for all j non-multiples of $2^{n/r}$. If the r period does not divide 2^n, the transformation is performed inaccurately, with a large amplitude concentrated near integer multiples of $[2^{n/r}]$.

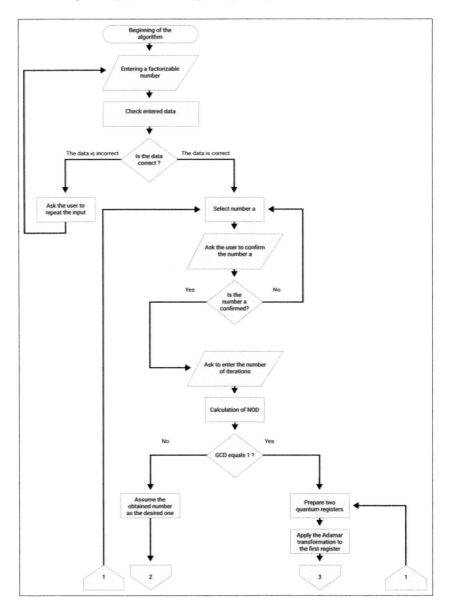

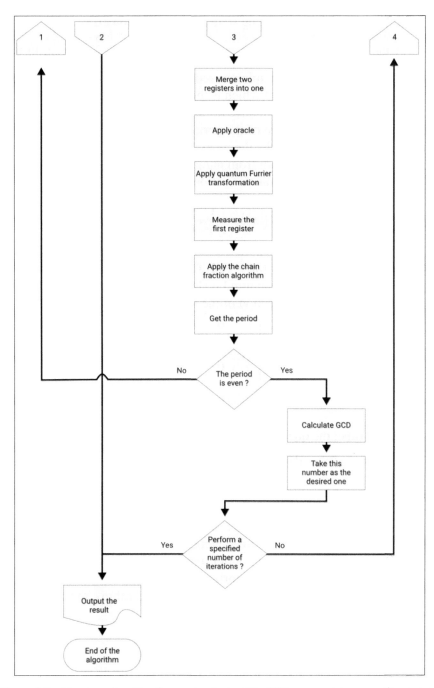

Figure 3.9 Quantum algorithm for cryptanalysis of the RSA asymmetric encryption system.

Let us measure the resulting state and get a v number.

If the period is equal to the power of 2, then $v = j\dfrac{2^n}{r}$. Since, in most cases, j and r are mutually simple, the reduction of the $v/2^n$ fraction will give a fraction, the denominator of which is the period.

In general, either we will have to run the entire algorithm several times until we get the correct value of the period (the maximum amplitude corresponds to it and, consequently, the maximum probability) or use the infinite fraction decomposition known from number theory [56].

The quantum Fourier transformation is defined as follows:

$$U_{QFT}\left(|x\rangle\right) = \frac{1}{\sqrt{2^m}} \sum_{c=0}^{2^m-1} e^{\frac{2\pi i c x}{2^m}} |c\rangle$$

P. Shor [85] showed that such a transformation can be constructed using only two types of quantum gates $(m + 1)/2$. One of them is a *Hadamard transformation* applied to j the quantum bit (let us denote it to H_j). Another gate implements a 2-bit transformation of the following form:

$$S_{j,k} = \begin{pmatrix} 1 & 0 & 0 & 0 \\ 0 & 1 & 0 & 0 \\ 0 & 0 & 1 & 0 \\ 0 & 0 & 0 & e^{i\frac{\pi}{2^{k-j}}} \end{pmatrix}.$$

At the same time, the quantum Fourier transformation can be set as follows:

$$H_0 S_{0,1} K S_{0,m-1} H_1 K H_{m-3} S_{m-3,m-2} S_{m-3,m-1} H_{m-2} S_{m-2,m-1} H_{m-1} =$$

$$= \prod_{k=0}^{m=1} H_k \prod_{t=k+1}^{m=1} S_{k,t}.$$

After this conversion, the bit order should be reversed. This can be done either by an appropriate quantum scheme or, if a measurement takes place immediately after the quantum Fourier transformation, in a classical way.

The considered quantum factorization algorithm has $O(n^3)$ complexity. At the same time, the best classical factorization algorithm – the number field sieve algorithm [85] has complexity:

$$O(\exp(c(\log n)^{1/3} (\log \log n)^{1/3})),$$

where $c = \sqrt{\dfrac{64}{9}}$. In other words, Shor's algorithm has polynomial complexity, and the best classical algorithm has superpolynomial complexity.

3.7 Development of an Algorithm for Cryptanalysis of the El Gamal System

El-Gamal system is based on the difficulty of calculating a discrete logarithm, i.e., if g is the forming element of a finite G group, then, knowing that $a \in G$, it is necessary to find $r \in G$ such that $a = g^r$. Most often, this system is used for a group Z_p and for a group of points of an elliptic curve.

There is a quantum Shor algorithm [85] for calculating the discrete logarithm (Figure 3.10). Here is its original version, which is intended for the group Z_p (where p is simple).

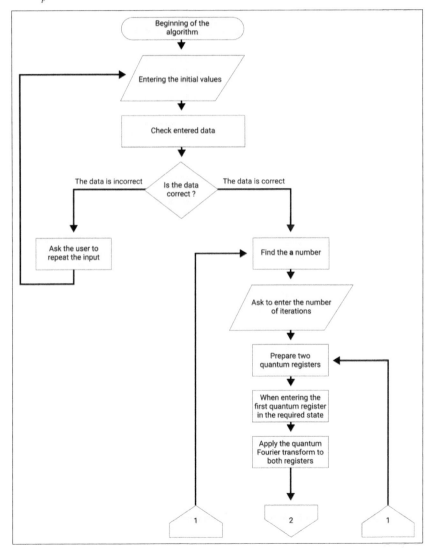

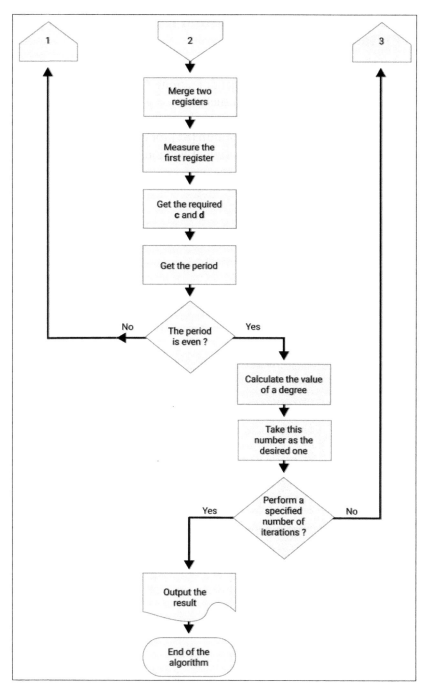

Figure 3.10 Quantum cryptanalysis algorithm of El Gamal system.

First, we will find q– the power of 2, such that $p < q < 2p$. Let us bring the quantum register to the state:

$$\frac{1}{p-1}\sum_{a=0}^{p-2}\sum_{b=0}^{p-2}\left|a,b,g^{a}x^{-b}\,(mod\ p)\right\rangle.$$

Applying the Fourier transformation to the first and second parts of the register, we obtain the state of the register:

$$\frac{1}{q(p-1)}\sum_{c=0}^{q-2}\sum_{d=0}^{q-2}e^{\frac{2\pi i}{q}(ac+bd)}\left|c,d,g^{a}x^{-b}\,(mod\ p)\right\rangle.$$

Let us measure the state of the quantum register. As a result, with a probability of at least 1/480, we will get c and d such that:

$$-\frac{1}{2q}\le\frac{d}{q}+r\left(\frac{c(p-1)-\{c(p-1)\}_{q}}{(p-1)q}\right)\le\frac{1}{2q}\,(mod\,1),$$

where $\{x\}_{q}$ is the number satisfying the relations:

$$\{x\}_{q}\equiv(mod\ q)\ \text{and}\ -\frac{q}{2}<\{x\}_{q}\le\frac{q}{2}.$$

In order to get a candidate for r, it is necessary to round a/q to the nearest multiple $1/p$–1, and then divide modulo p –1 on $\dfrac{c(p-1)-\{c(p-1)\}_{q}}{q}$. The complexity of this algorithm is estimated as $O(n^{3})$. Note that the complexity of the best classical algorithm for a discrete logarithm is estimated as superpolynomial.

Note that there is a variant of Shor's algorithm for a group of points of an elliptic curve over a field $GF(p)$ that has $O(n^{3})$ complexity, and it is also hypothesized that a similar algorithm exists for elliptic curves over other fields [29].

Thus, the appearance of existing samples of quantum computers will lead to the fact that many cryptosystems, primarily asymmetric, will become unstable, which will lead to the impossibility of using asymmetric crypto-systems and, consequently, to the impossibility of secure data transmission in dual-use and military systems. Electronic signatures and key distribution schemes will also cease to be secure. It means that it is already necessary to develop new asymmetric crypto algorithms. At the same time, symmetric encryption algorithms will remain stable, but the effective key length of such algorithms will decrease by half [29, 33].

Conclusions on Chapter 3

1. The stability analysis of the discrete algorithm (*DLP*) and the discrete algorithm with an elliptic curve (*ECDLP*) on the example of a number of applications improved the implementation of the original quantum Shor factorization algorithm. The algorithm is polynomial and is different from the known fundamental ability of software and hardware implementation in a hybrid computing environment (quantum computer *IBM Q* (16, 20, and 100 qubits), and/or Super-computer 5-generation *IBM BladeCenter (2020), PBC on FPGA Virtex UltraScale (2020), VS RFNC-VNIIEF (2021)*, and *SKIF P-0.5 (2018)*).

2. In the course of the work, a variant of the Grover quantum search algorithm was developed, the analysis of the limiting possibilities of which helped to establish that the overkill problem does not receive exponential quantum acceleration. However, it becomes possible to reduce the effective key length of symmetric encryption systems by exactly two times.

3. Modification of the Grover search algorithm for solving problems of cryptanalysis of symmetric encryption schemes developed an original quantum algorithm for restoring the symmetric encryption key from the message text and ciphertext. The proposed algorithm solves the mentioned cryptanalysis problems with acceptable complexity and labor intensity.

4. Analysis of the durability of RSA asymmetric encryption schemes based on the computational complexity of the integer factorization problem (DLP) allowed us to develop a polynomial quantum algorithm for cryptanalysis of the RSA asymmetric encryption system. The algorithm is polynomial and is different from the known fundamental ability of software and hardware implementation in a hybrid computing environment (quantum computer *IBM Q* (16, 20, and 100 qubits), and/or Super-computer 5-generation *IBM BladeCenter (2020), PBC on FPGA Virtex UltraScale (2020), VS RFNC-VNIIEF (2021)*, and *SKIF P-0.5 (2018)*).

5. Analysis of the strength of asymmetric encryption schemes, based on the computational complexity of the discrete logarithm problem (ECDLP), developed a polynomial quantum algorithm for cryptanalysis of the El Gamal system. This made it possible to determine the requirements for the length of quantum registers (from several hundred qubits), sufficient to solve cryptanalysis problems in practice.

4

Development of the "Q-Cryptanalysis" Platform

In Chapter 4, the "Q-cryptanalysis" platform is designed. The development environment of the "Q-cryptanalysis" platform is justified and selected. The structural and functional scheme of the "Q-cryptanalysis" platform is developed. An example of the work of the "Q-cryptanalysis" platform is described. The specific features of the development of the "Q-cryptanalysis" platform for working in a quantum computing model are revealed. A full-scale testing of the "Q-cryptanalysis" platform is carried out. The evaluation of the effectiveness of the "Q-cryptanalysis" platform is given. Possible directions of development of the "Q-cryptanalysis" platform are given. A feasibility study for the development of the "Q-cryptanalysis" platform is presented.

4.1 Features of the Implementation of the "Q-Cryptanalysis" Platform

4.1.1 Q-cryptanalysis platform development tools

During the design, the "Q-cryptanalysis" platform was developed to solve the problems of cryptanalysis of asymmetric encryption schemes (RSA or El Gamal) and digital signature (DSA, ECDSA, or RSA-PSS) in a hybrid computing environment; the "IBM Q quantum computer" is a "fifth-generation supercomputer" [22, 42–45, 48]. The "Q-cryptanalysis" platform was written primarily in the *Python* programming language using the *Jupyter Notebook* interpreter (included in the *Anaconda* development package), as well as using the IBM Qiskit library [110]. The choice of the mentioned "Q-cryptanalysis" platform development tools was due to the following.

Python is a modern object-oriented programming language with dynamic strict typing and automatic memory management. Despite the fact that Python is inferior to the well-known C++ and the rapidly gaining popularity Kotlin in terms of optimizing executable code, speed, and memory usage, this programming language has become widespread. The Python interpreter supports programs developed in procedural, functional, and logical programming styles. The Python library contains a well-developed set of functions that develop quite complex applications from text editors to specialized network security incident response applications. There are developed capabilities for mathematical modeling of physical processes, for the development of artificial intelligence (AI) and machine learning (ML) applications, for working with big data (Big Data) and for streaming data processing (ETL), etc. For this purpose, both proprietary and third-party libraries are used, including C or C++ libraries. There is a specialized Python software repository called PyPI. As of January 2022, Python occupies the third position in the popularity of programming languages with a share of 11.03% (TIOBE) [110, 111].

One of the Python distributions is Anaconda, which contains a developed set of thematic NumPy, SciPy, and Astropy modules (more than 1.7 thousand modules). The Dependency Resolution Manager with the Anaconda Navigator GUI allows you to opt out of using standard package managers. In addition, it is possible to simultaneously conduct several software developments projects in separate isolated environments with separate resolution of version dependencies in each.

Jupyter Notebook is a special toolkit (interpreter) for managing software projects, which is widely used for working with various types of data science. The interpreter integrates various software modules for data collection and processing in fairly complex software code development projects, for example, Kaggle Kernels (organization and holding of development contests on the Kaggle platform). Note that Jupyter is the successor of another well-known interpreter Notebook IPython from 2010. Currently, Jupyter Notebooks support a large number of programming languages, including the Python language we previously selected.

Qiskit (*IBM Research* developer) is an open framework for programming and debugging quantum programs both on real prototypes of IBM Q quantum computers and in the environment of corresponding emulators (*IBM Q Experience*) [48, 110, 111]. This framework also models quantum algorithms on quantum circuits (superconducting qubits and trapped ions). Qiskit also supports the Python programming language we selected earlier.

Thus, the considered programming environment for the development of the "Q-cryptanalysis" platform provided opportunities for the following:

- Work organization on real prototypes of IBM Q quantum computers for 16 (or more) qubits;

- Work organization with quantum emulators of high and ultra-high performance (up to 1 Exaflops) (Lomonosov-2 supercomputer, Tornado, SKIF, FPGA calculators, 61 department calculators, etc.);

- Operation under the control of a widespread line of operating systems of the MS Windows family and the Linux family (including Astra Linux);

- High-quality development of standard modules of the mentioned "Q-cryptanalysis" platform in a timely manner;

- Project development management of the "Q-cryptanalysis" complex as a whole;

- High-quality debugging of the "Q-cryptanalysis" platform;

- Operation and further maintenance of the quantum cryptanalysis "Q-cryptanalysis" platform.

4.1.2 Q-cryptanalysis platform architecture

During the design of the "Q-cryptanalysis" platform, the following main modules were developed [48]:

1. primary cryptosystem analysis module, designed to determine the cryptographic cipher and reduce the opening task of factorization;

2. searching module for the period of an indefinite function, designed to implement factorization on a quantum computing system;

3. secret key calculation module designed to process the factorization result obtained as a result of the previous module operation for the subsequent opening of the cryptosystem;

4. module for presenting results and analyzing them, designed to display the result obtained and analyze the characteristics of its receipt.

The structural and functional scheme of the "Q-cryptanalysis" platform is shown in Figure 4.1.

A typical algorithm of the "Q-cryptanalysis" platform is shown in Figure 4.2.

4.1.3 Example of "Q-cryptanalysis" platform operation

Let us consider an example of the "Q-cryptanalysis" platform launch and operation for solving problems of quantum cryptanalysis of asymmetric encryption and digital signature schemes in a hybrid computing environment "IBM Q quantum computer – fifth generation supercomputer" based on solving the factorization problem in polynomial time.

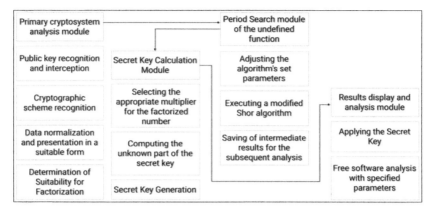

Figure 4.1   Structural and functional diagram of "Q-cryptanalysis" platforms.

At the beginning of operation, the "Q-cryptanalysis" platform, the user is asked to enter a factorizable number, the output window is shown in Figure 4.3.

Next, you need to confirm the number that will be used when finding the period, or enter it yourself (Figure 4.4).

After that, the platform outputs the required number of qubits for the operation and prompts the user to select the number of operation calculation (Figure 4.5). It is recommended to choose at least three calculations here, because due to the phenomenon of quantum decoherence, significant failures may occur on a few duplicate calculations on a quantum computer.

As a result, the "Q-cryptanalysis" platform visualizes the execution of the modified Shor algorithm step by step, along with an analysis of the work cycles and estimates of the accuracy of the intermediate and output results obtained (Figure 4.6).

A certificate of registration of the computer program No. 2020665981 in 2020 was received on the Q-cryptanalysis platform.

4.2 Features of the used Quantum Computing Model

First, a number of principles for cryptanalysis of asymmetric encryption and digital signature schemes were defined. In particular, the following typical sequence of actions is highlighted (Figure 4.7) for asymmetric encryption schemes (RSA or El Gamal) and digital signature (DSA, ECDSA, or RSA-PSS) [48]:

1.   based on the private key, *Subscriber A* public key is generated;

2.   public key is transmitted to *Subscriber B*;

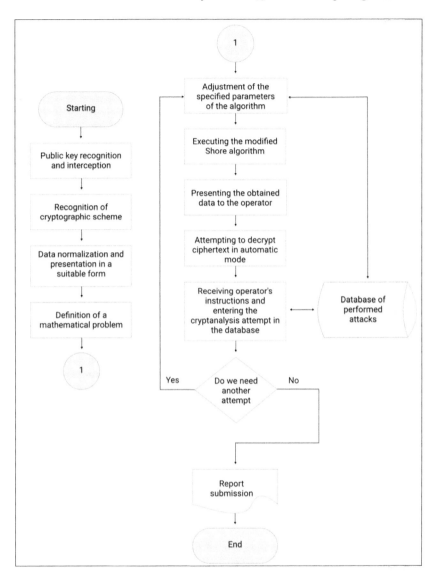

Figure 4.2   "Q-cryptanalysis" flowchart.

3. *Subscriber B* encrypts information using a public key for *Subscriber A*;

4. *Subscriber B* transmits the ciphertext to *Subscriber A* via the communication channel;

5. *Subscriber A* performs decryption of the ciphertext using his private key.

```
  Консоль 1/A
Python 3.7.4 (default, Aug  9 2019, 18:34:13) [MSC v.1915 64 bit
(AMD64)]
Type "copyright", "credits" or "license" for more information.

IPython 7.8.0 -- An enhanced Interactive Python.

In [1]: runfile('C:/Users/Alexey/untitled24.py', wdir='C:/Users/
Alexey')

Please insert integer number N:
```

Figure 4.3 "Q-cryptanalysis" output window when entering a factorizable number.

```
  Консоль 1/A
Python 3.7.4 (default, Aug  9 2019, 18:34:13) [MSC v.1915 64 bit
(AMD64)]
Type "copyright", "credits" or "license" for more information.

IPython 7.8.0 -- An enhanced Interactive Python.

In [1]: runfile('C:/Users/Alexey/untitled24.py', wdir='C:/Users/
Alexey')

Please insert integer number N: 15
input number was: 15

Not an easy case, using the quantum circuit is necessary


Is the number 2 ok for a? Press 0 if not, other number if yes:
```

Figure 4.4 Auxiliary number request window.

The basic principles necessary for the development of the quantum cryptanalysis platform "Q-cryptanalysis" included the following:

1. It is possible to generate a pair of very large numbers (public key and private key) so that knowing the public key, it is impossible to calculate

```
  Консоль 1/A ☒                                                    ■ ✎

Python 3.7.4 (default, Aug  9 2019, 18:34:13) [MSC v.1915 64 bit
(AMD64)]
Type "copyright", "credits" or "license" for more information.

IPython 7.8.0 -- An enhanced Interactive Python.

In [1]: runfile('C:/Users/Alexey/untitled24.py', wdir='C:/Users/
Alexey')

Please insert integer number N: 15
input number was: 15

Not an easy case, using the quantum circuit is necessary


Is the number 2 ok for a? Press 0 if not, other number if yes: 43
Using 2 as value for a

Total number of qubits used: 11


Number of times to run the circuit: |
```

Figure 4.5   Request window for the number operation calculations.

the private key in a reasonable time. At the same time, the generation mechanism is well known.

2.   There are reliable encryption methods that encrypt a message with a public key so that it can only be decrypted with a private key. The encryption mechanism is well known.

3.   The owner of the two keys does not disclose the private key to anyone but passes the public key to counterparties or makes it publicly known.

Here, factorization of a natural number means its decomposition into a product of prime factors. The existence and uniqueness (up to the order of the multipliers) of such a decomposition follows from the basic theorem of arithmetic. Unlike the problem of recognizing the simplicity of a number, factorization is presumably a computationally complex task. Therefore, finding an effective quantum algorithm for factorization of integers is relevant here (Figure 4.8). At the same time, there is no evidence that the solution of this problem in polynomial time does not exist [23, 25, 29, 44–48].

Note that the assumption that the factorization problem is computationally complex for large numbers is the basis of widely used algorithms.

```
  Консоль 1/А ☒                                                    ■ ◢
not an easy case; using the quantum circuit is necessary

Is the number 2 ok for a? Press 0 if not, other number if yes: 0

Is the number 4 ok for a? Press 0 if not, other number if yes: 2
Using 4 as value for a

Total number of qubits used: 11


Number of times to run the circuit: 3
Executing the circuit 3 times for N=15 and a=4

Printing the various results followed by how many times they happened
(out of the 3 cases):

Result "1 10000000" happened 3 times out of 3

------> Analysing result 10000000. This result happened in 100.0000 %
of all cases

In decimal, x_final value for this result is: 128

Running continued fractions for this case

Approximation number 1 of continued fractions:
Numerator:0                    Denominator: 1

Odd denominator, will try next iteration of continued fractions

Approximation number 2 of continued fractions:
Numerator:1                    Denominator: 2

The factors of 15 are 5 and 3

Found the desired factors!


Using a=4, found the factors of N=15 in 100.0000 % of the cases

In [2]:
```

Figure 4.6   Example of the result of the software cryptanalysis complex "Q-cryptanalysis."

The solution of a number of applied problems of mathematics and theoretical computer science depends on the completeness, consistency, and solvability of the mentioned factorization problem, including applications of *elliptic curves, algebraic number theory, quantum computing*, etc. As a rule, the input of such algorithms is a number that needs to be factorized, consisting

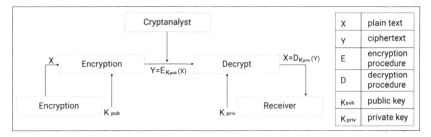

Figure 4.7   A typical scheme of asymmetric encryption.

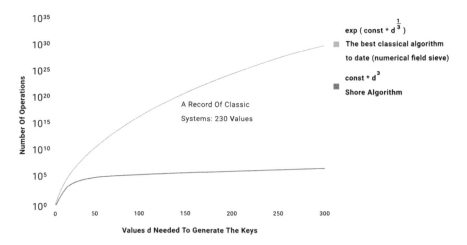

Figure 4.8   Explanations for assessing the durability of the studied cryptosystems.

of $N = [\log_2 n] + 1$ characters (if n presented in binary form). In this case, the first prime divisor is searched for first, after which, if necessary, the search is repeated for further factorization. Before starting factorization of a large number, you should make sure that it is not simple. It is sufficient to pass the appropriate number test for this. This problem is deterministically solvable in polynomial time [44–48].

Depending on the complexity, the factorization algorithms were divided into two groups. The first group includes *exponential algorithms* whose complexity exponentially depends on the length of the input parameters (that is, on the length N of the number itself in binary representation). The second group includes *subexponential algorithms*. It is clear that the strength of symmetric and asymmetric cryptography algorithms is based on the complexity of solving certain classes of problems on classical computers (enumeration, factorization, and discrete logarithm are in the NPP complexity class by key length in bits), in contrast to quantum cryptography, the strength of which is based on the laws of quantum physics. An estimate of the time complexity

Table 4.1 Time complexity of algorithms, solving factorization, and discrete logarithm problems.

Solving the factorization problem	
Title	**Complexity**
Farm method	$T(N) = O(N^{\frac{1}{3}})$
Lenstra method	$T = O(e^{\sqrt{2 \ln p \ \ln \ln p}})$
Dixon's method	$T = O(L(n)^2)$
Quadratic sieve method	$T = O\left(\exp\left((1 + o(1)) \sqrt{\log n \log \log n} \right) \right)$
Numerical field sieve method	$T(N) = O(n \log n \log N)$
Shor's method	$T = O(\log_3 M)$
Solving the discrete logarithm problem	
Title	**Complexity**
The Adleman method	$T = O\left(c^{\ln p^{\frac{1}{2}}} \right)$
The COS method	$T = O(\exp\left((\log p \log \log p)^{\frac{1}{2}} \right)$
Numerical field sieve method	$T(N) = O(n \log n \log N)$
Shor's method	$T = O(\log_3 M)$

of the main factorization and discrete logarithm algorithms is presented in Table 4.1.

Thus, typical schemes of asymmetric encryption (RSA or El Gamal) and digital signature (DSA, ECDSA, or RSA-PSS) are based on the complexity of computing a discrete logarithm in finite groups defined over various algebraic constructions or on the complexity of decomposing a natural number into simple factors. And the vulnerability of the mentioned schemes is based on the computational complexity of the factorization numbers.

The discrete logarithm and factorization problems have asymptotic complexity when solving quantum steps on a $O(n^2 \log n \log \log n)$ quantum computer. On a classical computer using the best-known algorithm – the numerical field sieve algorithm – the asymptotic complexity is $O(e^{cn^{1/3} \log^{2/3} n})$, where c is some constant. The polynomial solution of discrete logarithm problems on a quantum computer is also found in $O(n^2 \log n \log (\log n))$ [44–48].

1. $|0> |0>$ Initiating the condition

2. $\rightarrow \dfrac{1}{\sqrt{2^t}} \sum\limits_{x=0}^{2^t-1} |x> |0>$ Creating the superposition

3. $\rightarrow \dfrac{1}{\sqrt{2^t}} \sum\limits_{x=0}^{2^t-1} |x> |f(x)>$ Apply $U\, f(x) = ax(\mathrm{mod}N)$

$\approx \dfrac{1}{\sqrt{r2^t}} \sum\limits_{l=0}^{r-1} \sum\limits_{x=0}^{2^t-1} e^{2\pi i l x/r} |x> |\hat{f}(l)>$

4. $\rightarrow \dfrac{1}{\sqrt{r}} \sum\limits_{l=0}^{r-1} \left|\dfrac{l}{r}> |\hat{f}(l)>\right.$ Apply QFT to the first register

5. $\rightarrow \widetilde{l/r}$ Measure the first register

6. $\rightarrow r$ Apply chain fraction algorithm

Figure 4.9   The main stages of the proposed quantum Shor factorization algorithm.

As a result, the practical significance of quantum algorithms for solving factorization and discrete logarithm problems lies in the fact that with their help, when using a quantum computer with several hundred logical qubits (Figures 4.9 and 4.10), it becomes possible to crack cryptographic systems with a public key. For example, *RSA* uses an *M* public key that is the product of two large primes. One way to crack the *RSA* cipher is to find its multipliers. With a large enough *M*, it is almost impossible to do this using the well-known classical algorithms. The best-known classical factorization algorithms require $M^{1/3}$ order time. *Shor's algorithm*, using the capabilities of quantum computers, is able to factorize a number not just in polynomial time, but in a time slightly exceeding the multiplication time of integers (that is, almost as fast as the encryption itself occurs) [44–48].

It is clear that here we are speaking not only about *the RSA scheme* directly based on the difficulty of factorization but also about other similar schemes' asymmetric encryption (derived from RSA and El Gamal) and digital signature (DSA, ECDSA, or RSA-PSS), which become vulnerable to the "Q-cryptanalysis" platform developed by the author.

Now let us consider the software and technical implementation of the proposed algorithm for solving typical factorization problems with polynomial complexity in more detail [48].

First, it was taken into account that the proposed quantum Shor factorization algorithm (Figure 4.11) is characterized by a probabilistic nature [85–90]. Here, the first source of randomness is embedded in the classical

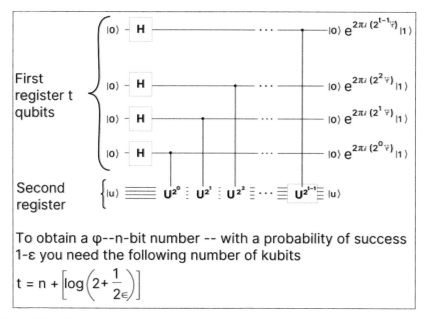

Figure 4.10   Finding the required number of qubits, as a criterion for the success of solving the cryptanalysis problem.

probabilistic reduction of factorization to finding the period of some function. The second source comes from the need to observe quantum memory, which also produces random results. Therefore, the following typical steps for solving the factorization problem were programmed:

1. choose a random *a* remainder modulo *N*;

2. check GCF $(a, N) = 1$;

3. find the *r* order of *a* remainder of *N* modulo;

4. if *r* is even, the GCF $(a^{r/2}-1, N)$ is calculated.

With high probability, the number obtained at the fourth step has always been a non-trivial *N* divisor. The third step turned out to be a rather difficult step to implement. Here, the minimum *r* is such that a $r \equiv 1 \bmod N$ is the *a* order on *N* modulo (the *r* order is the period of the $f(x) = a \times x \bmod N$ function).

   For example, let there be a *N* number. We will randomly select the number *a* so that it is mutually prime with *N*. Such a number will be found with a high probability. Repeating several times, we will find such a number (a number *a* is called mutually simple *b* if their greatest common divisor is 1). After that, we determine the *r* order of the *a* remainder *N* modulo. We will

$f(x) = a^x \bmod N.$

$7^4 \bmod 15 \equiv 1 \Rightarrow 7^4 - 1 \bmod 15 \equiv 0 \Rightarrow (7^2 - 1)(7^2 + 1) \bmod 15 \equiv 0 \bmod 15 \Rightarrow 15 \text{ divides } 48 \cdot 50$

$$\gcd(48, 15) = 3 \qquad\qquad \gcd(50, 15) = 5$$

$N = 15.$
$x = 7$
$t=11 \ \varepsilon=1/4$

$$\frac{1}{\sqrt{2^t}} \sum_{k=0}^{2^t-1} |k\rangle|0\rangle = \frac{1}{\sqrt{2^t}}\left[|0\rangle + |1\rangle + |2\rangle + \cdots + |2^t - 1\rangle \right]|0\rangle \qquad t = 11 \ \text{H:}$$

$$f(k) = x^k \bmod N$$

$$\frac{1}{\sqrt{2^t}} \sum_{k=0}^{2^t-1} |k\rangle|x^k \bmod N\rangle = \frac{1}{\sqrt{2^t}}\left[|0\rangle|1\rangle + |1\rangle|7\rangle + |2\rangle|4\rangle + |3\rangle|13\rangle + |4\rangle|1\rangle + |5\rangle|7\rangle + |6\rangle|4\rangle + \cdots \right]$$

$$FT^\dagger \qquad\qquad \widetilde{\ell/r}$$

Figure 4.11   An example of solving the factorization problem by quantum computing.

get: $a^r \equiv 1 \bmod N$. We want r to be even. If this is not the case, go back to the a number selection step. So, we have: $a \ r \equiv 1 \bmod N$, where r is even, and then we can write: $(a^{r/2} - 1) (a^{r/2} + 1) = cN$, where c is some positive integer. It is not difficult to prove that one of the brackets has a N common non-trivial divisor. Then, taking $\gcd(a^{r/2} - 1, N)$, we get one divisor N (it may turn out that the number N will have a common non-trivial divisor with the second bracket, and then we will have to repeat the choice of the number a again). Dividing N by the resulting number, we find the second divisor. The task of factoring a number N was reduced to quickly find the period r for a randomly selected a number.

Second, to determine the period of the r function using the *Fourier* transformation, it was not necessary to calculate all the $f(x)$ values. The problem was reduced to a solution similar to the solution of the Deutsch problem, which takes into account not all the values of the function but only some of its properties. As a result, the obtained representations of the *Fourier trans-formation* in the form of a product (Figure 4.12) made it possible to simulate the required quantum circuits (Figure 4.14) to work with the IBM Q quantum computer, which was selected for the engineering implementation and testing of the proposed quantum Shor factorization algorithm (Figure 4.13) [48].

Here, the *gate R_k* denotes a unitary transformation of the form:

$$\begin{bmatrix} 1 & 0 \\ 0 & e^{2\pi i/2^k} \end{bmatrix}.$$

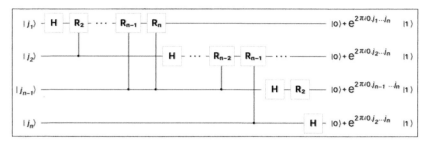

Figure 4.12   Gate representation of the quantum Fourier transformation.

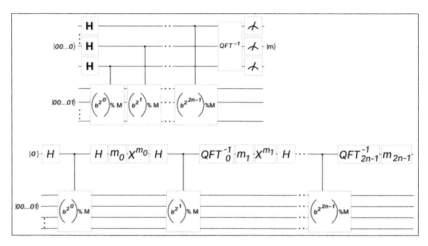

Figure 4.13   Quantum representation of the modified quantum Shor factorization algorithm.

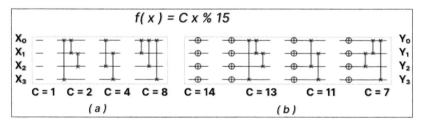

Figure 4.14   Example of quantum gate modeling.

Third, the scheme of direct connection to the *IBM Q* quantum 16-qubit system using the *IBM Cloud platform* was tested. The direct access to the *IBM Quantum Experience* was obtained and the corresponding application was launched to do this (Figure 4.15) on a quantum circuit to work with individual qubits [48].

Fourth, possible hybrid schemes from *IBM Q quantum computers and simulators on fifth-generation supercomputers (Lomonosov-2 supercomputers,*

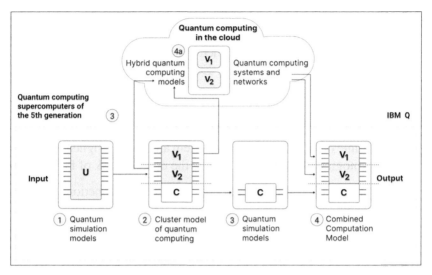

Figure 4.15 Testing of the developed "Q-cryptanalysis" platform in the *IBM Q System One* environment (16-qubit) and a fifth generation supercomputer.

Tornado, SKIF, and *FPGA computers*) were tested. At the same time, the author's *Python* applications were used, as well as a number of open libraries for modeling quantum algorithms on quantum circuits [48, 110, 111].

4.3 Testing of the "Q-Cryptanalysis" Platform

A testing plan for the "Q-cryptanalysis" platform was prepared and implemented during the development [48]. Here, the main testing goals were the following:

- verification of the fulfillment of functional and technical requirements for the "Q-cryptanalysis" platform;

- checking the operability of the "Q-cryptanalysis" platform in various operating conditions (including in the conditions of failures and system errors of the computing environment);

- identification and elimination of identified software defects committed at the stages of implementation of the "Q-cryptanalysis" platform;

- checking the operability of each "Q-cryptanalysis" platform module according to the specification of module requirements;

- checking the performance of the "Q-cryptanalysis" platform as a whole;

- checking the completeness and sufficiency of the "Q-cryptanalysis" operational documentation.

Brief description of the tested "Q-cryptanalysis" platform:
"Q-cryptanalysis" platform has been determined for the effective solution of cryptanalysis problems of asymmetric encryption schemes (RSA or El Gamal) and digital signature (DSA, ECDSA, or RSA-PSS) in a quantum computing model.

Tested modules of the "Q-cryptanalysis" platform:

1. the module of the primary cryptosystem analysis, designed to determine the cryptographic cipher and reduce the opening task of factorization;

2. searching module for the period of an indefinite function, designed to implement factorization on a quantum computing system;

3. secret key calculation module designed to process the factorization result obtained as a result of the previous module operation for the subsequent opening of the cryptosystem;

4. module for presenting results and analyzing them, designed to display the result obtained and analyze the characteristics of its receipt.

Test tasks:
The main tasks of testing the "Q-cryptanalysis" platform were defined as follows:

•   conducting functional testing of each module of the "Q-cryptanalysis" platform to ensure its compliance with functional requirements;

•   conducting comprehensive testing to ensure the interaction of the modules of the "Q-cryptanalysis" platform with each other;

•   determining and maximizing the performance of the "Q-cryptanalysis" platform and each individual module;

•   development of a sufficient set of control examples for testing new modules of the "Q-cryptanalysis" platform.

Registration of testing the "Q-cryptanalysis" platform:
During the testing process, "Q-cryptanalysis" was documented:

•   list of tests of modules and the complex as a whole;

•   task for testing each module of the complex;

•   list of tests for each module of the complex;

•   platform testing results in chronological order.

Table 4.2 Testing stages of the "Q-cryptanalysis" platform.

N/a	Deadlines of implementations	Tested modules of the "Q-cryptanalysis" platform	Mark of completion
1.	12.2021	The core of the "Q-cryptanalysis" software complex.	Done
2.	12.2021	The module of the primary cryptosystem analysis, designed to determine the cryptographic cipher and reduce the opening task to factorization.	Done
3.	12.2021	Searching module for the period of an indefinite function, designed to implement factorization on a quantum computing system.	Done
4.	12.2021	Secret key calculation module designed to process the factorization result obtained as a result of the previous module operation for the subsequent opening of the cryptosystem.	Done
5.	12.2021	Module for presenting results and analyzing them, designed to display the result obtained and analyze the characteristics of its receipt.	Done

The stages of testing the "Q-cryptanalysis" platform:
The stages of testing the "Q-cryptanalysis" platform are presented in Table 4.2.

4.4 The Evaluation of the Effectiveness of the "Q-Cryptanalysis" Platform

As a result, the "Q-cryptanalysis" platform was developed to solve the problems of cryptanalysis of asymmetric encryption schemes (RSA or El Gamal) and digital signature (DSA, ECDSA, or RSA-PSS) in a hybrid computing environment; the "IBM Q quantum computer" is a "fifth-generation supercomputer" (Figures 4.16 and 4.17). The quantum "Q-cryptanalysis" platform was written primarily in the *Python* programming language using the *Jupyter Notebook* interpreter (included in the *Anaconda* development package), as well as using the IBM *Qiskit* library.

The advantages of the developed quantum cryptanalysis platform "Q-cryptanalysis" include the following:

1. For the first time, a fundamentally new type of quantum cryptanalysis of asymmetric encryption schemes (*RSA* or *El Gamal*) and digital signature (*DSA*, *ECDSA*, or *RSA-PSS*) based on a modified Shor factorization algorithm is proposed for practical use.

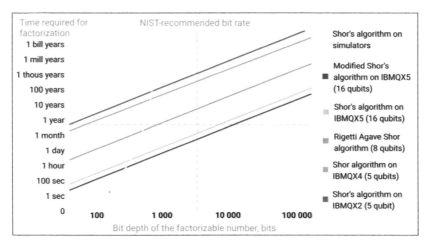

Figure 4.16   The total gain from the proposed quantum implementations of the Shor algorithm in the IBM Q hybrid environment and a fifth generation supercomputer.

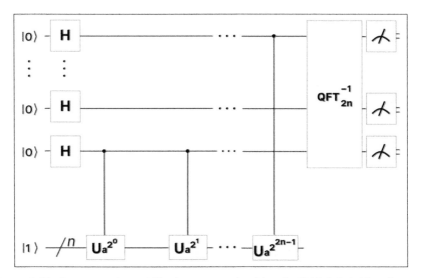

Figure 4.17   Representations of Shor's quantum algorithm for IBM Q hybrid environment and fifth generation supercomputers.

2. Improvement of the research efficiency of the reliability of circuits asymmetric encryption (*RSA* or *El Gamal*) and digital signature (*DSA*, *ECDSA*, or *RSA-PSS*) in **20%–30%** due to the automation of the first and second parts of the modified (quantum) algorithm of Shor's factorization in a hybrid environment, the IBM *Q* (16 or more qubits) and supercomputers fifth generation (Figure 4.18).

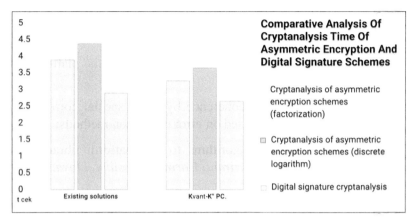

Figure 4.18 Comparative time analysis of cryptanalysis of schemes of asymmetric encryption (*RSA* or *El Gamal*) and digital signature (*DSA, ECDSA*, or *RSA-PSS*).

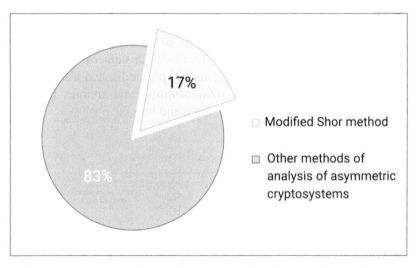

Figure 4.19 Increasing the share of quantum cryptanalysis algorithms of asymmetric encryption (RSA or El Gamal) and digital signature (DSA, ECDSA, or RSA-PSS).

3. Increasing the share of quantum cryptanalysis algorithms in the arsenal of cryptanalysis tools for asymmetric encryption schemes (*RSA* or *El Gamal*) and digital signature (*DSA, ECDSA*, or *RSA-PSS*) to **17%** (Figure 4.19).

4. Increasing the effectiveness of cryptanalysis of asymmetric ciphers of asymmetric encryption schemes (*RSA* or *El Gamal*) and digital signature (*DSA, ECDSA*, or *RSA-PSS*) by 10%–15% in general.

4.5 Possible Development Directions of the "Q-Cryptanalysis" Platform

Possible directions of development of the "Q-cryptanalysis" platform include the following (Figure 4.20):

1. reduction of quantum decoherence by using special correcting algorithms, including those based on error correction methods;

2. adding other quantum algorithms to the platform library (*Grover, Simon, Ecker, Berstein–Vazirani, Harrow, Hassilim, Lloyd, Denisenko, Klyuchkarev*, etc.);

3. improvement of methods for determining the suitability of cryptosystems for a crypto attack;

4. adding new cryptosystems to the Q-cryptanalysis library for cryptanalysis;

5. development of the Q-cryptanalysis platform interface for organizing the collective work of cryptanalysts based on cloud (access to other quantum computing systems, libraries with vulnerabilities of known implementations of cryptosystems and protocols, and libraries of other implementations of quantum algorithms) and mobile technologies (social networks, messengers, chats, and bots).

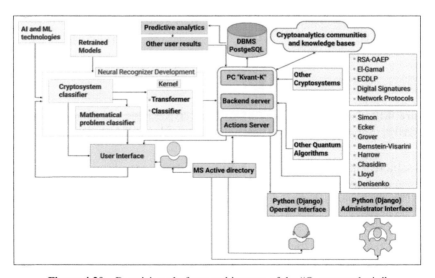

Figure 4.20   Promising platform architecture of the "Q-cryptanalysis."

4.6 A Feasibility Study for the Development of the "Q-Cryptanalysis" Platform

The feasibility study of the development of the "Q-cryptanalysis" platform was carried out using the following groups of indicators:

1. technical indicators, characterizing the functioning quality of the developed tools;

2. economic indicators characterizing the effectiveness of the funds use.

We will show the economic gain from the proposed development of a demonstration prototype (alpha and beta versions) of the "Q-cryptanalysis" platform in comparison with the problem formulation and solution of corresponding team of engineers, mathematicians, and programmers. We will calculate the development costs of the mentioned platform under two articles: developer remuneration and material resources for development in Table 4.3.

The first cost item will also include additional salary costs in the amount of 15% of the basic:

1 category of costs = Main + Additional = 770 000+115 **500 = 885,500** rubles.

2 category of costs includes the cost of all types of material resources required for the development of the platform (primarily the payment of licenses for development tools) (Table 4.4).

The total cost of developing the platform was

Σ = 1 Category + 2 Category = **885,500** + 78,000 = **963,500** Rub (**7,808,646** Euro).

It should also be taken into account that the main indicators determining the economic feasibility of the costs of creating software tools are the annual profit growth and the coefficient of economic efficiency of capital investments, compared with the normative value of 0.15.

Let us calculate the annual profit growth using the following formula:

$$\Pi = \frac{A_2 - A_1}{A_1 \cdot \Pi_1} + \left(C_1 - C_2\right) \cdot A_2$$

where A_1 and A_2 are the annual volume of products sold before and after the introduction of the software product (in cost terms); Π_1 is the profit from the products sold before the introduction of the software product; C_1 и C_2 are the costs per unit of products sold before and after the implementation of the software product.

Table 4.3   Remuneration of platform developers.

Stage of developments and the results	Executor	Labor intensity		Salary rub/m	The amount rub/m
		h/day	h/ms		
Analysis of requirements Technical task	Main designer	2	0.09	250,000	22,500
Preparatory stage	Programmer of the first category	10	0.45	200,000	90,000
Working Design (preliminary design technical project, technical, and economic project)	Programmer of the first category	20	0.9	200,000	180,000
	Programmer of the first category	35	1.8	150,000	270,000
Debugging and testing (testing program and methodology, testing plan, and act of eliminated comments)	Programmer of the first category	10	0.45	200,000	90,000
Technical report	Programmer of the first category	7	0.31	200,000	62,000
	Programmer of the first category	5	0.22	150,000	33,000
Commissioning of the project	Main designer	2	0.09	250,000	22,500

Total: 770,000 rubles

Table 4.4 Material costs for the development of the complex.

Name	Unit of measurement	Price, rub.	Standard ofexpenses, pcs.	Cost, rub.
Anaconda Team Edition Programming Environment	pc.	33400	1	74500
MS Windows 10 operating System	pc.	3500	1	3500

Total: **78 000** rubles

For the volume of products produced per year, you can take the time spent by the operator on the implementation of a particular task during the year.

We will assume that the time spent on completing tasks after automation has been halved ($A_1 = 264$ days, $A_2 = 132$ days).

Thus, the first term reflects an annual increase in profit due to a rise in the volume of products sold, and the second an increase due to a reduction in production costs.

The volume of production can be understood as the number of automated tasks. The cost of a task can be defined as the product of the cost of the staff's working time and the time spent by them on solving the corresponding task before and after the software product implementation. Suppose that after the PC implementation, the operator saves 5 hours in one working day, and then, knowing the cost of 1 hour of working time (437 rubles), we get

$$C_1 = 8 \times 437 = 3496;$$

$$C_2 = 5 \times 437 = 2185.$$

After the implementation of the software product, it is necessary to take into account the time costs of personnel and machine time of the computer used.

The cost of the machine time is made up of the cost of electricity spent on powering computing equipment. Taking into account the fact that the complex will be operated 3 hours a day, the operating time for the year will be 648 hours; with a power consumption of approximately 250 W, the electricity consumption for 1 year is 162 kW/h. With an average cost of 1 kW/h = 1 ruble 20 kopecks, we get 194.4 rubles.

The coefficient of economic efficiency is calculated by the following formula:

$$E = \frac{\Pi}{K}$$

where K is the capital investment (costs) for the creation of an information support system.

When calculating the costs of creating and implementing the system, it was obtained:

$$K = 155\ 450\ \text{rubles}.$$

The resulting coefficient should be compared with the standard value of 0.15. However, when solving important social and special, including military, tasks, the coefficient may be lower than the normative one and does not have a decisive value for a military platform.

Now let us calculate the economic efficiency.

Since the value of Π_1 (profit from the products sold before the introduction of the platform being developed) is zero, the formula for calculating the annual profit increase will take the following form:

$$\Pi = (C_1 - C_2) A_2 - \Theta_\pi.$$

Substituting this formula into the previous one, we get the final formula for calculating the annual economic efficiency coefficient:

$$E = \frac{(C_1 - C_2)A_2 - \Theta_\pi}{K}.$$

Thus, substituting numeric values into the last formula, we get

$$E = 0.271$$

The coefficient of annual economic efficiency is higher than the normative one, which indicates the feasibility of introducing this platform into the practice of cryptanalysis.

Conclusions on Chapter 4

1. During the work, a demonstration prototype of the "Q-cryptanalysis" platform was developed to solve the problems of cryptanalysis of asymmetric encryption schemes (*RSA* or *El Gamal*) and digital signature (*DSA, ECDSA*, or *RSA-PSS*). The platform is intended for operation in a hybrid computing environment (IBM Q quantum computer (16, 20, and 100 qubits) and/or fifth generation supercomputers: *IBM BladeCenter (2020), RVS on FPGA Virtex UltraScale (2020), VS RFNC-VNIIEF (2021)*, and *SKIF P-0.5 (2018)*). The corresponding certificate of registration of the computer program No. 2020665981 for the Q-cryptanalysis platform was received in November 2020.

2. The "Q-cryptanalysis" platform was written primarily in the *Python* programming language using the *Jupyter Notebook* interpreter (included in the *Anaconda* development package), as well as using the IBM *Qiskit* library [110]. The chosen development environment of the "Q-cryptanalysis" platform made it possible to solve the tasks and achieve the research goal. First time the scheme of direct connection to the *IBM Q* quantum 16-qubit system using the *IBM Cloud platform was tested*. For this, direct access to the *IBM Quantum Experience* was obtained and the corresponding *application* was *launched* (Figure 4.15) on a quantum circuit to work with individual qubits [48].

3. The structure and functional scheme of the "Q-cryptanalysis" platform includes four modules that proved sufficient for the purposes and objectives of the study. Namely, the modules: primary analysis of the cryptosystem, designed to determine the cryptographic cipher and reduce the opening task to the factorization; search for the period of an indefinite function, designed to implement factorization on a quantum computing system; calculation of the secret key, designed to process the factorization result, obtained as a result of the operation of the previous module for the subsequent opening of the cryptosystem; presentation of results and their analysis, designed to display the result obtained and analyze the characteristics of its receipt.

4. During the testing of the demo prototype of the "Q-cryptanalysis" platform, the operability of the Q-cryptanalysis complex was tested in various operating conditions (including the conditions of failures and system errors of the computing environment). A number of software defects committed at the programming stages of the Q-cryptanalysis platform were also identified and eliminated, checking the completeness and sufficiency of the "Q-cryptanalysis" operational documentation.

5. The advantages of the "Q-cryptanalysis" platform include: first proposed and justified fundamentally new type of quantum cryptanalysis of asymmetric encryption schemes based on modified algorithm of Shor's factorization; efficiency studies of the encryption schemes asymmetric encryption (*RSA* or *El Gamal*) and digital signature (*DSA*, *ECDSA*, or *RSA-PSS*) increased by **20%–30%** due to the automation of the first and second parts of Shor's algorithm; increased share of quantum algorithms for cryptanalysis in the arsenal of cryptanalysis tools for asymmetric encryption schemes to **17%**; improves the performance of cryptanalysis of asymmetric ciphers of asymmetric encryption schemes

(*RSA* or *El Gamal*) and digital signature (*DSA*, *ECDSA*, or *RSA-PSS*) at **10%–15%** in general.

6. The main development directions of the "Q-cryptanalysis" platform include: the use of artificial intelligence (AI) and machine learning (ML) methods to give the complex fundamentally new properties of adaptability and self-organization; the development of the functionality of the complex by adding other quantum algorithms to the platform library (*Grover, Simon, Ecker, Berstein–Vazirani, Harrow, Hassilim, Lloyd, Denisenko, Klyuchkarev,* etc.) as well as other cryptosystems of asymmetric and symmetric encryption for research; reducing the effects of quantum decoherence by using special correcting algorithms, including those based on error correction methods, etc.

7. During the feasibility study of the development of the "Q-cryptanalysis" platform, the annual profit growth and the economic efficiency coefficient of investments compared with the normative value of 0.15 were calculated. The coefficient of annual economic efficiency is higher than the normative one, which indicates the feasibility of introducing this platform into the practice of cryptanalysis.

Conclusion

Dear reader,

We hope that our book was interesting and beneficial to you!

In conclusion, I would like to note that the Russian School of Higher Education (the leading universities of Russia) and academic institutes of the Russian Academy of Sciences (RAS) pay sufficient attention to the scientific and engineering problems of cryptanalysis and cryptography considered in this monograph. Mainly to assess the quantum resilience of crypto-primitives of key ecosystems and platforms of the digital economy of the Russian Federation. In particular, for the development of new cryptosystems, algorithms and protocols of post-quantum cryptography for modern blockchain systems: *InnoChain (Innopolis University), Waves Enterprise (Waves, Vostok), Hyperledger Fabric (Linux, IBM), Corda Enterprise, Bitfury Exonum, Blockchain Industrial Alliance, Exonum (Bitfury CIS), NodesPlus (b41), Masterchain (Sberbank), Microsoft Azure Blockchain, Enterprise Ethereum Alliance*, etc.

Moreover, the "Roadmap for the Development of Quantum Technologies" in the Russian Federation (2019) was adopted at the government level in 2019.[1] The main goal of the mentioned roadmap is to achieve in the medium- and long-term practically significant world-class scientific, technical, and practical results in the following areas.

- *Quantum computers and computing.* Quantum computers and simulators are computing systems that use quantum phenomena to solve problems. Devices based on quantum computing can be many times superior to classical computers in solving cryptanalysis problems, modeling of complex systems, as well as machine learning and artificial intelligence. With the development of existing quantum computers, the appearance of the first applied results can be expected in the direction of accelerating machine learning tasks and modeling new promising materials. The most promising and leading platforms in

---

[1] https://digital.gov.ru/uploaded/files/07102019kvantyi.pdf

155

the world are three: superconducting chains, neutral atoms, and ions in traps. According to the *QTRL classification*, the development of companies in the world currently corresponds to QTRL levels *4–5*, i.e., the problem of implementing quantum error correction codes has not yet been solved in the computing systems of these companies and, accordingly, practically significant algorithms (including the Shor algorithm) cannot be fully implemented on them. In the Russian Federation, prototypes of quantum computers with 2 qubits (according to the DC FPI 2-10 qubits) and quantum simulators with 10–20 qubits have been implemented today. This corresponds to *QTRL levels 3–4*.

- *Quantum communications*. Technologies aimed at eliminating threats to information security, including quantum computers, include the use of properties of quantum systems for key transfer. The main technology is KRK. The main advantage of KRK is the security of information guaranteed by the laws of physics. The readiness level in the world is *TRL-9* both in point-to-point solutions and in networks with a trusted node. KRK equipment for networks with untrusted nodes is at the laboratory testing. Today, the level of readiness of domestic point-to-point solutions can be estimated as *TRL-8*. While in terms of quantum networks, based on trusted nodes, domestic developments of quantum networks lag far behind the level of China and the EU: *TRL-6* versus *TRL-9*.

- *Quantum sensors and metrology*. Quantum sensors are high-precision measuring devices based on quantum effects. It is expected that quantum sensors will have high spatial and temporal resolution, which will increase the accuracy of measurements in comparison with existing classical sensors, and the use of superposition, entanglement, and compression properties of quantum states, in turn, will provide in the future the maximum possible sensitivity of measurement by overcoming the standard quantum limit. The high degree of control over the state of individual microscopic systems provided by quantum technologies makes it possible to create quantum sensors with high sensitivity. The development of technologies of various sensors of a new generation can give a powerful impetus in several areas at once: defense and security, navigation (space, unmanned transport); construction, 10 oil production and exploration; medical diagnostics/therapy; industry 4.0, etc. General assessment of the level of readiness of quantum sensor technologies in the world *TRL 3-9* and in the Russian Federation *TRL 1-5*.

For a breakthrough in the field of quantum technologies, a course has been taken to support exploratory research and launch infrastructure projects on a national scale. For this purpose, a corresponding budget of *51.1 billion rubles* has been formed for the period 2019–2024, including extra-budgetary financing in the amount of *8.7 billion rubles*.[2]

The main tasks of the "Roadmap for the Development of Quantum Technologies" in the Russian Federation (https://digital.gov.ru/uploaded/files/07102019kvantyi.pdf) include:

- comprehensive support of breakthrough scientific and technological projects aimed at the development of CT;

- consolidation of the scientific and technological community within the framework of the creation of projects of national and global scale;

- the creation of an innovative ecosystem in Russia and the formation of conditions for the transition of quantum developments from laboratories to industry, as well as the formation of a business community;

- organization of cooperation between research units and potential consumers of quantum technologies from key industries;

- development of human resources in the field of quantum technologies through the introduction of new types of educational programs at all levels;

- carrying out a set of organizational measures aimed at reducing bureaucratic barriers.

Note that the "Roadmap for the Development of Quantum Technologies" in the Russian Federation corresponds to the "Strategy of Scientific and Technological Development of the Russian Federation (SNTR),"[3] as well as "Strategies for the Development of the Information Society of the Russian Federation (SRIO)."[4] Here, the support of all three main sub-technologies of quantum technologies is critically important for national security and ensuring the digital sovereignty of the Russian Federation.

The scientific and practical results of the author considered in this monograph indicate the expediency of continuing the development of promising quantum methods and algorithms for cryptanalysis of asymmetric

---

[2] https://digital.gov.ru/uploaded/files/07102019kvantyi.pdf
[3] https://sochisirius.ru/sntr
[4] http://www.kremlin.ru/acts/bank/41919

encryption schemes (*El Gamal* or *RSA-OAEP*) and digital signatures (*DSA*, *ECDSA*, or *RSA-PSS* signatures). The scientific and practical results of this monograph made it possible to evaluate the quantum resilience of a number of well-known blockchain projects: InnoChain (Innopolis University), Waves Enterprise (Waves, Vostok), Hyperledger Fabric (Linux, IBM), Corda Enterprise, Bitfury Exonum, Blockchain Industrial Alliance, Exonum (Bitfury CIS), NodesPlus (b41), Masterchain (Sberbank), Microsoft Azure Blockchain, Enterprise Ethereum Alliance and etc.).

I hope that this book will inspire you to continue research in the field of quantum cryptanalysis to solve the urgent cybersecurity problems of the digital economy.

I wish you success in this difficult but interesting work!

Alexei Petrenko

Associate Professor Innopolis University, PhD

fatawl1b@gmail.com

References

[1] Abdullin D.I. Shore factorization algorithm based on hardware IP cores in FPGA architecture/FPGA/ Proceedings of the conference. XXIV Tupolev Readings (School of Young Scientists), Kazan, November 07–08, 2019, Kazan National Research Technical University named after A.N. Tupolev-KAI (KNITU-KAI), pp. 573–575.

[2] Shor's algorithm, its implementation in Haskell and the results of some experiments [Electronic resource]/Programmer's Notes. Access mode: http://eax.me/shors-algorithm 14.05.2021 p.

[3] Andreev, D.Yu., Korzh O.V., Korobkov S.V., Chernyavsky A.Yu. A parallel algorithm for modeling Grover's ideal quantum algorithm. Parallel Computing Technologies (PaVT'2013): Proceedings of the International Scientific Conference (Chelyabinsk, April 1–5, 2013). SUSU Publishing Center, Chelyabinsk, 2013. pp. 38–48.

[4] Aho A., Hopcroft J., Ulman J. Construction and analysis of computational algorithms: Trans. from English. A.O. Slisenko. / Edited by Yu.V. Matiyasevich, M.: Mir, 1979. 536s.

[5] Biryukov D.N. Smart cybersecurity/ Biryukov D.N., Petrenko A.S., Petrenko S.A./ Journal: Information Protection. Inside. 2019. No. 4 (88). c. 14–24.

[6] Biryukov D.N., Lomako A.G., Rostovtsev Yu.G. The appearance of anticipating systems for preventing the risks of implementing cyber threats // Proceedings of SPIIRAN. 2015. No. 2(39). P.5–25.

[7] Biryukov D.N., Lomako A.G., Rostovtsev Yu.G. An approach to building information security systems capable of synthesizing scenarios of proactive behavior in an information conflict // Information Protection. INSIDE. 2014. No. 6. C. 42–50.

[8] Bogdanov A.Yu. Quantum algorithms and their impact on the security of modern classical cryptographic systems. / A.Yu. Bogdanov, I.S. Kizhvatov // RGGU. - 2005. 18 p.

[9] Valiev K.A. Quantum computers and quantum computations / K.A. Valiev. M.: Institute of Physics and Technology, 2005. 387c.

[10] Vasilenko O. N. Number-theoretic algorithms in cryptography / O. N. Vasilenko. - M.: ICNMO, 2003. 328 p.

[11] Wentzel, E.S. Probability theory and its engineering applications / E.S. Wentzel, L.A. Ovcharov. M.: Nauka, 1988 480 p.

[12] Vinberg E. B. Fermat's small theorem and its generalizations // Matem. prosv. M., 2008. vol. 12. pp. 43–53. URL: http: //mi.mathnet.ru/mp238.

[13] Wentzel E. S."Operations research: tasks, principles, methodology"- 2nd ed. Moscow: Nauka, 1988. 208 p.

[14] Gabidulin E. M., Pilipchuk N. I. Lectures on information theory: textbook. Moscow: MIPT, 2007. - 214 p—ISBN 5-7417-0197-3.

[15] Gultyaeva T. A. Fundamentals of information theory and cryptography. Novosibirsk: NSTU Publishing House, 2010. 88 p. ISBN 978-5-7782-1425-5.

[16] GOST R 51583-2014 "Information security". The procedure for creating automated systems in a protected version. General provisions". M.: Standartinform. 2014.

[17] Grishanov S.A. Hardware implementation of a typical module for performing the Shore algorithm in FPGA class FPGA architecture // materials of the scientific and practical seminar. Issue 1. Moscow: IPM named after M.V.Keldysh, 2014. p. 12–16.

[18] Denisenko D.V., Marshalko G.B., Nikitenkova M.V., Rudskoy V.I., Shishkin V.A. Evaluation of the complexity of implementing the Grover algorithm for sorting the keys of block encryption algorithms GOST R 34.12-2015, Journal of Experimental and Theoretical Physics, RAS, P.L. Institute of Physical Problems. Kapitsy RAS (Moscow), 2019, volume 155, issue 4, pp. 645–653, 2019.

[19] The Doctrine of Information Security of the Russian Federation [Electronic resource]: approved. By the Decree of the President of the Russian Federation of 5 Dec. 2016 No. 646. URL: https:// rg.ru/2016/12/06/doktrina-infobezobasnost-site-dok.html (accessed: 05/15/2021)

[20] Dupliy S.A., Shapoval I.I. Topological methods in quantum computing/ Bulletin of KhNU (ser. "Nuclei, Particles, fields"), 2007, Vol. 781. No. 3(35). c. 3–30. Journal of Kharkov National University, ser. "Nuclei, particles and fields". 2007. V. 781. N 3(35). p. 3–30.

[21] Dushkin R. Quantum computing and functional programming / R. V. Dushkin. M.: DMK Press, 2015. 232 p.

[22] Eremeev M.A., Moldovyan N.A., Moldovyan A.A. From primitives to synthesis of algorithms, Publishing House BHV-Petersburg, 2004, 448 p. 2004.

[23] Ishmukhametov Sh.T. Methods of factorization of natural numbers.: textbook / Sh.T. Ishmukhametov. Kazan: Kazan University. 2011. 192 p.

[24] Kalinin, V.N. Theoretical foundations of system research / V.N. Kalinin // St. Petersburg: Mozhaisky VKA. 2013. 278 p.

[25] Kitaev A., Shen A., Vyaly M. Classical and quantum computing / M.: ICNMO, Publishing House of Chero, 1999. 192 p.

[26] Clark, E.M. Verification of program models: Model Checking / E.M. Clark, O. Gramberg, D. Peled. Translated from English / Edited by R. Smelyansky. M.: ICNMO, 2002–416 p.

[27] Kolmogorov, A.N. Information theory and theory of algorithms. USSR Academy of Sciences, Moscow: Nauka, 1987.

[28] Kotelnikov V. A. The fate that engulfed the century. In 2 t. / comp. N. V. Kotelnikova. Moscow: Fizmatlit, 2011. 312 p.

[29] Korolkov A.V. On some applied aspects of quantum cryptography in the context of the development of quantum computing and the emergence of quantum computers. / A.V. Korolkov // Issues of cybersecurity No. 1(9) - 2015. M.: Journal "Issues of cybersecurity", 2015. pp. 6–13.

[30] Korzh O.B., Andreev D.Yu., Korzh A.A., Korobkov V.A., Chernyavsky A.Yu., Modeling of an ideal quantum computer on a Lomonosov supercomputer, Journal "Computational Methods and Programming", Ed. Research Computing Center of Moscow State University named after M.V. Lomonosov, 2013, No. 14, issue 2, pp. 24–34

[31] Korzh O.B., Chernyavsky A.Yu., Korzh A.A.,Simulation of the quantum Fourier transform with noise on the Lomonosov supercomputer, CollectionScientific service on the Internet: all facets of parallelism: Proceedings of the International Supercomputer Conference (September 23–28, 2013, Novorossiysk), Ed. of the Moscow State University. Lomonosova, Moscow, pp. 188–193.

[32] Korn, G., Handbook of Mathematics for Researchers and Engineers. Definitions, theorems, formulas. / g. Korn, T. Korn // Ed. 4 / Under the general ed. Aramanovich I.G. M.: Nauka, 1978– 832 p.

[33] Klyucharev P.G. Abstract of the dissertation for the Candidate of Technical Sciences. Algorithmic and software for modeling a quantum computer. Moscow State Technical University named after N.E. Bauman, 2009, 18 p.

[34] Knut D. E. The Art of Programming, Volume 2. Calculated methods, 3rd ed. - Williams, 2001— 832 p— ISBN 5-8459-0081-6.408

[35] Knut D. E. The Art of Programming, Volume 2. Sorting and searching., 3rd ed. Williams, 2001. 800 p.

[36] Cryptographic protection of information. The processes of forming and verifying an electronic digital signature [text]: GOST R 34.10-2001. Instead of GOST R 34.10-94, introduction. 01.07.2002. Moscow: IPK Publishing House of Standards, 2001. 16 p— (State Standard of the Russian Federation). — URL: http://protect.gost.ru/document.aspx?-control= 7&id=131131.

[37] Crandall R., Pomerance K. Prime numbers: Cryptographic and computational aspects / ed. N. Chubarikova; trans. a. V. Beguntsa [et al.]. M.: URSS: Book house "LIBROCOM", 2011— 664 p.

[38] Manin Yu. I. Computable and non-computable. Moscow: Sovetskoe radio, 1980. 128 p.

[39] Markov, A.S. The experience of identifying vulnerabilities in foreign software products / A.S. Markov, V.L. Cirlov // Questions of cybersecurity. 2013. No. 1(1) pp. 42–48.

[40] Matveev E.A. Dissertation for the Candidate of Physical and Mathematical Sciences. Application of quantum mechanical effects in information security systems. Penza, NTP Cryptosoft, 2019 157 p.

[41] Mesarovich, M. Theory of hierarchical multilevel systems / M. Mesarovich, D. Mako, I. Takahara. M.: Mir, 1973. p. 344.

[42] Moldovyan A.A., Moldovyan N.A. New forms of the hidden discrete logarithm problem. Proceedings of SPIIRAN 2019. Volume 18 No. 2. Pp. 504–529.

[43] Moldovyan N.A., *Introduction* to *Public Key Cryptosystems* / N.A. Moldovyan, *Moldovyan* A.A./, Publishing House of BHV-Petersburg, 2005, 286 p. 2005.

[44] Moldovyan N.A., Workshop on cryptosystems with a public key, Publishing House BHV-Petersburg, 2005, 298 p. 2007.

[45] Nikolenko S.I. New constructions of cryptographic primitives based on semigroups, groups and linear algebra. Dissertation for the Candidate of Physical and Mathematical Sciences. St. Petersburg, Institution of the Russian Academy of Sciences St. Petersburg Department of the Mathematical Institute named after V.A. Steklova RAS, 2008 120 p.

[46] Nielsen M., Chang I. Quantum computing and quantum information. Translated from English: Mir, 2006 824 p., ill.

[47] Fundamentals of cryptography. Textbook / A. P. Alferov [et al.]. - M.: Helios ARV, 2001. 480 p— ISBN 5-85438-137-0.

[48] Petrenko, A.S., Romanchenko A.M. A promising method of cryptanalysis based on the Shor algorithm// Information security. Inside No. 2 2020. St. Petersburg: Publishing house Athena, 2020. pp. 17–23.

[49] Petrenko A.S. On the implementation of the partially homomorphic El-Gamal cryptosystem. In the collection: The 2019 Symposium on Cybersecurity of the Digital Economy (CDE19). The third International Scientific and Technical Conference. Saint Petersburg, 2019. pp. 262–265.

[50] Petrenko A.S. On the implementation of the partially homomorphic RSA cryptosystem. In the collection: The 2019 Symposium on Cybersecurity of the Digital Economy (CDE19). The third International Scientific and Technical Conference. Saint Petersburg, 2019. pp. 266–268.

[51] Petrenko A.S. On the implementation of the partially homomorphic Paie cryptosystem. In the collection: The 2019 Symposium on Cybersecurity of the Digital Economy (CDE19). The third International Scientific and Technical Conference. Saint Petersburg, 2019. pp. 266–268.

[52] Petrenko A.S. On the implementation of a completely homomorphic Gentry-Halevi-Smart cryptosystem. In the collection: The 2019 Symposium on Cybersecurity of the Digital Economy (CDE19). The third International Scientific and Technical Conference. Saint Petersburg, 2019. pp. 272–275.

[53] Petrenko A.S. On the implementation of a fully homomorphic cryptosystem based on matrix polynomials. In the collection: The 2019 Symposium on Cybersecurity of the Digital Economy (CDE19). The third International Scientific and Technical Conference. Saint Petersburg, 2019. Pp. 276–279.

[54] Petrenko S.A., Stupin D.D. National early warning system about a computer attack: a scientific monograph / edited by S. F. Boeva. Publishing House "Athena", 2018– 440 p.

[55] Petrenko S. Cyber Resilient Platform for Internet of Things (IIoT/IoT)ed Systems: Survey of Architecture Patterns. Voprosy Kiberbezopasnosti [Cybersecurity issue]. 2021. No 2 (42). P. 81–91. DOI: 10.21681/2311-3456-2021-2-81-91

[56] Petrenko S. Self-Healing Cloud Computing. Voprosy Kiberbezopasnosti [Cybersecurity issue]. 2021. No 1 (41). P. 80–89. DOI: 10.21681/2311-3456-2021-1-80-89.

[57] Pravilschikov P.A. Quantum parallelism and the solution of equations in control problems based on a new model of computing / P.A. Pravoshchikov. M.: V.A. Institute of Management Problems. Trapeznikova, 2014. 179 p.

[58] Order No. 31 of the FSTEC of Russia dated 14.03.2014 "On Approval of requirements for ensuring the protection of Information in Automated Control Systems for Production and Technological Processes at Critical

Facilities, Potentially Dangerous Facilities, as well as Facilities that pose an increased danger to Human Life and Health and to the Environment". Access mode: http://fstec.ru.

[59] Order No. 235 of the FSTEC of Russia dated December 21, 2017 "On Approval of Requirements for the Creation of Security Systems for Significant Objects of the Critical Information Structure of the Russian Federation and Ensuring their Functioning". Access mode: http://fstec.ru.

[60] Order No. 239 of the FSTEC of Russia dated December 25, 2017 "On Approval of Requirements for Ensuring the Security of Significant Objects of the Critical Information Infrastructure of the Russian Federation". Access mode: http://fstec.ru.

[61] Preskill J. Quantum information and quantum computations / D. Preskill. M.: Izhevsk, 2008. 464 p.

[62] Rostovtsev, Yu.G. Fundamentals of building automated systems for collecting and processing information. - Ministry of Defense of the Russian Federation, 1992– 717 p.

[63] Guidance document. Computer equipment. Protection against unauthorized access to information Indicators of security against unauthorized access to information. Approved by the decision of the Chairman of the State Technical Commission under the President of the Russian Federation dated March 30, 1992. Access mode: http://fstec.ru.

[64] Guidance document. Protection against unauthorized access to information. Part 1. Information security software. Classification according to the level of control of the absence of undeclared opportunities. Approved by the decision of the Chairman of the State Technical Commission under the President of the Russian Federation dated March 30, 1992 Access mode: http://fstec.ru.

[65] Ruchkin V.N. Natural parallelism of quantum computers and neural calculators / V.N. Ruchkin, V.A. Romanchuk, V.A. Fulin. Ryazan.: Ryazan State University named after S.A. Yesenina, 2013 387 p.

[66] Ryzhikov, Yu.I. Computational methods / Yu.I. Ryzhikov // Ucheb. pos. - SPb: BHV-Petersburg. - 2007. 397 p.

[67] Saati, Vol. Decision-making. Method of hierarchy analysis // M: Radio and Communications. 1993. 278 p.

[68] Sachkov V.N., V.A. Kotelnikov and encrypted communication. Conferences and Symposiums, vol. 176, No. 7, UFN 2006, pp. 775–777

[69] Information processing systems. Cryptographic protection. Algorithm of cryptographic transformation [text]: GOST 28147-89. Introduction. 01.07.90. Moscow: Publishing House of Standards, 1989. 28 p— (State standard of the USSR). — URL: http://protect.gost.ru/document.aspx?control=7&id=139177.

[70] Dictionary of Cryptographic Terms. Edited by B. A. Pogorelova and V. N. Sachkova. Moscow State University named after M.V. Lomonosov Academy of Cryptography of the Russian Federation. Moscow ICNMO Publishing House. 2006– 50 p.

[71] The National Security Strategy of the Russian Federation (approved by Decree The President of the Russian Federation on December 31, 2015 N 683) // SPS "ConsultantPlus".

[72] Tokareva N.N. On the History of Cryptography in Russia, Historical Essays on Discrete Mathematics and its Applications, No. 4 (18), S.L. Mathematical Institute. Soboleva SB RAS Novosibirsk, 2012, pp. 82–107.

[73] Thomas H. Algorithms. Construction and analysis [Text] / X. Thomas - M.: Williams, 2016. 1328 p.

[74] Requirements for ensuring the security of significant objects of the critical information infrastructure of the Russian Federation, approved by the Order of the FSTEC of Russia No. 239 dated December 25, 2017 Access mode: http://fstec.ru.

[75] Federal Law No. 187-FZ of June 26, 2017 "On the Security of the Critical Information Structure of the Russian Federation". Access mode: https://rg.ru.

[76] Federal Law No. 149-FZ of 27.07.2006 "On Information, Information Technologies and Information Protection". Access mode: https://rg.ru.

[77] Kholevo A. S. Mathematical foundations of quantum computer science M.: MIAN, 2018. 118 p– (Lecture. REC courses, ISSN 2226-8782; Issue 30). ISBN 978-5-98419-080-7

[78] Kholevo A. S. Quantum systems, channels, information. Electronic edition. Moscow: ICNMO, 2014. 327 p. ISBN 978-5-4439-2092-4

[79] Kholevo A. S.. Introduction to quantum information theory. MCNMO, 2002 128 p.

[80] Cheremushkin A. V. Cryptographic protocols: basic properties and vulnerabilities // Applied Discrete Mathematics. 2009. Nov. issue 2. pp. 115–150.—URL: https://cyberleninka.ru/article/n/kriptograficheskie-protokoly-osnovnye-svoystva-i-uyazvimosti.pdf.

[81] Shalagin S.V. Implementation of the Shore algorithm based on IP cores in PLIS/FPGA //C architecture. V. Shalagin, S.A. Grishanov // Fundamental and applied problems of mathematics and computer science. Materials of the XII International Conference. Makhachkala: publishing house of DSU, 2017. pp. 202–205.

[82] Shannon K. Works on information theory and cybernetics / edited by R. L. Dobrushina, O. B. Lupanova. M.: Publishing House of Foreign Literature, 1963— 830 p.

[83] Schneier B. Applied cryptography: protocols, algorithms, source code in the C language. Williams Publishing House, 2016– 816 p.

[84] Ebbinhaus G.D. Turing machines and recursive functions/ G.D. Ebbinhaus. M.: Mir, 1972– 264 p.

[85] Shor P. Algorithms for quantum computation: discrete logarithms and factoring [Text] /Shor P.// Foundations of Computer Science.—1994.— No. 10. —134p.

[86] Aaronson, Scott (2013). Quantum Computing Since Democritus. Cambridge: Cambridge University Press.

[87] Aaronson S., Arkhipov A., The Computational Complexity of Linear Optics, Proceedings of the forty-third annual ACM symposium on Theory of computing, 333–342 (2011)

[88] Arute F., Arya K., Martinis John M., Quantum supremacy using a programmable superconducting processor, Nature, 574, 505–510 (2019)

[89] Bell, Philip (2018). Beyond Weird: Why Everything You Knew About Quantum Physics Is Different. Chicago: University of Chicago Press.

[90] Benioff P, The computer as a physical system: A microscopic quantum mechanical Hamiltonian model of computers as represented by Turing machines J. Statist. Phys. 22, 563–591 (1980)

[91] Bernhardt, Chris (2019). Quantum Computing for Everyone. Cambridge, MA: MIT Press.

[92] Bouland A., Fefferman B., Nirkhe Ch., Quantum Supremacy and the Complexity of Random Circuit Sampling, arxiv.org/abs/1803.04402 (2018)

[93] Carroll, Sean (2019). Something Deeply Hidden. United States: Dutton.

[94] Deutsch D., Quantum theory, the Church-Turing principle and the universal quantum computer, Proceedings of the Royal Society A. 400 (1818), 97–117 (1985)

[95] Deutsch D., Jozsa R., Rapid solution of problems by quantum computation, Proceedings of the Royal Society of London A, 439, (1907), 553–558 (1992)

[96] Diffie D, Hellman M. New directions in cryptography, IEEE Transactions on Information Theory, v. 22, Issue 6 (1976)

[97] Feynman R, Simulating physics with computers, Internat. J. Theoret. Phys. 21, 467–488 (1982)

[98] Grover L.K., A fast quantum mechanical algorithm for database search, In Proceedings of the twenty-eighth, annual ACM symposium on Theory of computing, 212–219, ACM (1996)

[99] Huang C, Zhang F., Newman M/, Classical Simulation of Quantum Supremacy Circuits, arxiv.org/abs/2005.06787 (2020) 19. A. Zlokapa, S. Boixo, D. Lidar, Boundaries of quantum supremacy via random circuit sampling, arxiv.org/abs/2005.02464 (2020)

[100] Johnston, Eric R., Nic Harrigan, and Mercedes Gimeno-Segovia (2019). Programming Quantum Computers: Essential Algorithms and Code Elements. Sebastopol, CA: O'Reilly.

[101] Kumar, Manjit (2011). Quantum: Einstein, Bohr, and the Great Debate about the Nature of Reality. New Delhi: Hachette India.

[102] Orzel, Chad (2009). How to Teach [Quantum] Physics to Your Dog. New York: Scribner.

[103] Orzel, Chad (2018). Breakfast with Einstein: The Exotic Physics of Everyday Objects. Dallas, TX: BenBella Books, Inc.

[104] Pednault E, Gunnels J., On "Quantum Supremacy", ibm.com/blogs/research/2019/10/on-quantum-supremacy (2019)

[105] Rhodes, Richard (2012). Hedy's Folly: The Life and Breakthrough Inventions of Hedy Lamarr, the Most Beautiful Woman in the World. New York: Doubleday.

[106] Shor, P.W. Polynomial-time algorithms for prime factorization and discrete logarithms on a quantum computer, SIAM J. Computing 26, 1484–1509 (1997)

[107] Simon D.R., On the power of quantum computation, SFCS '94: Proceedings of the 35th Annual Symposium on Foundations of Computer Science, 116–123 (1994)

[108] Zhou Y, Stoudenmire E.M., Waintal X., What limits the simulation of quantum computers?, arxiv.org/abs/2002.07730 (2021)

[109] Magomedov S., Gusev A., Ilin D., Nikulchev E. Used the Time of User Reactions to Improve Security and Control Access To Web Services // Applied Science. 2021. Vol. 11, No. 5. P. 2561.

[110] Magomedov S, Ilin D, Nikulchev E. Resource Analysis of the Log Files Storage Based on Simulation Models in a Virtual Environment. // Applied Science. 2021. Vol. 11, No. 11. P. 4718.

[111] Magomedov S., Lebedev, A. Protected network architecture for ensuring consistency of 2 medical data through validation of user behavior and DICOM 3 archive integrity // Applied Science. 2021, Vol. 11. No. 5. P. 2072.

[112] Magomedov S., Ilin D., Silaeva A., Nikulchev E. Dataset of User Reactions When Filling Out Web Questionnaires // Data. 2020. Vol. 5, No. 4. P. 108, 1–7.

[113] Nikulchev E., Ilin D., Silaeva A., Kolyasnikov P., Belov V., Runtov A., Pushkin P., Laptev N., Alexeenko A., Magomedov S., Kosenkov A., Zakharov, I.; Ismatullina, V.; Malykh, S. Digital Psychological Platform for Mass Web-Surveys // Data. 2020. V. 5, No. 4. P. 95, 1–16.

[114] Moody Dustin, NIST PQC team, NIST Status Update on the 3rd Round. Cryptographic Technology Group. Computer Security Division. 2021,

https://csrc.nist.gov/CSRC/media/Presentations/status-update-on-the-3rd-round/images-media/session-1-moody-nist-round-3-update.pdf

[115] Belenko V., Krundyshev V., Kalinin M. Synthetic datasets generation for intrusion detection in VANET // Proceedings of the 11th International Conference on Security of Information and Networks. 2018.

[116] Myasnikov A.V. Application of machine learning technologies to optimize the penetration testing process // Problems of information security. Computer systems. 2019. No. 2. p.9

[117] Dakhnovich A.D., Moskvin D.A., Zegzhda D.P. Analysis of threats to information security in digital production networks // Problems of information security. Computer systems. 2017. No. 4. pp.41–46.

[118] Zegzhda P.D., Rudina E.A. Fundamentals of information security. Textbook Publishing House of the Polytechnic University, St. Petersburg, 2008, 224 p.

[119] Poltavtseva M.A., Zegzhda D.P., Suprun A.F. Database security. Textbook Publishing House of the Polytechnic University, St. Petersburg, 2008, 224 p.

[120] Alexandrova E.B., Shkorkina. E.N., Oblogina A.Yu. Authentication of control devices in the Internet of Things network with the architecture of boundary computing // Problems of information security. Computer systems. – 2021. No. 2.

[121] Aleksandrova E. B., Shkorkina E. N. Using Undeniable Signature on Elliptic Curves to Verify Servers in Outsourced Computations // Automatic Control and Computer Sciences. 2018. V. 52. No. 8. P. 1160–1163.

[122] Zegzhda D.P., Alexandrova E.B., Kalinin M.O., etc. Cybersecurity of the digital industry. Theory and practice of functional resistance to cyber attacks. Publishing house: Hotline - Telecom, 2020, 560 pages.

[123] Vorobyev E.G., Khomonenko A.D. Mathematical model of binary-decimal conversion and algorithms of information compression based on linear functions. // "Information protection. Inside." 2019. No. 5. pp.15–21.

[124] Vorobyov E. G., Khomonenko A. D. Models of vector representation of multi-bit binary data based on pseudoregular numbers // Control, communication and security systems. 2019. No. 2. pp. 291–303.

[125] Vorobyov E.G. Mathematical models of management of the system for ensuring the availability of information and assessing the quality of its functioning // High-tech technologies in Earth space research (H&ES Research). - 2019. No. 2. pp. 51–64.

[126] Vorobyov E.G. Compression methods based on reversible calculations. // Izvestiya SPbGETU "LETI". 2015. No. 5. pp. 15–21.

[127] Vorobyov E.G. Compression of binary codes based on traditional methods and the use of pseudoregular numbers. // Izvestiya SPbGETU "LETI". 2015. No. 5. p. 23–28.

[128] Vorobyov E.G. The concept of ensuring the continuity of the functioning of distributed information and telecommunication systems based on quantum methods of information representation. // Izvestiya SPbGETU "LETI". 2015. No. 4. pp. 17–21.

[129] Vorobyov E.G. Using the fractal structure of fields formed by codes with different bases to solve the problem of creating a single information space. // Izvestiya SPbGETU "LETI". 2015. No. 3. pp. 11–16.

[130] Vorobyov E.G. Complex numbers and optimization of information storage facilities in global information systems. // Izvestiya SPbGETU "LETI". 2015. No. 2. pp. 22–25.

[131] Vorobyov E.G. Calculation of the effectiveness of information attacks by an external intruder on informatization objects with a distributed infrastructure. // Izvestiya SPbGETU "LETI". 2015. No. 1. p.23–28.

[132] Vorobyov E.G. Controlled polarization of electromagnetic waves as a means of increasing the secrecy of information transmission. // Izvestiya SPbGETU "LETI". 2014. No. 9. pp. 44–49.

[133] Vorobyov E.G. Tsekhanovsky V.V. Pseudoregular numbers in binary fields. // Izvestiya SPbGETU "LETI". 2014. No. 2. pp. 18–23.

[134] D. A. Nabokov, "Post-quantum electronic voting based on grids with the participation of several candidates", PDM. Appendix, 2021, No. 14, 95–100

[135] M. A. Kudinov, E. O. Kiktenko, A. K. Fedorov, Security analysis of the W-OTS+ signature scheme: Updating security bounds Mathematical Issues of Cryptography, 12:2 (2021), 129–145

[136] Grebnev S.V., Klyucharev P.G., Koreneva A.M., Koshelev D.I., Taraskin O.G., Tulebaev A.I. A post-quantum cryptographic protocol for generating a common key based on isogeny of supersingular elliptic curves. Proceedings of the XI International Scientific and Technical Conference "Secure Information Technologies". Moscow State Technical University named after N.E. Bauman, 2021.

[137] S.E. Yunakovsky, M. Kot, N.O. Pozhar, D. Nabokov, M.A. Kudinov, A. Guglya, E.O. Kiktenko, E. Kolycheva, A. Borisov, A.K. Fedorov. Towards security recommendations for public-key infrastructures for production environments in the post-quantum era. EPJ Quantum Technology (2021) arXiv: 2105.01324

[138] E.O. Kiktenko, M.A. Kudinov, and A.K. Fedorov. Detecting brute-force attacks on cryptocurrency wallets, Lecture Notes in Business Information Processing. 373, 232–242 (2019); arXiv:1904.06943

[139] E.O. Kiktenko, M.A. Kudinov, A.A. Bulychev, and A.K. Fedorov. Proof-of-forgery for hash-based signatures. arXiv:1905.12993

[140] E.O. Kiktenko, A.A. Bulychev, P.A. Karagodin, N.O. Pozhar, M.N. Anufriev, and A.K. Fedorov. SPHINCS+ digital signature scheme with GOST hash functions. arXiv:1904.06525

[141] M.A. Kudinov, E.O. Kiktenko, and A.K. Fedorov. Security analysis of the W-OTS+ signature scheme: Updating security bounds. arXiv:2002.07419S.

[142] S.V. Grebnev. Limonnitsa: making Limonnik-3 post-quantum. Mathematical Questions of Cryptography, 11:2 (2020), 25-42

[143] Grebnev S.V. Post-quantum cryptography: Trends, problems and prospects. Information Security. 2019, 2.

[144] E.O. Kiktenko, N.O. Pozhar, M.N. Anufriev, A.S. Trushechkin, R.R. Yunusov, Y.V. Kurochkin, A.I. Lvovsky, and A.K. Fedorov, Quantum-secured blockchain, Quantum Science and Technology 3, 035004 (2018); arXiv:1705.09258

[145] A.K. Fedorov, E.O. Kiktenko, and A.I. Lvovsky. Quantum computers put blockchain security at risk Nature 563, 465 (2018);

[146] M. A. Kudinov, A. A. Chilikov, E. O. Kiktenko, A. K. Fedorov. Advanced attribute-based protocol based on the modified secret sharing scheme Journal of Computer Virology and Hacking Techniques volume 16, pages 333–341 (2020) arXiv:1912.03009

[147] Grebnev S.V. On the cryptographic properties of the scheme for generating a common "Limonnik-3" key. Information technology security. 2019. 2(27). 6–20

[148] S. V. Grebnev, E. V. Lazareva, P. A. Lebedev, A. Yu. Nesterenko, A. M. Semenov. Integration of domestic protocols for generating a common key into the TLS 1.3 protocol. PDM. Appendix, 2018, 11, 62–65.

[149] S. V. Grebnev. On the feasibility of an ECDLP algorithm Cryptology ePrint Archive, Report 2018/399

[150] D.A. Kronberg, E.O. Kiktenko, A.K. Fedorov, and Y.V. Kurochkin, Analysis of coherent quantum cryptography protocol vulnerability to an active beam-splitting attack Quantum Electronics 47, 163–168 (2017); arXiv:1611.04112

[151] A.S. Trushechkin, E.O. Kiktenko, and A.K. Fedorov, Practical issues in decoy-state quantum key distribution based on the central limit theorem Physical Review A 96, 022316 (2017); arXiv:1702.08531

[152] E.O. Kiktenko, A.S. Trushechkin, C.C.W. Lim, Y.V. Kurochkin, and A.K. Fedorov, Symmetric blind information reconciliation for quantum key distribution Physical Review Applied 8, 044017 (2017); arXiv:1612.03673

[153] A.S. Trushechkin, P.A. Tregubov, E.O. Kiktenko, Y.V. Kurochkin, and A.K. Fedorov, Quantum-key- distribution protocol with pseudorandom bases Physical Review A 97, 012311 (2018); arXiv:1706.00611

[154] A. Farouk, J. Batle M. Elhoseny, M. Naseri, M. Lone, A.K. Fedorov, M. Alkhambashi, S.H. Ahmed, and M. Abdel-Aty, Robust general N user authentication scheme in a centralized quantum communication network via generalized GHZ states Frontiers of Physics 13, 130306 (2018).

[155] A.K. Fedorov, E.O. Kiktenko, and A.S. Trushechkin. Symmetric blind information reconciliation and hash-function-based verification for quantum key distribution Lobachevskii Journal of Mathematics 39, 992 (2018); arXiv:1705.06664

[156] E.O. Kiktenko, A.O. Malyshev, A.A. Bozhedarov, N.O. Pozhar, M.N. Anufriev, and A.K. Fedorov, Error estimation at the information reconciliation stage of quantum key distribution Journal of Russian Laser Research 39, 558 (2018); arXiv:1810.05841

[157] A.K. Fedorov, I. Gerhardt, A. Huang, J. Jogenfors, Y. Kurochkin, A. Lamas-Linares, J.-A. Larsson, G. Leuchs, L. Lydersen, V. Makarov, and J. Skaar. Comment on "Inherent security of phase coding quantum key distribution systems against detector blinding attacks" [Laser Phys. Lett. 15, 095203 (2018)], Laser Physics Letters 16, 019401 (2019); arXiv:1809.03911

[158] E.O. Kiktenko, N.O. Pozhar, A.V. Duplinskiy, A.A. Kanapin, A.S. Sokolov, S.S. Vorobey, A.V. Miller, V.E. Ustimchik, M.N. Anufriev, A.S. Trushechkin, R.R. Yunusov, V.L. Kurochkin, Y.V. Kurochkin, and A.K. Fedorov, Demonstration of a quantum key distribution network in urban fibre-optic communication lines Quantum Electronics 47, 798–802 (2017); arXiv:1705.07154

[159] A.V. Duplinskiy, E.O. Kiktenko, N.O. Pozhar, M.N. Anufriev, R.P. Ermakov, A.I. Kotov, A.V. Brodskiy, R.R. Yunusov, V.L. Kurochkin, A.K. Fedorov, and Y.V. Kurochkin. Quantum-secured data transmission in urban fibre-optic communication lines Journal of Russian Laser Research 39, 113 (2018); arXiv:1712.09831

[160] V.E. Rodimin, E.O. Kiktenko, V.V. Usova, M.Yu. Ponomarev, T.V. Kazieva, A.V. Miller, A.S. Sokolov, A.A. Kanapin, A.V. Losev, A.S. Trushechkin, M.N. Anufriev, N.O. Pozhar, V.L. Kurochkin, Y.V.

Kurochkin, and A.K. Fedorov, Modular quantum key distribution setup for research and development applications, Journal of Russian Laser Research 40, 221 (2019); arXiv:1612.04168

[161] A.K. Fedorov, A.A. Kanapin, V.L. Kurochkin, Y.V. Kurochkin, A.V. Losev, A.V. Miller, I.O. Pashinskiy, V.E. Rodimin, and A.S. Sokolov, Educational potential of quantum cryptography and its experimental modular realization, Proceedings of the Scientific-Practical Conference "Research and Development – 2016", 83 (2018); arXiv:1710.08090

[162] R. Shakhovoy, D. Sych, V. Sharoglazova, A. Udaltsov, A.K. Fedorov, and Y. Kurochkin, Quantum noise extraction from the interference of laser pulses in an optical quantum random number generator, Optics Express 28, 6209 (2020); arXiv:1910.00219

[163] I.S. Kabanov, R.R. Yunusov, Y.V. Kurochkin, and A.K. Fedorov. Practical cryptographic strategies in the post-quantum era, AIP Conference Proceedings 1936, 020021 (2018); arXiv:1703.04285

[164] V. S. Belsky, I. V. Chizhov, A. A. Chichaeva, V. A. Shishkin. Physically unclonable functions in cryptography. International Journal of Open Information Technologies ISSN: 2307-8162 vol. 8, no.10, 2020

[165] A.A. Garage, I.Yu. Gerasimov, M.V. Nikolaev, I.V. Chizhov. On the use of fully homomorphic encryption libraries. International Journal of Open Information Technologies ISSN: 2307-8162 vol. 9, no.3, 2021

List of Open Training Courses in WWW

— Scott Aaronson (2006). "Quantum Computing Since Democritus": www.scottaaronson.com/ democritus/

— Quantum Computing Report's list of online educational resources: https://quantumcomputingreport.com/resources/education/

— Kirill Shilov, "16 Best Resources to Learn Quantum Computing in 2019": https://hackernoon.com/16-best-resources-to-learn-quantum-computing-in-2019-e5d8b797aeb6

— Leonard Susskind (2011), professor of physics at Stanford University. Quantum Mechanics: "The Theoretical Minimum": http://theoreticalminimum.com/courses/quantum-mechanics/ 2012/winter

Websites of Manufacturers of Quantum Computers and Simulators

— Atos:https://atos.net/en/insights-and-innovation/quantum-computing/atos-quantum

— Cambridge Quantum Computing: https://cambridgequantum.com/

— D-Wave: www.dwavesys.com

— Google: https://ai.google/research/teams/applied-science/quantum-ai/

— Honeywell: www.honeywell.com/en-us/company/quantum

— Huawei: www.huaweicloud.com/en-us

— IBM: www.research.ibm.com/ibm-q/

— Intel:https://newsroom.intel.com/press-kits/quantum-computing/#quantumcomputing-news

— IonQ: https://ionq.co/ MagiQ Technologies: www.magiqtech.com

— Microsoft: www.microsoft.com/en-us/research/research-area/quantum/

— Quantum Computing, Inc.: https://quantumcomputinginc.com/

— Quantum Numbers Corp.: www.quantumnumberscorp.com

— Quintessence Labs: www.quintessencelabs.com

— Raytheon: www.raytheon.com/capabilities/products/quantum

— Rigetti: www.rigetti.com/qcs

— Toshiba:www.toshiba.eu/eu/Cambridge-Research-Laboratory/Quantum-Information/

Archives of Quantum Algorithms and Simulators

— List of quantum http://quantumalgorithmzoo.org/

— List of quantum computing simulators: www.quantiki.org/wiki/list-qc-simulators

— List of quantum open-source projects: https://arxiv.org/pdf/1812.09167.pdf

— List of quantum software: https://github.com/qosf/os_quantum_software

— IBM Quantum Q Experience: https://quantumexperience.ng.bluemix.net/qx/editor

— Microsoft Quantum Software Development Kit: https://marketplace.visualstudio.com/ items?itemName=quantum.DevKit

— Open Quantum Safe Project: https://openquantumsafe.org/

— Open-source and commercial quantum software projects and online quantum portals: https:// github.com/qosf/os_quantum_software

— Python quantum open-source library: https://github.com/rigetti/pyquil

— Quantum Open Source Foundation: https://qosf.org/

— Quirk, drag-and-drop quantum simulator: https://algassert.com/quirk

List of Well-known National Quantum Programs

— Australia, Australian Research Council's Centre of Excellence for Engineered Quantum Systems: https://equs.org/

— Australia, Center for Quantum Computation & Communication Technology: www.cqc2t.org

— Barcelona, Catalonia, Spain, Institute of Photonic Sciences: http://quantumtech.icfo.eu/

— Barcelonaqbit: www.barcelonaqbit.com/

— Beijing Academy of Quantum Information Science: www.baqis.ac.cn/en/

— Berkeley Quantum: https://berkeleyquantum.org/

— Brookhaven National Laboratories: www.bnl.gov/compsci/quantum/

— China, CAS Key Laboratory of Quantum Information: http://lqcc.ustc. edu.cn/

— Entanglement Institute, Newport, Rhode Island: www.entanglement. institute/

— Fermilab Quantum Information Science Program: https://qis.fnal.gov/

— France, Grenoble Quantum Silicon: www.quantumsilicon-grenoble.eu/

— German Research Foundation's Matter and Light for Quantum Computing: https://ml4q.de/

— IARPA's Coherent Superconducting Qubits: www.iarpa.gov/index.php/ research-programs/csq

— IARPA's Logical Qubits: www.iarpa.gov/index.php/research-programs/ logiq

— IARPA's Multi-Qubit Coherent Operations: www.iarpa.gov/index.php/ research-programs/mqco

— IARPA's Quantum Enhancement Optimization: www.iarpa.gov/index. php/research-programs/qeo

— India, Light and Matter Physics: www.rri.res.in/light-matter-physics. html

— Korea, Center for Quantum Information: http://quantum.kist.re.kr/

— Leti, France: www.leti-cea.com/cea-tech/leti/english/Pages/Applied-Research/StrategicAxes/Quantum-leti-initiative.aspx

— Los Alamos Quantum Institute: https://quantum.lanl.gov/about.shtml

— NASA Quantum Artificial Intelligence Laboratory: https://ti.arc.nasa. gov/tech/dash/ groups/quail/

— National Science Foundation's Enabling Practical-Scale Quantum Computing: www.epiqc.cs.uchicago.edu/

— National Science Foundation's Quantum Information Science: www. nsf.gov/funding/pgm_summ.jsp?pims_id=505207

— Netherlands, QuSoft Research Center for Quantum Software: www. qusoft.org

— Netherlands, QuTech Academy: http://qutech.nl/

— NIST Joint Center for Quantum Information and Computer Science: http://quics.umd.edu/

— NIST Joint Quantum Institute: https://jqi.umd.edu/

— NIST Post-Quantum Cryptography contest: https://csrc.nist.gov/ Projects/Post-Quantum-Cryptography

— NIST Quantum Information Science: www.nist.gov/topics/quantum-information-science

— Oak Ridge National Laboratory Quantum Computing Institute: https:// quantum.ornl.gov/

— Oak Ridge National Laboratory Quantum Information Science Group: https://web.ornl.gov/sci/ qis/index.shtml

— Paris Centre for Quantum Computing: www.pcqc.fr

— Perimeter Institute for Theoretical Physics Quantum Information Research Group: http:// perimeterinstitute.ca/research/research-areas/ quantum-information

— Russian Quantum Center (Российский квантовый центр): https:// rqc.ru/

— Singapore, Centre for Quantum Technologies: www.quantumlah.org

— Singapore, Quantum Technologies for Engineering Programme: www.a-star.edu.sg/imre/Research/Programmes-Centres/Quantum-Technologies-for-Engineering-Programme

— Spanish National Research Council: https://qst.csic.es/

— Swiss National Science Foundation's Quantum Science and Technology: https://nccr-qsit.ethz.ch/

— United Kingdom's National Quantum Technology Programme: www. nqit.ox.ac.uk/

— Universities Space Research Association: www.usra.edu/quantum-computing

Index

About the Author

Associate Professor at the Innopolis University, Ph.D.

Postdoctoral researcher at the Saint Petersburg Electrotechnical University "LETI," Russia.

Previously, Alexei Petrenko was a Postdoc and a Ph.D. student with the Innopolis University in the group of Professor Sergei Petrenko.

Alexei Petrenko prepared the Ph.D. thesis "Quantum-Resistance in Blockchain Networks" (2020).

Alexei Petrenko has been closely following the blockchain space since late 2014. His main research interests include quantum cryptanalysis in Bitcoin and off-chain protocols. Earlier, he was researching secure development practices on the Ethereum platform and domain-specific languages for smart contracts.

During 2016–2020, Alexei Petrenko was a researcher on code vulnerabilities blockchain networks.

The main scientific interests of Alexei Petrenko are as follows:

- quantum cryptanalysis;

- quantum computers and computing;

- quantum communications (near-term perspective);

- quantum key distribution (QKD) and quantum encryption in fiber-optic communication channels and in open space;

- quantum hashing and quantum digital signature;

- quantum super-dense encoding of information using "entangled" and "hyper-entangled" particles (one quantum bit (qubit) can carry up to two ordinary bits), which increases the bandwidth of the quantum communication channel;

- encoding in quantum information transmission systems;

- quantum and post-quantum cryptography, etc.

Publications[1]

Author and co-author of two monographs and more than 175 articles on information security issues (Proceedings of ISA RAS and SPIIRAS and journals *"Cybersecurity Issues," "Information Security Problems," "Open Systems," "Inside: Information Protection," "Security Systems," "Electronics," "Communication Bulletin," "Network Journal," "Connect World of Connect,"* etc.), including monographs and practical manuals of publishing houses Springer Nature Switzerland AG, Athena, and DMK-Press: *"Methods of Cryptographic Protection of Information in Modern Digital Platforms," "Big Data Technologies for Monitoring of Computer Security: A Case Study of the Russian Federation," "Methods and Technologies of Information Security of Critical Objects of the National Infrastructure,"* and others.

Projects

2018..2021: project number 18-47-160011 p a (Russian Foundation for Basic Research, RFBR) "Development of an early warning system for cyber-attacks on the critical infrastructure of enterprises of the Republic of Tatarstan based on the creation and development of new NBIC cyber-security technologies."

2018..2021: grant of the "Academy of Sciences of the Republic of Tatarstan" for financial support for the implementation of the project for conducting scientific research on the topic "Models and methods quantum cryptanalysis."

2020..2022: project number 20-04-60080 (Russian Foundation for Basic Research, RFBR) "Models and methods for ensuring the sustainability of society's social and technical systems in the face of viral epidemics such as the COVID-19 pandemic based on acquired immunity."

---

[1] https://www.scopus.com/authid/detail.uri?authorId=57200260915, https://scholar.google.com/citations?user=s11uZoYAAAAJ

9788770227933